# THE DOUBLE IN NINETEENTH-CENTURY FICTION

# The Double in Nineteenth-Century Fiction

## The Shadow Life

John Herdman

St. Martin's Press    New York

First published in the United States of America in 1991

Printed in Great Britain

ISBN 0–312–05311–8


Library of Congress Cataloging-in-Publication Data
Herdman, John, 1941–
    The double in nineteenth-century fiction: the shadow life/John
Herdman.
        p.   cm.
    Includes bibliographical references and index.
    ISBN 0–312–05311–8
    1. Fiction—19th century—History and criticism.   2. Romanticism.
3. Doubles in literature.   4. Split self in literature.   5. Multiple
personality in literature.      I. Title.
PN3500. H47   1991
809'.927—dc20                                              90–42641
                                                              CIP

*For*
*Arthur Sale*
*Teacher and friend*




*Je* est un autre
*Rimbaud*

# Contents

# Preface

The genesis of this study lies in the personal interest in – or, better, haunting by – the idea of the double which has been mine since childhood. This seems to have begun when, at the age of about eight, I listened on the wireless to a story about a man who is pursued by the footsteps of an invisible being: eventually he comes to believe that he has succeeded in excluding it from his room, perhaps killed it, only to find that it is still with him. The details are now hazy in my memory and I cannot identify the tale – possibly it was a dramatisation of Maupassant's story 'The Horla' – but the terror with which it inspired me is still vivid. Perhaps about the same time I learned of the folk belief that to see one's double presages an early death. Two or three years later, at school, I watched as a line of a dozen or more boys followed a friend of mine, imitating in unison, or as near to it as could be managed, his every word and gesture; and I experienced vicariously the horror of the reproduction of one's own personality, which is at the same time its loss.

Much later I discovered that I was quite a good mimic, and enjoyed becoming through mimicry the double of another, and simultaneously I became deeply interested in the aesthetic status of mimesis in art. Then I read James Hogg's *The Private Memoirs and Confessions of a Justified Sinner*, and later E. T. A. Hoffmann's *The Devil's Elixirs*, and myself wrote a short novel that was intended at once as a respectful pastiche of these classic tales of the double, and as a modest attempt to make a new use of the genre. Some years later again I had a series of dreams which involved violent struggles between identical twins, and became fascinated by the psychological dimension of the double and by Jung's concept of the shadow. Finally I made a study of dualism in orthodox Christianity and in early and medieval heresy, and became vividly aware of the religious provenance of the literary double.

When the idea of the present book was suggested to me by one of the co-editors of this series, I was aware that certain aspects of the subject had had a fair amount of previous attention. In 1949 Ralph Tymms published a pioneering study, *Doubles in Literary Psychology*; as its title indicates, this work is centred on the psychology of the double, and it is also heavily weighted towards

German literature. Masao Miyoshi, in the Preface to his excellent *The Divided Self* (1969), while disclaiming any intention on his own part to deal simply with the genre of the 'supernatural double', points out in a footnote that 'There is no satisfactory or comprehensive treatment of this subject' (p. xii). Karl Miller's most stimulating *Doubles* (1985) does not attempt this either, being instead a very eclectic and wide-ranging study of literary duality in a much broader sense, seen from a perspective of cultural history.

It seems to me that the *content* expressed by the device of the fictional double (not necessarily supernatural, though often possessing a supernatural dimension) has been comparatively neglected. The subject-matter of this literature is highly characteristic, and certain motifs recur again and again and with an astonishing consistency. The ideas which are articulated by means of the double are essentially moral and religious, and the psychological perspective cannot properly be separated from this content. My approach, then, has been to attempt to show how theology and psychology interpenetrated in the formation of the image of the double and to suggest that moral–religious and psychological understandings of what is being given form in these works of fiction are not alternatives but necessary to each other and indeed mutually supportive. Many of these novels and stories have very intricate plots and it has proved necessary to attend to the action in a fair amount of detail. The significance of the double is always unfolded in action, and is often intimately associated with the idea of fate which reverberates through the ramifications of the plots. An adequate understanding of what is being said through the image of the double can be derived only from close attention to what actually *happens*.

The double is a central Romantic image. Its heyday corresponds approximately to the span of the nineteenth century, but its immediate literary roots are in late-eighteenth-century Romanticism, and the earliest works which I discuss belong to the 1780s and 1790s. The motif does not die with the nineteenth century, but its treatment in the last decade shows it in a state of declension from the fullest development of its potential; its survival in altered form and with different emphases during the present century is a different story which I have not attempted to treat. This study limits itself to prose fiction, and I have tried to deal with the most important works falling within the relevant period in which the double is a central theme. What is or is not a 'true' double, as distinct from an example of some other species of literary duality, is of course not capable of precise determination, and some of my decisions have no doubt been arbitrary. I have not, for instance, dealt with Mary Shelley's *Frankenstein*, partly because although it is possible to view the monster as a double of his master it seems to me that this is not the primary aspect under which he is to be understood, and partly because what there is to be said about the monster as double has already been very well discussed by others. Nor have I ventured into the vast hinterland of Victorian popular fiction in which doubles roam in abundance, as these are invariably derivative in origin and break no distinctive new territory of their own.

I should like to express my warm thanks to John Orr, who suggested this project and who has been unfailingly interested and sympathetic; to Mrs Drue Heinz and the Hawthornden International Writers' Retreat for the incalculably helpful award of a Hawthornden Fellowship in the early months of 1989, during my tenure of which the greater part of this book was written; to David Black, Ian Campbell, Ellis Nadler, Richard Rayner and Arthur Sale (to whom this volume is dedicated) for invaluable help and suggestions; and finally to my wife for her encouragement and support.

J.H.

# 1
# The Psychological and Theological Background

The experience of duality can be described as the foundation stone of human consciousness. This consciousness, in what makes it distinctively human, rests upon our recognition of the distinction between the 'I' and the 'not-I'. Of one, nothing can be said or thought: 'One is one and all alone and ever more shall be so.' The existence of two, and the recognition of its existence, is necessary to the basic dialectic upon which the possibility of language rests. Consciousness develops in the child through a progressive acknowledgement of the other and its claims. The 'not-I', however, is not always experienced as external to the individual; it can also be experienced as existing within the self. The experience of self-division, or at least the potential for it, is almost an inseparable condition of consciousness.

The human being sees in nature and the world, either objectively or subjectively, a proliferation of dualities: light and darkness, sun and moon, night and day, sleeping and waking, conscious and unconscious, positive and negative, mind and matter, body and soul, spirit and flesh, man and woman, good and evil, Heaven and Hell, God and the Devil. All of these polarities, and countless others, can become figures for self-division; but some can also be, or be related to, the actual content of that self-division. Duality, again, can be contrast or opposition, but it can also be likeness. It can be complementarity, as in the Platonic conception of twin souls which seek each other in order to make a whole out of their sundered halves; sympathy between individuals, even human love, can be seen under one aspect as ultimately the search for wholeness or integration within the self.

The subject of this book is the double as a literary, and specifically a fictional, device for articulating the experience of self-division. Its variations include the duplication, supernatural or phantasmal, or through likeness or affinity to another, of the individual; and the division of a personality, by supernatural or fantastic means,

or through the opposition or complementarity of separate characters who can be looked upon as differing aspects of a sundered
whole. In all its variations, the double arises out of and gives
form to the tension between division and unity. It stands for
contradiction within unity, and for unity in spite of division, the
likeness expressing the unity of the individual, the doubleness or
complementarity expressing division within the personality.

The double can be approached by the twin avenues of form and
content, though, as is characteristic of dualities, these contrasting
aspects reflect each other. The form that is chosen is related to the
nature of the division. Language itself exemplifies the relation.
Take, for example, the colloquial phrase, to 'be beside oneself'. St
Augustine uses it in his famous description in the *Confessions*,
which we shall shortly look at in some detail, of his state of self-
division in the period immediately preceding his conversion. Here
we have the image of the double in its simplest and most vivid
form: Augustine envisages himself as two people, both of them
himself, standing beside each other: 'I was beside myself.'[1] Clearly,
this is not regarded as a permanent, inherent condition of his
individuality; it is an event, one occasioned by a moral and spiritual
conflict within his will, between the claims of the spiritual and the
natural man. One is not always beside oneself: the condition stems
from conflict, and that conflict has content.

With respect to form, the double as a literary device has its
roots in human experience, natural, religious, psychological and
parapsychological, and in the reflections of such experience in
legend and folklore.[2] The human shadow and reflection have
always been seen as extensions of the personality and have carried
a numinous charge. They were long regarded as in some sense
spiritual doubles, ultimately perhaps representing the soul, and
vital to the wholeness and integrity of the individual. Another
obvious natural phenomenon suggesting doubleness is that of
physical resemblance between individuals, particular family
likeness, and most of all the likeness of identical twins. It is scarcely
surprising that brother (less often, sister) and twin are constantly
recurring motifs in the literature of duality.

The folkloric belief that the encounter with one's double presages
death is linked to that in the 'wraith', or visible (though not
tangible) counterpart of a person seen approximately at the time
of death. This, and the related belief in the 'errant' soul that can
separate from the body and be seen by its owner (or alternatively,

can itself see the body), have received some substantiation this century from parapsychological investigation, and have been classified as 'duplication phenomena' by the Jungian psychologist Aniela Jaffé.[3] The notion of the Guardian Angel appears to be derived from such belief and experience, and has its negative counterpart in that of the individual's 'evil daemon'.

The Christian belief in the final resurrection of the body, a body different in substance from the physical body, and the appearances of Christ after the Resurrection in a form that was somehow not immediately recognisable, could not fail to be richly suggestive. In the various forms of the Docetist heresy which arose in Gnostic and other heterodox circles during the early Christian centuries, Christ's existence on earth was held to have been lived in an illusory or phantasmal body. The doctrines of the occultists, again, made much of the so-called 'astral body', another variant of the spiritual double.

It was the occultists, also, who developed notions derived from Neoplatonism of 'like souls' linked by mutual sympathy in a spiritual affinity which might reach such heights as to give rise to a physical resemblance amounting to complete identity. With the eighteenth century, and Mesmer's theory of the 'magnetic union of souls', these ideas are carried to the verge of modern scientific enquiry.[4] At the beginning of the nineteenth century G. H. Schubert further developed the notion of 'animal magnetism', described by Ralph Tymms as 'an incalculable force [which] bridges all physical division, linking together two souls as one'.[5] In the magnetic trance, the forerunner of hypnosis, there was often startlingly revealed a second personality arising from the dark side of the mind, its 'shadow-side' or 'night-side'. The teachings of Schubert had a profound influence on German Romanticism, and especially on the work of E. T. A. Hoffmann, in whose stories and novels the supernatural double approaches its most developed form.[6] Thereafter science, proto-science and pseudo-science have a significant though fluctuating part to play in determining the form in which writers of fiction handle the device of the double.

I have given a brief summary of the main historical sources of the double motif, considered as form, before turning to the comparatively neglected question of its content. This content, in the work of the nineteenth-century novelists and short-story writers which we shall be examining, is predominantly concerned with moral conflict, with conflict in the human will, with the dialectic of spiritual pride, and especially with the problem of evil and the issue of free will. These moral and theological questions can never be separated from their psychological context, and to attempt to distinguish one aspect from the other would be not only unrealistic, but unreal. Yet it is impossible to deal adequately with the use of the double by Romantic and post-Romantic novelists without some understanding of the complex history of moral duality in the Western Christian tradition, and of the elements of dualism as a metaphysical position within orthodox, and even more markedly within heterodox, Christian theology.

The prototype of all Christian moral conflict is Christ's prayer in the Garden of Gethsemane on the eve of his Passion: 'Father, if thou art willing, remove this cup from me; nevertheless not my will, but thine, be done.'[7] This passage raises the theological issue of whether there were two *will*s in Christ, corresponding respectively to his human and his Divine natures; it is clear, however, that he is here speaking out of his human nature, and that his victory in preferring his Father's will to his own can properly be regarded as the type of all such subsequent choosing by Christians, since it is in and through Christ that the Christian is enabled to subdue the natural to the spiritual in any conflict of the will.

The theology of the moral conflict between the opposing wills in man, natural and spiritual, was developed by St Paul in the Epistle to the Romans:

> We know that the law is spiritual; but I am carnal, sold under sin. I do not understand my own actions. For I do not do what I want, but I do the very thing I hate. Now if I do what I do not want, I agree that the law is good. So then it is no longer I that do it, but sin that dwells within me. For I know that nothing good dwells within me, that is, in my flesh. I can will what is right, but I cannot do it. For I do not do the good that I want, but the evil I do not want is what I do.[8]

In his 'inmost self' Paul delights in the good, but he sees 'in my members another law at war with the law of my mind', making him captive to the law of sin. He can be freed from this captivity only by the grace of God through Jesus Christ. Many of the Romantic heroes who will receive the visitation of a double will find, with St Paul, that 'when I want to do right, evil lies close at hand'.[9]

Such division in the will is dependent upon more fundamental dualities in Christian theology: those between spirit and flesh, good and evil, God and the Devil. Very early in the development of Christian thought groups arose which saw these divisions far more starkly than did orthodox Catholic theology. St Paul himself was strongly dualist; but when he says in the passage quoted above that 'nothing good' dwells in his flesh it is not clear how strictly he is using the phrase, whether he regards human nature as wholly subverted by original sin and the fall of man, or merely damaged.

In the thought of the Gnostics, the duality is far more radical.[10] The term 'Gnosticism' is applied generically to the systems of belief of the multiplicity of sects which emerged towards the end of the first century AD on the fringes of Christianity (perhaps having their origins in pre-Christian ways of thought), and flourished in the second century and into the third; and which differentiated themselves from other Christians by their claim to the possession of a saving knowledge (*gnosis*) of a supreme hidden God, given by private revelation. This knowledge conferred salvation through the adherent's recognition of his own true nature as a spiritual being imprisoned in the fleshly body given him by an alien creator. In spite of the bewildering variety of Gnostic systems, there are certain constant factors which bind the diversity of their beliefs into something like a common doctrine. All reject the material world, which is the work not of the supreme hidden God but of an evil or ignorant demiurge, or of a series of intermediate creators. In this world are imprisoned sparks of the Divine nature, embedded in certain individuals by a predetermined fate, and these sparks alone are capable of salvation.

To explain the existence of evil, for which the true God could not have been responsible, the Gnostics postulated the existence of a system of spiritual beings, or 'aeons', through whose sin or shortcomings the world came into being, somehow encapsulating within it the Divine sparks sent down by the supreme God. To free them, the Redeemer descends to reveal to spiritual men their true nature, thus making it possible for them to ascend to reunion with God. In many systems, this Redeemer, or 'Revealer', is Jesus; but as he came from God he could have no connection with the flesh or the material world, hence his human nature was only apparent and illusory. Many Gnostics expressed their alienation from human existence by a rigid asceticism, but there were other groups who found in it a justification for licence.

The lucky few who contained within their bodies the saving seed or spark of Divine substance were designated the 'spiritual', as opposed to the 'fleshly' or 'material' mass, though with some sects there was an intermediate 'psychic' class.[11] Gnostic knowledge derived solely from individual revelation and was comprehensible only to those who believed or 'knew' that they were spiritual beings. The Gnostic's faith was therefore individualistic, spiritually élitist and, above all, self-centred rather than God-centred. His approach to life has been described by R. M. Grant as one of 'passionate subjectivity'. The individualism of the doctrines tended towards a rejection of authority, resulting in doctrinal anarchy and a seemingly endless multiplication of sects. Redemption came from destiny, not from the choice of free will, and was available only to a predetermined elect.

Thus there arose very early on the fringes of Christianity groups of people given to self-assertion and to a high conception of their personal destiny, whose teaching, as Irenaeus, the foremost anti-heretical writer among the early Church Fathers, claimed in his *Adversus Haereses*, had no other basis than their own imaginations, and who were 'puffed up by knowledge'.[12] Irenaeus traces all Gnostic doctrines to the heresy of Simon Magus, the Samaritan Messianist and sorcerer mentioned in Acts 8.9–24. Although it seems that Simon was not himself a Gnostic, a sect deriving from his teaching certainly became so. These Simonians or Samaritans adored Simon as first God and linked him with a certain Helen, conceived variously as a reincarnation of Helen of Troy and as a Tyrean prostitute, who appears as 'first Thought'. Simon Magus is believed to lie at the root of the ancient and medieval legends from which evolved the story of Faust, that archetypal figure of spiritual pride.[13]

It is clear that the *hubris* involved in the beliefs of such religious groups as the Gnostic 'Spirituals', the complete and unqualified self-identification with the spiritual and the good, and the consequent denial and suppression of all natural impulses and of the darker sides of the personality, would make them peculiarly prone to sudden and unexpected moral reversals – the phenomenon which C. G. Jung has called 'enantiodromia', the conversion of a thing into its opposite.[14] Such groups continued to flourish sporadically in late antiquity and into the Middle Ages, and, it may plausibly be argued, eventually found a new home on the extremes of Reformation theology. Persons given to just such a view of themselves, we will find, are subject in the fiction of the Romantic period to astonishing moral reversals, and it is precisely in this kind of soil that the double pre-eminently flourishes.

In the third century the Gnostic tendency had a fresh resurgence in the form of Manichaeism, a syncretistic Gnostic dualism founded by the Persian Manes (*c.*216–76), strongly influenced by Zoroastrianism and based on a belief in primeval conflict between light and darkness.[15] Manichaeism spread widely and lasted long. In the fourth century it was strong in Africa, and at the age of about twenty Augustine became a Manichee 'Hearer' (the grade below the 'Elect'), and remained so for about nine years. It was probably the Manichaean solution to the problem of evil that had attracted Augustine, but the failure in 383 of the celebrated Faustus to answer adequately some of the questions which had been troubling him initiated a gradual disillusion which culminated three years later in his conversion to Christianity.

From his own experience, Augustine tells us in the *Confessions* (p. 164), he came to understand the words of St Paul that 'the impulses of nature and the impulses of the spirit are at war with one another.'[16] The analysis of his state of mind in the months before his conversion is one of the seminal documents of Western consciousness. 'My inner self', he writes, 'was a house divided against itself.' In this 'fierce struggle, in which I was my own contestant', he felt himself 'beside myself with madness that would bring me sanity'. Knowing in his bones what he ought to do, he found himself unable to do it, incapable of making the necessary act of will. How was it that, though he wanted to make this act, and so in a sense willed it, his will did not obey him? It could only be that his willing was not 'wholehearted'. 'For in this case the power to act was the same as the will. To will it was to do it. Yet I did not do it.' When the mind gives an order to the body, it is instantly obeyed, yet when it gives one to itself it is resisted. Already he begins to suspect that this weakness is part of the punishment of Adam. But the cause of the phenomenon becomes clear to him: 'The reason, then, why the command is not obeyed is that it is not given with the full will.' It appears to Augustine to be a 'disease of the mind' that habit, the lower nature, pulls down the mind from its aspiration to truth. 'So there are two wills in us, because neither by itself is the whole will, and each possesses what the other lacks' (pp. 170–2).

Augustine immediately rejects, however, the Manichaean conclusion that we have two minds of different natures, one good and
the other evil. 'These people want to be light, not in the Lord, but
in themselves, because they think that the nature of the soul is the
same as God.' He argues that there can be a multiplicity of
conflicting wills in us, which cannot correspond to an equal number
of conflicting natures. 'It was I and I alone' who both willed to
serve God and willed not to do so, but could will neither fully.
When he was thus as odds with himself, 'It was part of the
punishment of a sin freely committed by Adam, my first father'
(pp. 172–5).

Augustine's subsequent conversion, which he experienced as
effected as it were from outside himself, left him with a conviction
of man's utter dependence on Divine grace which became the
mainspring of his theology. Only by the aid of grace had he been
enabled to will entirely and rightly. The key text for Augustine is,
'apart from me, you can do nothing'.[17] Against the Manichees he
maintained the creation of all things by God and the essential
goodness of all creation; evil had, properly speaking, no existence
in itself (a view first promulgated by Origen), but was a privation
of good resulting from the imperfection and incapacity to will
rightly which were the fruits of original sin.

Against Pelagius (who, ironically, was motivated in his insistence
on the absolute, unfettered freedom of the will by reaction against
Manichee determinism), Augustine argued in *On Nature and Grace*
(415) that the power to choose good by the unaided action of the
free will presupposed a human nature which had not been damaged
in its essential constitution. During the course of the Pelagian
controversy Augustine's attitude hardened to an extent that in
effect blotted out any contribution of the will to salvation and
entailed a predestinarian conception of the operation of grace. He
valued freedom rather than free will, true freedom consisting in
the will's regaining, through grace, the capacity to choose good
rather than evil. Christian freedom depends on a willingness to
surrender utterly to God, but that willingness is itself a gift of
grace.[18]

The more extreme implications of Augustine's position towards
the end of his life were never universally endorsed by the mind of
the Church, and the system of St Thomas Aquinas, based on the
rediscovery of Aristotle in the thirteenth century, represented

in some degree a reaction against Augustinianism. Augustine's formulations continued to be highly influential, however, and a resurgence of predestinarianism occurred with the writings of Calvin and other of the Reformers. Luther had already denied the possibility of free will after the fall of Adam; Calvin hardened this position with the development of the doctrines of the inamissability of grace, the certitude of salvation, and absolute predestination.

A result of this thinking was to establish within Calvinist Protestantism an emphasis on the Elect as a favoured group perfectly assured of eternal salvation, and in this respect directly analogous to the 'Sprititual' of Gnosticism, the 'Elect' among the Manichees and their successors (by way of an obscure and debatable line of descent via the Paulicians of the Byzantine Empire and the Balkan Bogomils of the tenth century), the 'Perfect' of the late medieval Cathar or Albigensian heresy. These last were set apart even physically by the donning of a black robe or, later, a cord worn next to the skin.[19]

A further and crucial question arising from Calvinist views on predestination related to the status, and indeed the possibility in any real sense, of repentance, hitherto absolutely central to the Christian conception of the working of redemption. The implication of extreme predestinarian views could only be to limit God's mercy, and since the knowledge of whether or not one was numbered among the Elect could finally be a matter only of subjective conviction, those not certain of their status must be equally uncertain as to the possibility of their repentance and hence of their redemption. Moreover, it was precisely this mass of mankind who stood in need of redemption through repentance and God's mercy, since the Elect have already received justification and are assured of salvation through 'faith'. One could only repent if one was free to repent, and if one was free to repent, that repentance was already implied by and subsumed in one's justification and salvation.

For the dramatists of the Renaissance, these questions had already become pressing. In particular, it is precisely this dilemma which animates the action of Marlowe's *Dr Faustus*, a work which is seminal to the later development of the theme of the double, in relation to both form and content. Faustus is the absolute type of spiritual and intellectual pride, the impulse to gratify the thirst for knowledge and power which involves an aspiration to emulate the Deity and attempt 'more than heavenly power permits'.

Mephistophilis is a prototype of the demonic tempter who in Romantic literature will often take the form of a double, since although he is an emissary of Lucifer he can also, and without contradiction, be viewed as an embodiment of the dark and evil tendencies which emerge from within the self. The pact with the Devil, again, will become one of the commonplaces of the Gothic novel.

'Protestant theology', T. R. Wright has written, 'provides the dominant discourse of the play, contributing to its almost Manichean division between the spiritual powers of good and evil. Faustus seems quite literally torn between rival pictures of the world.'[20] These rival pictures are the Calvinist and the traditional Catholic views of repentance and redemption. It is clear that the sinful pride of Faustus exemplifies the fallen state of man and repeats the original fall, again through pride, of his ultimate tempter Lucifer, who in turn was responsible for the fall of Adam. Is Faustus free to repent, however? The Good Angel urges that he is, while the Bad Angel insists that repentance is vain and that he is doomed to persist in the path he has chosen. In the end, Faustus does not repent; but does this failure result from a contrary predestination, or only from his *belief* in his own irredeemability, in which the Bad Angel encourages him? The dramatic suspense of the play, as Wright points out, depends upon the audience feeling that Faustus is free to repent at any time. Marlowe's own emotional position is sufficiently indicated by the fact that it is the *Good* Angel who tells the protagonist, 'never too late, if Faustus will repent'; while it is Lucifer who insists that 'Christ cannot save thy soul, for he is just.' The conclusion seems irresistible that the latter advice is devilish.

This theological excursus has been necessary in order to outline the history of consciousness of division in the will in Western Christian thought, and some of the implications of the problem of evil, the ambiguous role of free will and the controverted issue of predestination, and the impulse of spiritual pride in determining the content of such division. Marlow's *Dr Faustus* brings us to the literary involvement with these questions, and assembles on stage some of the most important elements that will contribute to the character of the Romantic double.

# 2

# The Emergence and Development of the Double Theme

Before we proceed to examine individual works, it will be useful to provide an outline of the emergence of the theme of the double in Romantic fiction and its development, traceable in several intertwining strands, through the course of the nineteenth century. The preoccupation with duality which characterises the age took no monolithic form; the double was only one way, though an important one, of giving expression to the consciousness of self-division, opposition, contradiction and ambiguity, and it often shades off into, or interpenetrates with, related approaches and forms. The theme also developed differently and on a different time-scale in the various national cultures of Europe and America, though the degree of common consciousness and experience transcending national divisions is often more remarkable and important than the variations.

In the latter half of the eighteenth century the European sensibility began to grow restive under the rule of Reason which held such powerful sway during the Enlightenment. As Edwin M. Eigner has noticed, 'the romantic dualism of the end of the eighteenth century and the beginning of the nineteenth is often an answer to the skeptical optimism of the perfectibilinarians.'[1] The old features and concerns of the theological tradition of dualism outlined in Chapter 1 rose to the surface once more, but attached themselves to preoccupations peculiar to the new age. The concept of moral evil became associated with the primitive, the savage and the untamed in the human spirit, which contact with the native cultures of newly explored or colonised lands was forcing upon the collective attention, and still more upon the collective unconscious of Enlightenment man. The savage of the unconscious housed within the European breast became associated with evil because of the threat it posed to the values of rationalism, to the

11

ideals of progress and human perfectibility.

The Romantic obsession with the arbitrary and the irrational found its most characteristic symbolisation in the idea of Fate. No concept is more central to the theme of the double. Again and again protagonists, confronted with an embodiment of the dark forces from within their own natures, attribute their possession to the inscrutable workings of a destiny which they are powerless to evade. The notion of Fate as understood in the pagan classical world now attaches itself to the Augustinian and Calvinist theology of predestination, which carries with it, as we have seen, the attendant questions of the status of free will and the possibility of repentance and redemption. Philosophy added its voice to those which spoke of a threat from within to the rule of reason and goodness in the heart and mind, and hence in the society, of man. Kant subscribed to the view that good and evil were equally real and equally at home in the human soul, and spoke of a struggle between reason and the evil and irrational, in which reason must prevail if the good is to survive and flourish.

In the Romantic consciousness, then, a strong rationalist and realistic element persisted which sought to control and order the emergent extravagances of fantasy and imagination. The psychological impulse appealed to both of these conflicting tendencies. While it offered ample scope for the exploration of the vague longings and affective aspirations of the individual soul, it also provided the opportunity to learn more about the constitution of the human mind through close and realistic observation. Such observation, however, was no longer confined to the rational, conscious layers of the psyche. The investigations and theories of such influential figures as Mesmer and, later, G. H. Schubert, were providing access to the night-side of the mind where a second, shadowy self might be discovered.

As it happens, St Augustine, once more, had been there before. In Book x of the *Confessions* he asks how it is that in sleep the urges of the flesh imprinted on his memory by his former habits return to him so strongly as almost to amount to acquiescence in the acts that are imaged: 'The power which these illusory images have over my soul and body is so great that what is no more than a vision can influence me in sleep in a way that the reality cannot do when I am awake. Surely it cannot be that when I am asleep I am not myself, O Lord my God?' (p. 233).

To dream and religious vision were now added, for the early

Romantics, the more startling and disturbing divisions and dissociations within and of the mind occasioned by mesmeric trance and – witness the experience of Coleridge and De Quincey – opium. The second selves thus suggested or revealed interacted with the old Platonic and occultist yearning for the unification of the severed twin souls of man in the work of the early German Romantics. It was in Germany, in the thrills and terrors and sensations of the *Schauerroman* and the Romantic drama, that the supernatural double, the mainstream of the device which was to be employed with such psychological power and depth by Hoffmann, Hogg and Dostoevsky, had its humble fictional source.

The term *'Doppelgänger'* was invented by Jean-Paul Richter (who used the *nom-de-plume* 'Jean Paul'), but Ralph Tymms, the first chronicler of the psychological provenance of the double as a literary device, rightly asserts that 'Jean Paul's conception of the double is never profound, and sometimes it is quite trivial.'² In such works as *Siebenkäs*, Richter presents us with 'pairs of friends (in the original sense of "fellows, two of a pair"), who together form a unit, but individually appear as a "half", dependent on the *alter ego*'.³ Richter's main importance lies in the strong influence which he exerted upon E. T. A. Hoffmann, who was to exploit the potentialities of the *Doppelgänger* much more profoundly and with a far surer imaginative and psychological grasp.

Goethe was similarly interested in contrasting and complementary pairs of characters who may be taken as the divided parts of a single personality. Early works such as *Wilhelm Meister* prepare the way for the relationship between Faust and Mephisto, who in embodying respectively emotional and rational qualities of personality suggest the sundered elements of an ideal whole: 'Two souls, alas, are housed within my breast.' Yet in spite of the immense and pervasive influence of Goethe's *Faust* it cannot be said that his treatment of the archetypal Faust theme advances specifically the development of the double as a literary device greatly beyond the point attained in Marlowe's drama. Far more influential in terms of dualistic fashion was Schiller's drama *Die Räuber*, with its brother-doubles Franz and Karl Moor, a play whose shock-waves were still registering in 1880 when Dostoevsky made Fyodor Karamazov ironically compare his sons Dmitry and Ivan to the dual heroes of the drama.

Duality was everywhere in evidence in the last decade of the eighteenth century. The Marquis de Sade went so far as to write two separate novels, *Justine* (1791) and *Juliette* (1797), which, as Angela Carter has noticed, 'mutually reflect and complement one another, like a pair of mirrors'. Justine is the good girl whose story illustrates the misfortunes attendant upon virtue, while the history of her sister Juliette, 'Justine-through-the-looking-glass, an inversion of an inversion', drives home the corollary proposition that vice leads to happiness and prosperity.[4]

We have seen that the double proper had its birth, as a fictional device, in Germany. It is necessary to be clear about the nature of the true double, or *Doppelgänger*. The *Doppelgänger* is a second self, or *alter ego*, which appears as a distinct and separate being apprehensible by the physical senses (or at least, by *some* of them), but exists in a dependent relation to the original. By 'dependent' we do not mean 'subordinate', for often the double comes to dominate, control, and usurp the functions of the subject; but rather that, *qua* double, it has its *raison d'être* in its *relation* to the original. Often, but not always, the subject and his double are physically similar, often to the point of absolute identity. Brothers (sisters are a rarity in this literature), and especially twins, may be doubles, but where this is the case there is always an element, whether overtly supernatural, numinous or otherwise extraordinary, which goes beyond the merely natural relationship. The most characteristic *Doppelgänger* always have a supernatural or subjective *aspect*, which does not imply that, within the scheme of the fictions they inhabit, they have no objective existence. On the contrary, the psychological power of the device lies in its ambiguity, in the projection of the subject's subjectivity upon a being whose reality the structure of the novel or story obliges the reader to accept. It was above all E. T. A. Hoffmann who brought this procedure to maturity.

A second kind of double is that which, in relation to some of the characters of Dostoevsky, has been called by Joseph Frank the 'quasi-double'.[5] Quasi-doubles come in various forms, but always have an unambiguously independent existence within the fictional scheme. Frank cites 'characters who exist in their own right, but reflect some internal aspect of another character in a strengthened form'. In the work of Dostoevsky (whose novels furnish examples of almost every kind of double), Smerdyakov in *The Brothers Karamazov* has such an intensive relation to Ivan. Quasi-doubles may also, however, be complementary opposites, whether Platonic soul-mates or, more often, characters whose unlikenesses and contradictions reflect hostility and conflict, yet at the same time mutual dependence and interlocked destinies. Such a pair are Myshkin and Rogozhin in *The Idiot*, who represent a bifurcation and division of an originally conceived single character. Such characters are sometimes inaccurately referred to as 'mirror-images', which implies an identical likeness, though an inverted one; they should rather be thought of as the interlocking pieces of a two-piece jigsaw puzzle, whose oppositeness and complementarity imply a fractured or severed unity.

It is clear that such quasi-doubles may be hard to distinguish from the merely opposite (or congruent) characters who are bound to crop up in the work of even the most naturalistic novelists, since all characterisation involves an element of dialectic; that is, characters may testify to duality without in the least being doubles. We must then ask whether the likeness, opposition or complementarity in question is sufficiently marked to have a clear symbolic function. Dostoevsky, once again, affords an example of the distinction. In *The Brothers Karamazov* Ivan and Alyosha both have their origins in a single character in the original plan for *The Life of A Great Sinner*, whose attributes came to be divided between them; they are brothers and they stand for opposite values, but they are in no sense doubles – Ivan has two doubles, and neither of them is Alyosha. With Myshkin and Rogozhin the case is quite different In their relation there is a consistently developed numinous dimension, something that goes beyond any natural or realistic correspondence: Rogozhin *haunts* Myshkin, and the haunting is clearly developed in such a way as to point to their interwoven destinies and their underlying identity.

Divided, split or schizophrenic characters are, again, not in themselves doubles or *Doppelgänger*, though these terms may become appropriate if and when their division gives rise to a second, sensibly apprehensible personality (even if apprehensible only to the subject), which can occur for instance in the case of a hallucination fictionally presented as a distinct personage. The loose use of the term '*Doppelgänger*' to refer to split personalities, fictional or otherwise (Eigner persistently uses the word in such a sense) is to be avoided, since it blurs important distinctions. Clearly, however, the phenomenon of the double life is closely *related* to the device of the double, and several dualistically inclined writers deal in both types. Often the one can throw revealing light on the other, and we shall have occasion to refer in passing to several stories involving dramatically divided personalities.

The diverse variants of the double flourished unevenly on different national soils. The central stream of the supernatural double was developed by Hoffmann to the point at which the device became a precision tool of psychological penetration, and it quickly became naturalised in Scotland and Russia. That such a small country as Scotland should have contributed, in James Hogg and R. L. Stevenson, two of the foremost masters of the double is a remarkable fact, but though the ultimate reasons for the heightened Scottish awareness of duality may lie deep in the national psyche and history, a proximate causation in the schematic polarities of Calvinist theology can scarcely be in doubt. In Russia dualism became something of a literary fashion through the immense influence of Hoffmann; the Hoffmannisers were selective in what they borrowed from the German romancer, but the double was high on their list of priorities. Dostoevsky took up the theme in the late 1840s at a time when many others, whose concern with it was primarily fashionable, were dropping it; thenceforth it remained central to his apprehension of reality, and in his later work the various strands of the tradition come together and find their culmination.

In England the supernatural double was never truly at home. It is remarkable that Gothic romances such as M. G. Lewis's *The Monk* and Mrs Radcliffe's *The Italian* employ almost every supernatural device except that of the double. The English Gothic novel is none the less important for the development of the theme, because so many of its characteristic preoccupations and motifs are taken up by later works which harness them to the device of the double. *The Monk*, for instance, is a crucial model for Hoffmann's *The Devil's Elixirs*. Some of the earliest examples of quasi-doubles occur in English works, although here there is no clear line of transmission or development. William Godwin's *Caleb Williams*, a work at once affected by and critical of the 'Italian' tale of terror, provides two types of double: a complementary opposite whose character after his death is taken on by his rival, and an externalised embodiment of conscience. Charles Maturin's *Melmoth the Wanderer* (of Irish Protestant provenance, but clearly in the tradition of *The Monk*, though with more considerable claims to literary distinction) features a shadowy doubling between brothers and also an evil second self who is however a clearly independent character.

In America a characteristically materialist and rationalist cast of mind exists in tension with a strong consciousness of the 'other', and a heightened sensitivity to the power of unconscious forces, which is connected with the proximity of the wilderness and the closeness of the irrational and the untamed. Charles Brockden Brown was an enlightened admirer of Godwin but his novels are set on the frontier between civilisation and savagery, and his doubles reflect this dichotomy, in that while they are susceptible of rational explanation, they evoke and coax into activity dark and sinister unconscious powers. Hawthorne and Melville are dualists, but true doubles are not prominent in their work. Poe was obsessively concerned with the mysterious, the eccentric, the other-worldly and the horrible, but he strives to assimilate these preoccupations to an ultimately materialist perspective. His mental temper is profoundly dualistic, and gave rise to at least one classic of the double, 'William Wilson'.

The first *floreat* of the double achieves its consummation by the end of the first quarter of the nineteenth century. *The Devil's Elixirs* appeared in 1814, as did Chamisso's *Peter Schlemihl*, which initiated the sub-genre of 'shadow' romances. *Melmoth*, the last major work of the Gothic tradition, appeared in 1820; Hogg's *Private Memoirs and Confessions of a Justified Sinner* followed in 1824. To 1818 belongs Mary Shelley's *Frankenstein*, one of the great mythic constructs of the century, which, though not a novel about a double in the usual sense, contains strong intimations of a quasi-doubling relationship between creator and monster to which attention has been vividly drawn by Muriel Spark and Masao Miyoshi. To Frankenstein the 'daemon' he has introduced into the world appears 'nearly in the light of my own vampire, my own spirit let loose from the grave'. Spark examines these two characters as 'both complementary and antithetical beings' who are 'bound together by the nature of their relationship', ultimately 'facets of the same personality'.[6] In this they anticipate the symbiotic relationship between the later monster-maker Dr Jekyll and his stunted shadow-self Mr Hyde, the originator locked in symbolic conflict with the sinister power he has unleashed from within his own being.

In the 1830s the double was kept alive by Poe in America and by Gogol and the minor Hoffmannists in Russia, but in Western Europe the theme goes more or less into abeyance as a serious fictional concern for nearly fifty years. Dickens, it is true, sometimes hovers on the verge of creating characters who are at least quasi-doubles. Jonas Chuzzlewit, and Jasper in *Edwin Drood*, are certainly split personalities, murderers with double lives in the tradition of Hoffmann's Cardillac in 'Mademoiselle de Scudéry', but their inner division is not dramatised in terms of the appearance of a fully embodied second self. Various pairs of Dickensian opposites who have been proposed as doubles are scarcely developed in ways which justify the description; the only true exception lies in the dual heroes of *A Tale of Two Cities*. John Gross, writing of this novel, remarks that 'the theme of the double has such obvious attractions for a writer preoccupied with disguises, rival impulses, and hidden affinities that it is surprising that Dickens didn't make more use of it elsewhere'.[7] But, as Gross observes, the device is not very satisfactorily handled here. Charles Darnay and Sidney Carton are, however, doubles in a real sense: strikingly alike in appearance but divergent in character, they symbolically appear together in reflection in the mirror above the dock after Darnay's acquittal at the trial at the Old Bailey; Carton's mingled attraction and dislike for Darnay reflect his own self-hatred and self-love. Henceforth their destinies are inseparable, and it will be Carton's fate to give up his life for the other to whom he is so ambiguously related.

The mid-century decline in the literary double was almost certainly connected with the loss of intellectual respectability of the Romantic psychology on which it was founded. The ideas of Mesmer and Schubert had been taken with great seriousness both by creative artists and by the educated general public, and had found their philosophical counterpart in the idealist metaphysics represented most notably by Schelling; much later they were to regain a measure of recognition as foreshadowings of psychoanalysis and Jungian psychology. But in the middle of the nineteenth century mesmerism and its associated systems of psychological understanding seemed decidedly dated and cranky. It is perhaps significant that Dostoevsky, who alone of major writers carried the techniques of the double forward into the third quarter of the century with renewed vitality and power, had discovered for himself a satisfying intellectual foundation in the psychology of C. G. Carus, who advanced ideas very consistent with those of G. H. Schubert, and who, while enjoying the highest scientific repute as a physiologist, remained devoted to Schelling's idealist understanding of the world. We shall later have occasion to discuss the ideas of Carus in relation to their influence on Dostoevksy.

During these decades of comparative neglect of the double theme by novelists writing with a 'serious' intent – writers, that is, who would use it to shed light on the inner workings of the human mind and soul – it was enthusiastically taken up by other novelists who exploited it for sensational effects. This tradition, in fact, goes all the way back to Jean-Paul Richter and other practitioners of the *Schauerroman*. G. W. M. Reynolds, for instance, in his *Mysteries of London* (1847) describes the protracted haunting by a bad brother of a good brother; Wilkie Collins put the double to sensationalist use in *The Woman in White* (1859–60) and especially in *Armadale* (1864–6); and by the end of the century the theme and other motifs related to it had percolated deeply into the hinterland of popular fiction, as witness the work of the renowned Marie Corelli, who in *The Sorrows of Satan* (1895) paints an engaging devil who haunts the hero and is seen through only by a beautiful popular novelist. No hard-and-fast line, however, can be drawn between serious and sensationalist use of the theme. Stevenson, for example, adopted both approaches in different stories, and we may feel that there was on occasion a significant overlap.

In the last quarter of the century the work of the new French psychologists, led by the radically materialist Taine, reinstated the concept of double personality in the world of scientific psychology. The clinical work in mental institutions of the two Janets, of Charcot and Binet, largely endorsed the theories of the Romantic psychologists in revealing, as they believed, a second personality (activated, for instance, in somnambulism) eternally at war with the first, and liable to usurp and take possession of the entire life of the subject. But the crucial difference between the Romantic psychologists and their successors the 'nerve doctors' lay, as Eigner observes, 'in the connections or lack of connections which they made between psychology and theology. The psychologists at the end of the century, as one might expect, fought shy of making moral value judgments'.[8] This disjunction was to prove fatal to the central tradition of the supernatural double, which was pre-eminently a device at the service of a *moral* psychology, essentially anti-determinist in spirit, though usually concerned with protagonists who see their own history deterministically as a product of Fate. To put it at its crudest, the anti-heroes of this tradition go mad because they are bad (usually proud), rather than behaving badly because they are mad.

The dilemma faced by a writer contemplating a work in the tradition of the supernatural double in the new cultural climate is typified by the case of Stevenson. He was a profound admirer of the new psychology and actively interested in psychic research, yet his mind was cast in the ineradicable mould of a morally conceived dualism. If he were to develop the theme of the supernatural double in terms of the new clinical understanding of the divided personality he would be obliged, if he were to remain intellectually respectable, to eschew the moral dimension. Yet it was precisely the moral dimension which – and most unequivocally in *Dr Jekyll and Mr Hyde* – he aimed at. In order to attain his end he must, therefore, approach his theme allegorically, thus making it clear that his viewpoint was different from (though not necessarily opposed to) the scientific one; and this is the path which in fact he chose. Yet the allegorical approach was not capable of the subtlety of penetration which was available to the mode of the supernatural double as practised by Hoffmann and Hogg, and supremely by Dostoevsky, with its unique blend of psychological realism and supernatural, or at least numinous, symbolism, an approach committed to a moral–spiritual understanding of the mind and soul of man.

The alternative route involved bowing to the spirit of the age and dissociating the double from any application to a morally or spiritually based view of the world. This course was chosen by Chekhov when he pointedly described his story 'The Black Monk' as 'the case history of a disease', the disease in question being megalomania. Thus at the close of the nineteenth century we can observe a bifurcation of the broad river of the supernatural double into two streams, the allegorical and what may be called the 'clinical', neither of them capable of the artistic centrality available to the undivided tradition. With this division, the present study will reach its terminus.

# 3

# Terror, Pursuit and Shadows

The double reaches full maturity in the work of Hoffmann, but there are three distinct preliminary strains which can be distinguished apart from the work of the early German Romantics alluded to in the previous chapter. Two of these are preliminary in both a chronological and a developmental sense, the third only in the latter. The first is the English Gothic romance: although the seminal early works in this genre do not contain doubles in any strict meaning of the term, they deal with themes of moral reversal, of evil and remorse and of the divided will and spiritual pride, in ways which will crucially influence and be taken up by later books which, while perpetuating Gothic conventions, harness these themes to the device of the double. The second strand is the rationalistic but psychologically quite profound treatment of complementarity and role reversal in the work of William Godwin and his American disciple Charles Brockden Brown. The third strain is the special genre of 'shadow' fiction initiated and primarily exemplified by Chamisso's *Peter Schlemihl* (1814), which, although exactly contemporary with Hoffmann's *The Devil's Elixirs*, essentially belongs to an earlier, less developed conception of the double which is much closer to the folk tale than to the psychological novel. We shall look at each of these groups of fictions in turn.

## THE GOTHIC ROMANCE

There are two novels in variants of the Gothic genre in its earlier stages which show especially strong preoccupations with themes which interlock with that of the double. The backgrounds of these two works have a great deal in common but in character they are most diverse. William Beckford's *Vathek* (1786) and *The Monk* (1796) by Matthew Lewis were both written by very young and very wealthy men; their authors were twenty-one and nineteen respectively at the times of their composition. Both later became Members of Parliament, though scarcely devoted politicians, and both soon turned to other forms of literary expression, Beckford to travel writing and Lewis to the drama. The two romances reflect in a very direct way their authors' personalities, which in spite of their superficial resemblances could scarcely have been more contrasting.

*Vathek* belongs to a distinct sub-genre of the eighteenth-century romance, the Oriental tale, and reflects the young Beckford's absorption in the stories of the *Arabian Nights*. His temperament was detached and ironical, though in his earlier years he was very much subject to the temptations of the flesh; and his novel (with its attendant 'episodes', which were never, as originally intended, integrated into the main text), exhibits a curious mixture of passionate involvement with the underlying themes, and mocking, almost parodic reduction of the conventions within which he chooses to work. This duality of mood, which sometimes manifests itself in fluctuations of tone, as in the powerful and climactic scene in the Hall of Eblis (the Arab equivalent of Satan), in which the ironical mask is dropped and a sense of almost numinous awe invoked, is more continuously embodied in the novel's double-layered character, by which the reader can respond to both the humorous pastiche of the surface treatment and the deeper seriousness, without any consciousness of a contradiction between these elements.

In *Vathek* Beckford handles, with great narrative *élan* and agility of touch, a quite conscious transposition to an Oriental setting of the Faust theme. The 'unquiet and impetuous disposition' of the Caliph combines sensuality with an insatiable thirst for knowledge (extending even to 'sciences that did not exist'), an appetite which embraces unorthodox theological speculation.[1] He builds, 'from the insolent curiosity of penetrating the secrets of heaven', a tower in imitation of Nimrod's, from the heights of which he sees men and cities as ants and beehives. Mahomet permits this vaulting pride only to humble the Caliph to the dust. Inevitably Vathek swears allegiance to the Prince of Darkness, and the narrative charts his fluctuating devotion to his new master.

Pride always carries with it, in the Gothic romance, attendant secondary sins, and in Vathek's case these are cruelty and sensuality. The triangle formed by the Caliph, the beautiful Nouronihar and her childlike cousin and lover, Gulchenrouz, reflects, in a transposed ordering, the tangle of illicit attraction in which the bisexual Beckford had been scandalously involved with his cousin's wife, Louisa Beckford, and the young boy, William Courtenay. The catastrophe of *Vathek* consigns the Caliph and Nouronihar to everlasting anguish, 'whilst the humble and despised Gulchenrouz passed whole ages in undisturbed tranquillity, and in the pure happiness of childhood' (p. 255). The Faustian moral is continually enforced (though never except in a tone which conveys the mockingly superior stance assumed by the author), and is finally confirmed in Vathek's eternal perdition:

> Such shall be the chastisement of that blind curiosity, which would trangress those bounds the wisdom of the Creator has prescribed to human knowledge; and such the dreadful disappointment of that restless ambition, which, aiming at discoveries reserved for beings of a supernatural order, perceives not, through its infatuated pride, that the condition of man upon earth is to be – humble and ignorant.   (p. 254)

The second sentence of *Vathek* contains a pointed parody of a feature which will become an almost invariable badge of the proud and demonic spirit. The Caliph has the characteristic that 'when he was angry, one of his eyes became so terrible, that no person could bear to behold it; and the wretch upon whom it was fixed instantly fell backward, and sometimes expired. For fear, however, of depopulating his dominions and making his palace desolate, he but rarely gave way to his anger' (p. 151). This passage could be taken as a direct parody of the description of the eyes of Schedoni in Ann Radcliffe's *The Italian*, did not this post-date *Vathek* by eleven years. In relation to the 'glittering eye' of Coleridge's Ancient Mariner, John Livingston Lowes has speculated on the ancestry of these 'terrible eyes' which pursue such a lengthy career through Romantic and post-Romantic literature.[2] Lowes, while acknowledging the ultimate source of the image in Milton's Satan, plausibly suggests a more immediate derivation from the Armenian in Schiller's *Der Geisterseher*; but it seems equally likely that this prototype was reinforced for the eighteenth-century Romantics by the commanding and hypnotic eye of the mesmerist, with its terrifying assault on the unity and integrity of the personality. However that may be, the 'black and sparkling' eyes of the monk Ambrosio in Lewis's novel are invoked without a trace of Beckford's irony: 'few could sustain the glance of his eye at once fiery and penetrating'.[3]

In place of Beckford's ironical detachment, Lewis in *The Monk* exhibits a kind of exulting involvement in his hero's descent into depraved sensuality. Ambrosio is at the outset pictured as a man of commanding presence, of oustanding natural gifts and of unexampled holiness. The admiration in which he is held by the populace of Madrid is surpassed only by his own self-regard and the overweening confidence which he places in his inviolability to temptation.

That he is a monk and an abbot exemplifies the developing convention by which it is a Catholic priest who gives himself over to crime and licence. In relation to the portrait of Mrs Radcliffe's monk Schedoni, Mario Praz has indicated the historical context: 'Illuminism had pointed to the Roman Catholic monk as an infamy which must be crushed, and the recent campaign against the Society of Jesus had disclosed a sinister background of material interests.'[4] While this convention certainly reflects the strong anti-Catholic bias which pervades *The Monk*, and many other English Gothic productions (as Masao Miyoshi quite correctly maintains, the novel documents 'the Protestant dualism of flesh and soul projected onto imagined Catholic orgies'),[5] it also establishes the more general principle that it is those who are most proud of their unimpeachable sanctity who are most subject to the possibility of utter moral reversal.

The hypocrisy of the religious environment is blatantly emphasised at the very outset. Ambrosio has been left at the monastery gate as a young child and brought up in an atmosphere which Lewis represents as completely hypocritical and entirely devoted to the life-denying pursuit of power and influence under the mere appearance of holiness. Some sympathy is expressed for the perversion of his fine potential entailed by this upbringing with its unnatural suppression of his natural impulses; but this sympathy is quite overridden as we are made acquainted with the unrestrained vanity of this 'Man of Holiness' in whom 'Humility's semblance combated with the reality of Pride': 'He looked round him with exultation, and Pride told him loudly, that he was superior to the rest of his fellow-Creatures' (pp. 39–40).

In this spiritual condition, he is of course intensely vulnerable to temptation. Lorenzo, one of the novel's insipid heroes, has already been at pains to make this point: 'He is just at that period of life when the passions are most vigorous, unbridled and despotic; His established reputation will mark him out to Seduction as an illustrious Victim' (p. 21). This seduction is not slow to assail him, in the shape of Matilda, who is an emissary of Lucifer, although this only becomes clear to the reader much later.

It is part of the novel's salaciousness that Ambrosio is first attracted to Matilda while she is still under the disguise of a young novice. Matilda is no real sense a double, but in acting as temptress and calling up the repressed dark and sensual side of his nature she fulfils two roles which in subsequent novels in the tradition will find unified expression in true doubles. Ambrosio succumbs to Matilda's charms with unseemly promptitude; and while he is for a time subject to moods of remorse and self-doubt, these are never strong enough to subdue the imperious demands of his appetites.

Matilda is only the fleeting occasion of Ambrosio's fall. He soon tires of her, and starts to lust for the innocent young flesh of Antonia. Here we have to see unmistakably the hand of fate, that intervention of the arbitrary so beloved of the Romantics, for unknown to him Antonia is his sister, and his brutal and unrelenting determination on her violation is to involve him in the unspeakable crimes of rape, incest, murder and matricide. The novel's tension depends on the dialectic of evil and remorse; while early giving way to temptation, Ambrosio remains very reluctant to take the final step of selling his soul to the Devil, which is not, as with Faust, the precondition of his wickedness. It is only at the very close of the novel that he gives way when urged on by the second personal appearance of Lucifer, who dupes him mercilessly. Yet the strength of the influence exerted by fate ensures that the final outcome is never really in doubt, and behind the inevitability of Ambrosio's final commitment to the powers of evil we can detect the influence of predestinarian theology. It is his final despairing belief that he is 'doomed to perdition' which induces him to make the terrible compact which will rescue him from the vengeance of the Inquisition – only to receive, at the hands of Satan, a death yet more horrible.

*The Monk,* strongly influenced by the German *Schauerroman* or 'tale of terror', contains within the scope of the main plot and of the sub-plot, which deals with the popular theme of the enforced religious vow, almost every characteristic and device of the Gothic romance. The subterranean dungeons, the fearful backdrop of the Inquisition, the person of Lucifer and the compact with the Devil, the figures of the Wandering Jew and the Bleeding Nun, clerical perfidy and crime, evil and penitence, passion and reason, every kind of sexual perversion, the terrible eyes, the thrill of horror. Many of these themes are recapitulated in the last major Gothic novel, *Melmoth the Wanderer* (1820), by the Irish Protestant clergy-man Charles Maturin, a work endowed, in the words of Mario Praz, with 'a subtlety of penetration into the terrors of the souls such as is elsewhere only found in Poe'.[6] *Melmoth* is also the only considerable Gothic novel in English, until we come to the Gothic resurgence at the end of the nineteenth century, which embodies certain of its preoccupations in the figure of a double.

Maturin's romance shares with *The Monk*, upon which it is considerably dependent, a virulently anti-Catholic viewpoint, which is imparted with even less lightness of touch than that attained by Lewis. A priest's profession, for instance, is said to have 'torn every tie of nature and passion; and if it generates malignity, ambition, and the wish for mischief, it is the system, not the individual, we must blame'.[7] Yet the main story contained by the frame of the history of Melmoth the Wanderer, the story of Monçada, which concerns the latter's adventures and terrors in seeking to escape lifelong condemnation to a monastic religious life which he abhors, turns out, perhaps in spite of Maturin's conscious intentions, to take a very far from straightforward, and in some respects a very subtle, attitude to the issue of the broken religious vow.

The containing frame of the novel concerns the Promethean figure of Melmoth, born in the seventeenth century, who has sold his soul to the Devil in return for extended life, and who travels the world restlessly and agelessly as he seeks to trick or tempt others, always when they are *in extremis*, into accepting the transfer to them of his hated obligation. He is thus a variant of the figure of the Wandering Jew. His nineteenth-century descendant first recognises him from a portrait, which, reflecting a folkloric belief, functions as a kind of rudimentary double. Melmoth is a proud, commanding, mocking presence; his eyes, both in the portrait and in the flesh, shine with 'an infernal and dazzling lustre' (p. 54); Monçada, in the darkness of his prison, has to hold up his hand to shield himself from their 'preternatural glare'. All his efforts to exchange destinies with a victim fail, however, and as the hour at last approaches when he must pay his debt to the infernal powers, 'that appalling and supernatural lustre of the visual organ' is dimmed, and 'the lines of extreme old age were visible in every feature' (pp. 535, 540). (The motifs of the portrait and the sudden ageing were later to be combined in a famous novel of the double life, *The Picture of Dorian Gray*, by Maturin's great-nephew Oscar Wilde.[8]) Monçada and the younger Melmoth listen in horror as, with the hour of midnight, the appalling sounds commence which tell them that the Wanderer is, like Dr Faustus, being carried off by demons to eternal torment.

It is the story of Alonzo Monçada, however, in which the role of doubles is employed to suggest the convolutions of the protagonist's divided will. This young man of aristocratic origin has been assigned to the monastic life in infancy by his parents because he was born out of wedlock, although they have subsequently married. His condemnation to this hated life is represented as vital in their own eyes to their spiritual well-being and peace of mind, as it represents a vicarious atonement for their sin and also removes from their lives a presence which served as a rebuke. They weep for his suffering, but insist on its necessity. The monastic life which he endures is, of course, a nightmare of hypocrisy and oppression, of meanness, pettiness, vindictiveness and intrigue.

Monçada has a younger, legitimate, brother, who enjoys all the material advantages which are denied to the hero, as well as being taller, more confident, more brilliant. At first he is an object of envy and resentment to his brother, whom he has been taught to despise, but when Alonzo discovers his sympathy for his plight and his determination to help him escape from the monastery, Juan becomes endowed by him with every virtue and the recipient of his passionate affection. Juan, for his part, longs to be recognised by his brother as benefactor and patron, and becomes obsessed with the injury being done to him, for which he feels personal guilt. Alonzo becomes his double, his 'visionary companion': 'A figure like yours sat beside me in the carriage, alighted when we stopped, accompanied me where I remained, assisted me when I was placed again in the carriage. So vivid was this impression, that I was accustomed to say to my attendants, "Stop, my brother is assisting me"' (p. 123).

Juan, having fled from his parents' mansion, dedicates himself to his brother's liberation, and enlists the help of a conspirator within the monastery, 'a wretch whom nature must revolt from', a monk who has been guilty of parricide. The relationship between the brothers, however, is ambiguous: 'In proportion as Juan's confidence increased, mine appeared to diminish' (p. 179); yet he feels too that 'The precipitate vigour of Juan's movements seemed to impel mine without my own concurrence.' As the hour of his projected escape approaches, Monçada reflects on 'a destiny thus singularly entrusted to a being whose affections honoured humanity, and a being whose crimes disgraced it'. Gradually he moves from the dominance of one double to that of an opposite one, who is an 'incarnate devil', 'a monster who had tried to hide the stains of parricide, by casting over their bloody and ineffaceable traces the shroud of monasticism' (p. 181). The symbiotic identity between Monçada and the monk becomes established: 'I said in passing, "I am in your power." A hoarse repulsive voice answered, "No, I am in yours." I murmured, "Well then, I understand you, we belong to each other"' (p. 182).

The acquisition of this new and diabolical double comes at a significant moment. Hitherto, Alonzo has made no question of his motivation in seeking to escape from the monastery, and given no thought to the wider moral implications. He has been unjustly consigned to perpetual immuration in an institution which he loathes, and feels that he has right wholly on his side in his determination to free himself. Juan in his impetuous confidence, and as representing a vision of what Alonzo himself might have been had his fate been different, has been the flattering embodiment of this proud self-assurance. But now, at the moment of crisis, Alonzo falters. He enters the church to pray but cannot do so: 'I sought the church with a purpose of imposture and deception and abused the hour allotted to divine worship in contriving the means to escape from it. I felt I was a deceiver, shrouding my fraud in the very veils of the temple' (p. 183). A little later, in a similar situation, his self-doubt reaches new heights: 'As I knelt, I trembled at my own hypocrisy. I was profaning the altar of God . . . I was the worst of all hypocrites, a hypocrite on my knees, and at the altar' (p. 189).

The dark side of Monçada's aspirations now emerges. He is breaking a vow, refusing the service of God, destroying the peace of mind of his parents. He is later to learn that his conduct has resulted in their separation, his father's descent into alternating voluptuousness and penitence, his mother's retiral to a convent. Morally and symbolically he may be said to be a parricide, and this darkness in his character, which has hitherto been concealed by its morally self-assured surface, is now expressed in his identity with the parricide monk, and by their mutual dependence, for they must escape together. In the perilous attempt, their differing capacities complement each other: 'He possessed active, and I passive fortitude' (p. 190). In spite of their mutual loathing, they are bound together by 'the iron link of necessity' as they await in the horrors of the monastery's underground labyrinths the hour of their escape. When at last this is effected, the monk stabs Juan, who has been waiting without to complete Monçada's liberation. The evil double has slain the good.

Alonzo awakes after a long period of unconsciousness to find himself in a cell, attended by a figure who turns out to be the companion who has betrayed him. The latter reveals to him his murder of Juan, how the convent had bribed him with the promise of salvation. When Monçada reviles him as a traitor and murderer, his double replies with a masterful extended volley of rhetorical invective. Monçada has reclaimed his vows, seduced his brother from his duty to their parents, intrigued against monastic sanctity, callously and without conscience clung to the aid of one whom he knew to be an irreligious parricide, and whom in turn he was seducing from his vows. Coldly and deliberately he has struck at the hearts of father and mother: 'You killed by inches, – I murdered at a blow; – which of us is the murderer? – And *you* prate of treachery and murder?' He is the poisonous Upas tree and 'the erosions of the poison, having nothing left to consume strike inward, and prey on your heart' (p. 221). Then he reveals his own nihilistic faith, 'the theology of utter hostility to all beings whose sufferings may mitigate mine. In this flattering theory, your crimes became my virtue . . . your guilt is my exculpation, your sufferings are my triumph . . . I have literally worked out *my* salvation by *your* fear and trembling' (p. 225). With this parody of two famous Scriptural passages the parricide expounds the nature of their symbiotic relation;[9] and he reveals that Monçada is now in the prison of the Inquisition.

There he suffers horrors analogous to those undergone by Agnes in the sub-plot of *The Monk*. He escapes during a fire which destroys the prison building, just as the convent in which Agnes had been immured was also destroyed; he unwittingly rests on the grave of his brother and double; and from the window of the Jew's house where he has taken refuge witnesses the parricide torn to pieces by a furious mob, a fate identical to that of the Domina, the tormentress of Agnes in the earlier novel. The story of Monçada opens on to further tales in the series of open-sided Chinese boxes which forms the curious and clumsy structure of *Melmoth the Wanderer*; but his own history has already attained its moral climax.

Maturin has achieved in this tale a subtle interplay of two doubles who can be taken as personifying contrasting ways in which the hero's conduct may be viewed. His brother represents the daylight vision of himself as a wronged victim nobly endeavouring to reverse his fate; but when in plotting his escape he begins to be assailed by doubts and fears, there arises before him in the role of his accomplice a fearful, magnified and distorted reflection of an absolutely contrary aspect of his conduct and personality, and this double rebukes his complacency and presumption.

## WILLIAM GODWIN AND CHARLES BROCKDEN BROWN

William Godwin began to write *Caleb Williams* (1794) shortly after the publication of his *magnum opus, Enquiry Concerning Political Justice* (1793). It was intended by its author as 'a study and delineation of things passing in the moral world . . . a general review of the modes of domestic and unrecorded despotism by which man becomes the destroyer of man'.[10] It is thus a fictional expression of the philosophical anarchism of the earlier work, and an indictment of the tyrannies of the aristocratic government of his day and of the administration of justice in Britain.[11] Godwin, however, had always felt 'some vocation towards the composition of a narrative of fictitious adventure'; he planned one that would be 'distinguished by a very powerful interest', dealing with themes of flight and pursuit, and he was quickly caught up in the psychological implications of his chosen plot. In planning the novel he worked backwards from this idea of flight and pursuit towards the situations from which such an adventure might have arisen.[12]

Compared with the extremities of emotion, expression and situation characteristic of the Gothic romance, *Caleb Williams* may appear pervaded with a calm and rational spirit; but beneath this more civilised surface lurk passions no less irrational and frightening. The doubling in this novel is usually seen in terms of the pursuer-who-becomes-the-pursued relationship between Caleb and his employer Mr Falkland, with Caleb, as Hazlitt was quick to notice, functioning as Falkland's externalised conscience; but there is a prior use of the device on which the other depends, and which is no less interesting.

Godwin's plot required the murder on which it hinged to have been committed by one not only favoured by fortune in terms of material advantages and intellectual resources, but also of the highest virtue, 'so that his being driven to the first act of murder . . . should be seen in some measure to have arisen out of his virtues themselves'; the reader, in fact, 'should feel prompted almost to worship him for his high qualities' (p. 349). The character of Mr Falkland is indeed developed in just such a way. He is a man whose ruling passion is honour, and its offshoot, an honourable reputation. To begin with, however, Falkland's conception of honour is not limited to its narrower social meaning; it comprises what may be called in the broadest sense rectitude and natural justice. His weakness, however, is pride, which makes him react in a fiery, though initially also in a highly controlled and restrained manner, to any possible imputed slur on his personal honour.

Mr Falkland returns from a sojourn abroad, having distinguished himself for gallantry and virtue and with his honour unspotted and unstained, to take up the management of his estates. Immediately he falls foul of a neighbouring squire, Barnabas Tyrrel, who is remarkable for the barbarity and tyranny of his conduct. Hitherto Tyrrel has been undisputed cock of the local midden, but now finds himself displaced by the admiration universally bestowed on Falkland. In everything they are opposites: Tyrrel is coarse-grained where Falkland is refined, uneducated where Falkland is cultured, violent and unrestrained in his passions where his rival is cool and controlled, vengeful and malicious where the other is just and upright, physically powerful and brutal where Falkland is small and delicate. Tyrrel acquires an intense jealousy and hatred of Falkland, who without any intention of malice shows himself superior on every occasion, bests him in everything and crosses him in the evil and tyrannous designs he entertains on his social inferiors and any whom he has in his power. 'This Falkland', he exclaims, 'haunts me like a demon. I cannot wake but I think of him. I cannot sleep but I see him. He poisons all my pleasures' (p. 33). Projecting on to Falkland qualities of his own character, he sees in him his 'rival and persecutor', an embodiment of 'that blind and malicious power which delighted to cross his most deep-laid schemes' (p. 83).

Relations between the rival squires reach a point of crisis when

Falkland thwarts Tyrrel in his brutal attempt to force his cousin and ward, Emily Melville, into a hated match. Tyrrel's response is to have Emily cast into jail as a debtor; she dies there, and Tyrrel suffers complete social ostracism. When, enraged and baffled, he attempts to force his way into a local gathering, he is publicly rebuked and dismissed by Falkland. He returns drunk and batters his rival to the ground in the presence of all. To Falkland, for whom 'Reputation has been the idol, the jewel of my life', this represents the most appalling imaginable stain on his honour, an indelible and unendurable humiliation. He follows Tyrrel into the street, and, unwitnessed, stabs him to death.

From the moment of Tyrrel's murder, Falkland's character begins to degenerate. He becomes gloomy, melancholic, withdrawn, and subject to fits of violent anger. This is generally attributed to the effects of the terrible stain on his reputation which he has suffered from the assault of Tyrrel; and Caleb, once he knows the secret, perceives it as resulting from the weight of guilt and concealment by which his master is oppressed. It is clear, though, that it is not so much the fact of his being a murderer that oppresses him as the terror of the final loss of his reputation which would result from exposure. His ideal has degenerated from a conception of honour based on rectitude to one of honour based solely on reputation, without any recognition of a necessary relation between the two.

The decline of his moral consciousness appears most fatally in his allowing the Hawkinses, oppressed tenants of Tyrrel whose cause he had previously championed, to go to the gallows for his crime, without raising a finger. On any normal judgement this would, in the light of Falkland's established character, be incredible; but if Falkland and Tyrrel are regarded as complementary opposites, then we can see that Tyrrel represents the submerged dark side of Falkland's personality, which, after the former's death, surfaces and asserts itself within the murderer's character. By the murder of Tyrrel he releases the Tyrrel in himself. While Tyrrel lived, Falkland seemed like the accusing, external conscience which that tyrant lacked within himself; dead, Tyrrel is reincarnated as a part of Falkland.

Such a moral reversal in the character of Mr Falkland would only be possible, however, on the assumption that his admirable qualities were vitiated by an underlying pride, the false pride of the Gothic romance tradition. It is always overweening pride which prepares the way for such a psychic influx of evil impulses. Such a view is borne out by a comment of Mr Collins, who has related the history of his employer to Caleb Williams. From the moment of his loss of reputation at the hands of Tyrrel, Collins explains (he is, of course, unaware that Falkland is Tyrrel's murderer), life has become a burden on him: 'No more self-complacency, no more rapture, no more self-approving and heart-transporting benevolence!' (p. 101). Falkland's complacent self-regard acquires a far more sinister colour when, obsessed by the endeavour to protect what remains of his good name, he becomes – taking on the implacable persecuting character of the slain Tyrrel – the pursuing tormentor of Caleb. Caleb and Falkland, however, are also doubles.

Caleb represents the spring of action which draws him into the investigation of Falkland's past as being curiosity. Curiosity is his obsession and his Achilles' heel, as reputation in his master's. He early admits also to a certain vanity and 'love of praise' (p. 6). This is mentioned only in passing, and his pride is certainly not of the same order as Falkland's. It has to be remembered, however, that Caleb is, like Monçada, his own narrator, and his own view of his conduct is somewhat offset by Falkland's view of it, just as Monçada's is offset by that of the parricide monk. In the same way that Falkland takes over, or allows to become active in himself, the character of Tyrrel, so do the characters of Caleb and Falkland, as their involvement and animosity deepen, undergo various interchanges of personality, and each acquires some of the other's characteristics.

Taken into Falkland's employment and confidence as his secretary, Caleb soon begins to suspect that his master is the murderer of Tyrrel. His inveterate curiosity is whetted by the mystery and his spirit roused by the danger of the enterprise: 'To be a spy upon Mr Falkland!' (p. 112). His suspicion in no degree lessens his unbounded admiration for Falkland, and actually increases the 'magnetical' sympathy between them. This sympathy does not inhibit Caleb from tormenting his employer with probing questions. 'I have always tried to stop myself,' he confesses, 'but the demon that possessed me was too strong for me' (p. 125); like so many other heroes of the period, he projects his weakness on to a malevolent fate. Feelings of guilt and insatiable curiosity vie in him in 'a contention of opposite principles' (p. 128). Aware of his secretary's prying nature, Falkland in turn becomes watchful and suspicious, so that 'we were each of us a plague to the other' (p. 128). When Caleb becomes finally convinced of Falkland's guilt, his conviction induces in him a 'state of mental elevation'; and at this juncture Falkland's shadow passes him in the garden. The two are about to exchange roles.

Caleb now breaks into a chest in his efforts to find evidence, but is caught in the act. Falkland presents a pistol at his head, but draws back from another murder; that night he sends for him and confesses that he is the murderer of Tyrrel, swearing him to secrecy under the threat of death or worse. Too late, Caleb realises that he must live henceforth in the shadow of Falkland's insatiable vengeance, a prisoner of his untiring vigilance: 'All my actions observed; all my gestures marked' (p. 149). The hunter is now the hunted, and as he struggles to free himself from his master's stranglehold, the later reacts with all the persecuting malevolence of a Tyrrel, even using the kind of language previously employed by that 'devil incarnate': 'Begone, miscreant! reptile! and cease to contend with insurmountable power!' (p. 160).

Falkland forms the determination to save his own reputation by utterly blackening that of Williams; he frames him on a serious charge of theft which could lead Caleb to the gallows. The latter is now fighting for his life; but ironically he also begins to resemble Falkland in the concern which he shows for his reputation, 'the whiteness of my name'. Imprisoned on this false charge, he positively basks in the contemplation of his innocence: 'Blessed state of innocence and self-approbation! The sunshine of conscious integrity pierced through all the barriers of my cell' (p. 192).

The novel now develops into a taut and compulsive adventure of escape and pursuit, a cat-and-mouse game in which Caleb is always allowed just enough leeway to escape the gallows, but never enough to free himself from his hunted condition. All this has been planned by the malice and the 'colossal intelligence' of Mr Falkland, aided by the diabolical spy Gines, a second Falkland in relentless animosity. But Caleb gains strength and resolve through persecution: 'I would show myself bitter and inflexible as he had done' (p. 284). He has come to resemble his tormentor in other ways, too. As a fugitive in London he is given shelter and comfort by a benevolent lady, Mrs Marney, who he later learns has been sent to Newgate on a charge of abettting him. 'My sympathy for Mrs Marney however was at this moment a transient one', he casually remarks (p. 279). He is content to let another suffer for him, and his selfishness in this respect is an analogy to Falkland's far wickeder consignment of the Hawkinses to the gallows for his crime.

At last, after suffering for years the shadowing of the 'execrable Gines', which he likens to 'the eye of Omniscience pursuing the guilty sinner', Caleb resolves to do what he has always mysteriously shrunk from doing: denounce Falkland to the authorities. At their final confrontation before the magistrate Falkland appears like a corpse, all but eaten away by the spiritual cancer that is destroying him. As Caleb, utterly dismayed at this sight, begins his story, he immediately condemns his own purpose in accusing his former master as 'diabolical'. A complete emotional *renversement* takes place within him. While telling the truth of the story, he affirms the 'noble nature' of Falkland and expatiates on his admirable qualities, while condemning himself as 'the basest and most odious of mankind' (p. 334). Falkland then responds in kind, throwing himself into Caleb's arms: '"Williams," said he, "you have conquered! I see too late the greatness and elevation of your mind . . . My name will be consecrated to infamy, while your heroism, your patience and your virtues will be for ever admired . . . I am the most execrable of all villains"' (p. 335).

This speech does nothing to relieve Caleb's remorse. Falkland dies before he can be brought to justice, and Caleb condemns himself as his murderer: 'But, atrocious, execrable wretch that I have been! I wantonly inflicted on him an anguish a thousand times worse than death.' The misery of the past years is utterly forgotten as he extravagantly eulogises Falkland: 'A nobler spirit lived not among the sons of men.' As for himself, he condemns his self-regard as the root of the whole tragedy: ' – self, an overweening regard to which has been the source of my errors!' (p. 336).

What are we to make of this? Where before each protagonist could, at least by this stage in their relation, see only virtue and justification in himself, and wickedness and malignity in his adversary, now, at the catastrophe, each condemns himself as execrable and lauds the nobility of his foe. If we regard Falkland and Caleb simply as two separate characters whose destinies have become interlocked through fate, this reversal might seem unrealistic or even absurd, or at best as satisfying a demand for symmetry and reconciliation which would be merely dramatically appropriate but not psychologically persuasive. If, however, they are seen as opposing mirror-images of a single complex and self-divided personality, then their embrace can be discovered to acknowledge their identity and their mutual dependence.

Their long confrontation has been, for each man, a painful struggle towards self-knowledge. Each, in pride and complacency, has been unwilling to recognise his own failings. Each has required the opposition of the other in order to know and confront the darkness in himself. Caleb has set out to vindicate his own character, but ends with no other concern than to elevate that of Falkland. Master and servant have each come to know themselves only by gazing long at their reflection in each other. Reconciliation with the other within has been made possible by recognition of the other without.

In the interlocking pairs of doubles, Tyrrel and Falkland and Falkland and Caleb, Godwin has found a way of dramatising complexities and contradictions and dualities of personality which could only have been realised in a single character by employing much wider resources: a richer canvas, much more complex interaction with others, and greater psychological depth. With Falkland the pivot, we have in *Caleb Williams* two kinds of double: Tyrrel the externalisation of an unacknowledged fragment of personality, Caleb the modified mirror-image. For Caleb, whose path to self-knowledge the novel, in its psychological aspect, charts, Falkland becomes himself writ large, and it is only when he can salute once more the good in Falkland that he can acknowledge the negative elements in himself.

Charles Brockden Brown, the first important American writer of fiction, was a deep admirer of Godwin, and admired by him in turn. A pronounced rationalist, he was fascinated by new discoveries bearing on the underside of the human psyche, and took pleasure in laying bare the natural and 'scientific' determinants of those mysterious and obscure aspects of mind and behaviour which delighted the Romantic idealists. He remained very open, however, to the reality of the perverse and irrational as a determining factor in human action.

All of Brockden Brown's fiction is shot through with duality, but two of his novels in particular play interesting variations on the theme of the double: *Wieland* (1798), the plot of which hinges on

the phenomenon of ventriloquism, and *Edgar Huntly* (1799), which
similarly takes somnambulism as the spring of its action. The plot
of *Wieland* is highly complicated and convoluted, but the underlying
idea is simple. It concerns two brother-and-sister pairs, Wieland
and his sister Clara, who is the narrator of the story, and Wieland's
wife Catherine and her brother Henry Pleyel.

The Wielands are the offspring of a religious obsessive, an
immigrant from Europe (and said to be kin to the German Romantic
poet Wieland), who imagines himself 'beset by the snares of
a spiritual foe', and dies mysteriously of what appears to be
spontaneous combustion. His death prompts in Clara gloomy
thoughts on fate and predestination, which centre on fears for her
brother, who considerably resembles his father in character. The
younger Wieland is presented however as something of a human
paragon, a man of 'forethought and sobriety' and refined sensibility, a Classical scholar and admirer of Cicero, though also deeply
religious.

The happiness of the little family group is unexpectedly disturbed
by a series of apparently supernatural incidents: a voice, identical
to Catherine's but which cannot be hers, enunciates mysterious
warnings. These emanate from the summer house which was the
private temple of the elder Wieland, and seem to be associated
with his fate. Shortly after this a rough, uncouth figure makes his
appearance at Clara's door; she feels a mingled repulsion and
attraction for him, moved to tears by the 'force and sweetness' of
his accents and fascinated by a picture of him which she acquires,
which reveals features which, though odd, 'betoken a mind of the
highest order'.[13] The family become friendly with this Carwin,
an Englishman and former Catholic convert in Spain, who for
mysterious reasons has assumed in America the garb of a rustic.
Clara cannot decide whether Carwin is good or evil, and wonders
whether his mysteriousness is prompted by the shame of some
guilt.

Meanwhile the voices continue and become more sinister, and
their suggestions cause a disastrous rift between Clara and her
lover Pleyel. Clara now regards Carwin with fear and horror,
suspecting him to be 'in league with some infernal spirit' until she
reminds herself that 'There are no devils but those which are
begotten upon selfishness, and reared by cunning' (pp. 148, 150).
When he sends her a note urging her to a meeting, she feels
herself 'divested of the power to will contrary to the motives

that determined me to seek his presence' (p. 159). Rationalist psychology and Romantic determinism thus struggle for primacy in Clara's consciousness. The horrific and unexpected catastrophe occurs when the pacific and civilised Wieland brutally murders his wife and children, at the prompting of a voice which has enjoined this sacrifice upon him as a religious duty – a voice which has 'changed him who was the glory of his species into worse than brute' (p. 222).

Carwin now confesses that he is the cause of all these disasters. He has used his art of ventriloquism to sow havoc in the lives of the Wieland family out of some unexplained impulse of perverse curiosity and experimentation. From the point of view of Clara he is indeed diabolical, the 'enemy of man': who has urged Wieland to his terrible deed, she asks, 'but thou and the devil, with whom thou art confederated?' (p. 220). Carwin himself, who has indeed a dark past, can only admit that 'some daemon of mischief seized me', that he is pursued by some 'perverse fate': 'for the sake of creating a mysterious dread, I have made myself a villain' (pp. 227, 231, 235).

If mystery attaches to the motivation of the devilish Carwin, the irruption of evil in Wieland is ultimately even more inexplicable. While he seems to others to be 'leagued with hell', he himself protests that 'If a devil has deceived me, he came in the habit of an angel' (p. 251). While the parallel religious delusion of his father suggests that he is the victim of heredity and fate, his own spiritual blindness and infatuation are not the less blameworthy. As Clara recognises, 'If Wieland had framed juster notions of moral duty, and of the divine attributes . . . the double-tongued deceiver would have been baffled and repelled' (p. 273). Once more, in an outwardly exemplary character a dark and irrational inner force has been summoned up by an external agency which personifies it. A disastrous moral revolution has occurred in a character apparently virtuous and saintly, but perhaps blinkered and self-complacent to the point of madness; and the previously unsuspected negative dimension of the personality is expressed and drawn out by the figure of a diabolic double.

*Edgar Huntly* is strongly influenced by *Caleb Williams* in being an adventure of pursuit, of the hunter hunted, in which the action is initiated by the hero's 'ungovernable curiosity'.[14] Edg. r, determined to discover the truth about the murder of his friend Waldegrave, finds his suspicions aroused by the curious nocturnal behaviour of one Clithero Edny, an Irish worker on a neighbouring farm, whom he observes digging under the elm which has been the scene of the killing. On successive nights he follows Clithero on his rampages through the wilderness, and it becomes apparent to him that the mysterious figure is sleepwalking.

After a time he confronts Clithero and demands an explanation. The Irishman exculpates himself from any blame in the murder of Waldegrave but narrates his curious and fateful history; he believes himself controlled by a 'daemon' and his calamities to have resulted from 'the scheme of some infernal agent' (p. 29). The son of peasant parents in Ireland, he has been taken up by a benevolent patroness, Mrs Lorimer, raised as a second son, and favoured by the promise of the hand of her niece, Clarice. But his fair fortune is reversed by the return of Mrs Lorimer's twin brother, Wiatte, identical to her in looks but utterly opposite in character, a figure of 'pure unadulterated evil' (p. 44). She feels an invincible love of her twin, and an identity with him which extends to a belief that they will die at the same time; and when Clithero kills the devilishly scheming Wiatte in self-defence, his mind, already obsessed by the notion of fatality, is turned by the belief that 'The fate of Wiatte would inevitably draw along with it that of his sister' (p. 74). Believing himself to have caused her death (she is actually still alive) as the result of actions instigated by the 'evil genius' by whom he feels himself possessed, 'of whose malice a mysterious destiny had assigned me to be the sport and prey' (p. 81), Clithero has escaped to America to while away his remaining days in unappeasable sorrow and melancholy.

Shortly after telling Edgar his story, Clithero disappears. Now filled with sympathy for the sufferings of the man he has been pursuing, Huntly seeks him out, exploring the underground cave system into which he has once seen him disappear; in pursuit of his double he is venturing into the abysmal caverns of the unconscious. One night Edgar goes to bed as usual, and wakes to find himself lying, fearfully battered, in the total darkness of a pit in the depths of the cave. His subsequent terrifying adventures occupy a considerable portion of the novel. He struggles out only to find himself the prey of Indians, for the town where he lives is close to the frontier and the tribes from the interior are raiding the European settlements (it transpires that they were the killers of Waldegrave). There follows an intensely gripping, if wildly improbable, tale of pursuit and escape, at the conclusion of which the solution of many complicated mysteries is revealed.

Edgar, like Clithero, is a somnambulist, and while asleep has entered the cave and fallen into the pit. 'What but this solution ought to have been suggested by the conduct I had witnessed in Clithero?' (p. 252). The identity between the two is revealed in extraordinary parallels. Clithero's devotion to Euphemia Lorimer's memoirs is matched by Edgar's to Waldegrave's letters. Each removes them during sleep from a hiding-place of his own contrivance and hides them again; and each rediscovers them in what seem like miraculous circumstances which each attributes to supernatural intervention. The correspondence is not lost on Huntly, nor the implications of the somnambulistic acts of himself and his double: 'Disastrous and humiliating is the state of man! By his own hands is constructed the mass of misery and error in which his steps are for ever involved' (p. 268).

Edgar now believes he can rehabilitate Clithero by revealing that Mrs Lorimer is still alive; her husband Sarsefield (Edgar's former teacher) vehemently disagrees, believing Clithero to be a wicked madman whose faculties have been mastered by an 'agent from Hell' – which was, of course, Clithero's own belief. Rashly, the hero persists in his purpose, with disastrous results. Clithero is in fact a maniac, and Edgar remembers too late his earlier insight: 'How little cognizance have men over the actions and motives of each other! How total is our blindness with regard to our own performances!' (p. 268). As a result of his wilful rashness and blindness Mrs Lorimer loses the child she is carrying, and Clithero his life. Edgar is left bitterly to regret the evil caused by his 'unfortunate temerity'.

The pervasive theme of *Edgar Huntly* is blindness and unconsciousness. These are powerfully symbolised by sleepwalking and by the absolute darkness of the caves — natural symbols of the unconscious – in which so considerable a part of the action takes place. Burying and hiding, too, suggest wilful repression of consciousness. Edgar and Clithero are equally implicated in lack of insight and self-knowledge. Clithero allows himself to be taken over by Mrs Lorimer's irrational and delusory obsession concerning the identity of her fate with that of her twin brother. He believes himself the victim of an evil daemon, but fails to see that it is this conviction which itself constitutes his possession and determines his fate. Edgar is wilfully blind to the madness of Clithero with whom he has come to be identified, and no more sees the consequences of his own actions than he sees the pit into which he falls while sleepwalking. The pryings of his early curiosity are like his gropings in the cave while awake, the impetuosity of his later conduct like his somnambulistic descent into the abyss. Each is ruled by his unconscious passions and the more fearful blindness of Clithero is a magnified reflection of Edgar's self-delusion.

Brockden Brown's variations on the double are less organic and more mechanical and contrived than those of his master, Godwin, but they are of very considerable interest among those manipulations of the motif which eschew any supernatural dimension.

## CHAMISSO AND ANDERSEN

None of the examples of the double that we have so far examined has included a true supernatural element. In the pages of the Gothic romance the fantastic and the supernatural proliferate on every page, yet the one important use of the device in the English Gothic novel, that of Maturin in the Monçada tale, happens not to have any overtly supernatural aspect. Godwin and Brockden Brown were rationalists who had no resort to anything outside conceivable natural experience in teasing out the psychological interrelations of their double characters. Yet the central tradition of the double was to develop through strategies to which the supernatural element was indispensable, and this element, by a paradox that is perhaps more apparent than real, was greatly to enhance the psychological depth and potential of the device. It is in the German tradition that this development originates.

We have seen that the shadow was primordially regarded as an extension of the self and perhaps even as a representation of the soul. No good, then, may be expected to follow for the man who sells his shadow to the Devil; and this is the fate of the hero of *Peter Schlemihl* (1814), by Adalbert von Chamisso. Chamisso was a typical Romantic divided man, his particular duality exacerbated by an uncertain national identity: born in France but raised in Berlin after his family had fled the French Revolution, he came to regard Germany as his spiritual fatherland, but was always deracinated and never fully at home in either country. At last he found himself, as his translator describes, 'without a shadow – that is to say, without established or recognised background, a born Frenchman, a former Prussian officer, an exile in his own homeland – a sorry figure, a "Schlemihl"' – which, in Yiddish, means an 'unlucky, ridiculous person'.[15]

Karl Miller has underlined the closeness of the tale to folklore.[16] There is a curious feeling of insubstantiality to this fable, appropriate to its subject, but it has, too, a haunting, ethereal quality that remains in the mind. Peter Schlemihl, as rootless as his creator, meets the Devil at a garden-party, in the form of a 'man in grey', a quiet, elderly, thin man with magic pockets from which he can produce any number of weird and wonderful objects. Shadowed by this 'ghostly' and 'sinister' figure, the hero feels 'like a bird hyponotised by a snake' (p. 21). The offer made by the grey man is the acquisition of Schlemihl's shadow in return for the lucky purse of Fortunatus, an exchange which turns out to be far from fortunate. The deal done, he puts the shadow in his pocket, and Peter hears him 'softly laughing to himself' (p. 23).

The symbolism of the story may be variously interpreted, and there can be different understandings of what it is that Schlemihl loses when he sells his shadow: probably it is the psychic wholeness on which he depends to function in the world. The horror of being shadowless is assumed by all whom he meets; the loss is shameful and even reprehensible. It is something vital which he has given up, and his character without it is one of extreme defectiveness. Having traded away his shadow he must live in the shade, condemned to avoid the sun which would pitilessly betray his secret. The false exchange implies moral subversion: 'as I had previously held my conscience higher than wealth, I had now given up my shadow for the sake of gold' (p. 25). He is soon weary and disgusted with his limitless wealth, and steals away like a criminal. The man in grey has 'vanished like a shadow, leaving no trace behind', but promises to return in a year and a day.

If a shadow is an annexe of the self, so is a portrait, and Peter asks a painter to provide him with a new shadow, but the artist will have nothing to do with the proposal. The world has rejected the shadowless man and he has to keep on fleeing, pursued by the Devil in the form of a mysterious stranger who continually thwarts his designs. For a time he settles in a watering-place where, because of his vast riches, he is thought to be a visiting potentate, 'Count Peter', perhaps the King of Prussia in disguise. (This is a recurrent motif in Romantic tales of the period: the Wandering Jew, in his brief appearance in *The Monk*, is believed to be 'The Great Mogul', and James Hogg's justified sinner will later labour under the illusion that his devilish double is the Czar Peter of Russia.) Here Schlemihl falls in love with the beautiful Mina, but in spite of all his efforts to conceal his condition by appearing in public only in the evening, or when he can hide in the shade, she begins to suspect his secret, and at last he is betrayed by his rascally servant, Rascal.

Schlemihl has two servants, a good and a bad, who function in his life rather like the Good and Bad Angels of medieval folk belief. The good servant, Bendel, is unshakeably faithful, and devotes himself to protecting his master's interests and pursuing the grey man whenever he has an opportunity. The latter reappears at the promised hour, and at the crucial moment at which Mina's father has given Peter three days in which to acquire a shadow, and offers Schlemihl his shadow back in return for his soul after death, a compact to be signed in his own blood. It is apparent, then, that the previous deal has been only as it were provisional; he has compromised himself, but not fatally. The possibility of redemption still exists; and in spite of being shown his shadow he refuses the bargain.

After various further adventures, including the 'despicable theft' of a magic bird's nest which confers invisibility, he returns, pursued by the man in grey, to Mina's father's garden, only to find that his lover is about to marry the usurper, Rascal. The Devil provokes him into agreeing to sign the compact: 'Believe me, my friend, he who carelessly steps off the straight and narrow path, soon finds himself impelled step by step down a very different road, along which he will be led further and further astray' (p. 67). While preparing to sign, however, he swoons; when he awakes Mina is married to Rascal. He flees, pursued by his tormentor who tells him, 'man cannot escape his fate' (p. 69). He sets off again to wander restlessly through the world: 'I had no goal, no wish, no hope on earth.'

The dramatic tension of the tale hinges, as so often in stories of moral division, on whether the protagonist will succumb to the suggestions and persuasions of his tempter (whether internal or external) that he is powerless in the hands of fate, that he cannot resist his destiny, that he is beyond repentance and redemption. To believe this is, of course, to enforce its truth. In the case of Schlemihl, this fatal suggestion is resisted. The Devil appears to him in a new metamorphosis as a travelling companion whose philosophisings convince Peter's mind but not his heart. He lends him his shadow back, with the proviso that it will only stick to him when he is once more its legal owner; and, dogging him as his valet ('I hold you by your shadow – you cannot escape me'; p. 74), drives him back to earthly vanities. In spite of all, however, Schlemihl determines not to transfer his soul. At last 'I could no longer endure my inner conflict and the decisive struggle began.' He hurls the fatal purse into the abyss and the power of the man in grey is broken. 'He rose darkly and left me. His figure seemed to vanish immediately behind the masses of savage rocks' (p. 78).

A load has dropped from Peter's heart, but he can redeem himself only at a price, which is solitariness and isolation. He can never again fully re-enter the world of men. Abandoning his possessions he sets out alone, and unknowingly buying seven-league boots is enabled to pass at a stride from land to land, determined to study the glories of nature which he finds wherever he goes. Thus expiating his sin, he is another type of the Wandering Jew. So he lives on as a scientist, a 'solitary man of learning', his experience a terrible warning to others who may find themselves seduced by externalities from their true path. 'But if you choose to live for your inner self alone, you will need no counsel of mine' (p. 93).

*Peter Schlemihl* is unusual among stories of the double in that it is a tale of privation rather than of duplication or division. Without his shadow, Peter is less than a whole man; but his second, complementary self is known only by its absence. It is only by losing it that he becomes aware of its reality, and the shadow never acquires a separate life of its own. It is quite otherwise with Hans Christian Andersen's 'The Shadow' (written in the early 1840s), the most interesting of the many shadow-romances to be inspired by Chamisso's original. It picks up the unasked question that can be derived from *Peter Schlemihl* – what happens to the shadow when it separates from its owner? In this obverse of the earlier story, the lost shadow takes on the character of a true double, and the theme is not one of privation, but of usurpation.

The hero is a young, 'learned man' from a cold country living in a hot country, who is exhausted by the heat, so that, like the original shadowless man, he is happiest out of the sun. There is a suggestion in this that he is abstracted from the warmth and the human relatedness of the living world, devoted as he is to the artistic representation of the good and the true and the beautiful. He falls in love with a lovely but elusive maiden who dwells in a room on the opposite side of the street, in an atmosphere of flowers and captivating music. One moonlit night, as his shadow rests on her balcony, he asks it to go in and observe what it finds there, and then return with its tidings. But next morning it has failed to return. The scholar decides to say nothing because, as Andersen explains in a self-conscious reference to his model, 'he knew there was a story about a man without a shadow which everyone at home in the cold countries knew; and if the learned man went there and told them his own story they would say he was merely imitating the other, and that he had no business to do'.[17]

He tries without success to get his shadow back, but soon a new one sprouts in its place. He returns home; many years pass. One evening an extraordinarily thin man appears at his door. 'Don't you recognise your old shadow?' he asks (p. 78). He is extremely well dressed, has done very well, and wants to buy himself out of service; but the scholar will not hear of payment. The former shadow explains his success. It was Poetry who lived opposite, and in Poetry's antechamber he has turned into a man and learned to know his 'innermost nature'. He has retained his shadow-like mobility, however, which enables him to see 'what everybody wants very much to know, that is their neighbours' wrong-doings. . . . They were terribly afraid of me, and they became amazingly fond of me' – hence his worldly success (p. 79). He goes off, but returns in a year and a day. The scholar is now in despair, for he continues to write about the good and the true and the beautiful, about which nobody wants to hear. The Shadow, on the contrary, is growing fat.

The learned man and his shadow are now exchanging roles. The former is fading into a shadow; and the shadow, who of course has no shadow of his own, suggests to his former master that he travel with him in that capacity. The scholar indignantly rejects the proposal as 'absolute madness', but this is in effect what happens: 'The Shadow was the master and the master was the shadow' (p. 80). They stop at a watering-place where there is a Beautiful Princess who astutely notices that the Shadow casts no shadow. The usurper claims that the scholar is his shadow, 'smartened up into a man', and obtains the credit for the wisdom of his erstwhile master. The Princess falls in love with him, and they marry, and the learned man is offered a pension on the most humiliating conditions: 'you must allow yourself to be called a shadow by everyone, you must never say that you were at one time a man, and once a year . . . you must lie at my feet as a shadow ought to do' (p. 81). He threatens to tell the truth, but no one will believe him. He is shut away as mad, and eventually executed.

This evocative fable symbolises the dreamy aesthete's incapacity to live. Rather than approach the girl in the room opposite himself, he sends his shadow to do the work for him, the shadow who embodies the active life which he can only yearn for. In this he anticipates the aestheticism of Pater: 'As for living, our servants will do that for us.' What the dreamer can do only in imagination the shadow does in reality, thus stealing from him the substance of his dreams just as he usurps the substance of his body. His dissociation is imaged in the separate life of this second self, which achieves its breakthrough into reality by attaining to that knowledge of its 'innermost nature' which is denied the artist and thinker, seduced as he is by phantoms, the abstractions of his unrealised ideals. As a cautionary tale it has a different meaning from *Peter Schlemihl*, but both are concerned with the ambiguities of shadow and substance, with the insight that the psyche is incomplete without its shadow-side, and with the conclusion that wholeness is possible only when these complementary aspects of the personality are bound together in harmony.

After Andersen's tale no further important additions were made to the shadow romance as a distinct sub-genre, but shadow imagery was to have a permanent part to play within the wider literature of duality.

# 4

# E. T. A. Hoffmann

E. T. A. Hoffmann has been described by one commentator, R. J. Hollingdale, as 'a two-sided, schizophrenic kind of man; by day a decent citizen and lawyer, by night a fantasist with a strong penchant for the freakish and the weird'.[1] He even invented for himself an *alter ego* in the person of Kapellmeister Johannes Kreisler, who obsessively reappears in Hoffmann's stories and finally comes to dominate his last, unfinished novel, *Kater Murr*. Kreisler has been described as being 'as faithful and complete an author's self-portrait as literature has to offer'.[2] Hollingdale develops his summary of the romancer's life and character in terms of this Jekyll-and-Hyde opposition. Hoffmann's tales are full of madness, supernatural happenings and fantastic developments, and repeatedly they depict minds divided against themselves to the point of pathology and possession, conjuring up the darkness within as palpable phantasms and fantastic realities which irrupt disastrously into the calm, civilized life with which they are satirically contrasted.

A typical double life is that of Master René Cardillac, the brilliant and pious master jeweller of 'Mademoiselle de Scudéry' (1819), who so identifies himself with his own creations that he cannot tolerate being separated from them and is consumed by hatred and resentment of their owners.[3] Driven on by what he believes to be his 'evil star', 'the whispering Satan at my ear', he becomes, in order to regain possession of the glittering masterpieces that are the indispensable adjuncts of his identity, compulsively addicted to robbery, violence and murder. While acting out of his second personality he experiences his compulsion as a fate which he is powerless to resist; but the tendency of Hoffmann's fictions is repeatedly to undermine the suggestion made by his protagonists that the forces which exert pressure on them truly deprive them of free will. However hard may be the choices with which they are confronted, the decision between good and evil is always ultimately their own. Where this appears not to be the case, it will be because there has been a prior unconscious collusion of the will which causes it to succumb to the powers of darkness.

A creative intelligence such as Hoffmann's, imbued with the idealism of Schelling, permeated with duality and greatly affected by the dualistic fantasies of Jean-Paul Richter, could not fail to be drawn to the concept of the double for the embodiment of its ingrained dividedness. It fell to Hoffmann, acute psychologist that he was, to bring to maturity the device of the supernatural double as a representation of the second self, 'the physical projection', as Ralph Tymms has put it, 'of the second of the mind's twin inmates'; 'the projection', that is, 'of the unconscious, and hitherto latent second self as a physical *Doppelgänger*, apparent to the senses'.[4]

Kenneth Negus has identified the years 1814–17 as Hoffmann's 'Satanic' period, when he was haunted by the diabolical and repeatedly reverted to demonic figures;[5] and in almost every case such figures relate to the central protagonist as a species of *Doppelgänger*. The central episode of 'Die Abenteuer der Sylvester-nacht' (1815) strongly echoes Chamisso's *Peter Schlemihl*: the hero, Spikher, allows his mirror-image to be stolen by the *femme fatale* Giulietta, whose master is Spikher's Satanic tempter, Dapertutto. This story was parodied by Gogol in 'The Nose' and was one of the models for Dostoevsky's *The Double*.[6] The device of the identical double is developed most fully in *The Devil's Elixirs* (1814); but we shall look first at the slightly later and very remarkable story 'The Sandman' (1816), because in the course of relating this tale Hoffmann puts into the mouth of two of his characters his subtlest elucidation of this psychological principle of projection.

## 'THE SANDMAN'

'The Sandman' concerns the disastrous obsession of a young student named Nathaniel with the figure of the aged advocate Coppelius, whom in his childhood he has come to identify with the hated and feared bogeyman 'the sandman', who throws sand in the eyes of children and picks them out. The imagery of this fairy tale provides the thematic *leitmotiv* of Hoffmann's subtly elaborated parable. Eyes are the dominant image of 'The Sandman', blazing terrifically and twinkling seductively, and the sand may be thought to symbolise the blindness of delusion which allows Nathaniel to be mastered by his obsessive fears. The 'loathsome' and 'diabolical' Coppelius has 'a pair of green cat's-eyes [which] blaze out piercingly' and he behaves towards the children with horrible cruelty and malice.[7] He is also associated in the young Nathaniel's mind with the terrible death of his father, whose partner he has been in alchemical experiments.

The happy youth of Nathaniel, enjoying the love of Clara and the friendship of her brother, Lothario, is hideously disturbed by the appearance at his door of a Piedmontese barometer dealer, Giuseppe Coppola, whom he identifies unhesitatingly with the repulsive Coppelius. Clara, seeking to reassure him, asks whether he does not believe that within any heart 'there may dwell the presentiment of a dark power which strives to ruin us within our own selves?' She goes on to elaborate this insight with great perception:

Perhaps there does exist a dark power which fastens on to us and leads us off along a dangerous and ruinous path which we would otherwise not have trodden; but if so, this power must have assumed within us the form of ourself; indeed have become ourself, for otherwise we would not listen to it, otherwise there would be no space within us in which it could perform its secret work.   (p. 96)

Refusal to give admittance to this power will force it to go under before it can achieve the form of a 'mirror-image of ourself'. Lothario adds to this that this dark psychic power, once surrendered to, can assume the chance forms which the outer world throws in our path, enkindled and animated by ourselves into a condition of 'inner affinity with us'. Their power over us lies precisely in the fact that they are 'phantoms of our own ego'. (p. 97). Clara, promising to become Nathaniel's guardian spirit and to laugh his phantoms out of court, begs him: 'banish the repulsive Coppelius and the barometer man Giuseppe Coppola from your mind altogether. Be assured that these forms from without have no power over you; only a belief that they have such a power can bestow it upon them.' In these passages Clara and Lothario enunciate the essential doctrine of the double as it is found in Hoffmann's own work and in that of his most notable successors in the tradition, especially Hogg and Dostoevsky. Repeatedly it will be found to have expressed with great exactness the relation of a protagonist to his double.

This seems to be the appropriate juncture at which to try to lay to rest the naive point surprisingly often raised by commentators on novels or stories containing a supernatural double, that the double may exist 'only' in the imagination of the character. This might be a valid possibility to explore if we were dealing with case histories, but applied to works of fiction it is, of course, absolutely meaningless. To suggest that Coppelius, or Gil-Martin in James Hogg's *Justified Sinner*, or the second Mr Golyadkin in Dostoevsky's *The Double*, are purely interior beings, mere projections of the subjectivity of the original, is not only to over-psychologise but to rob the device of the double of all its potency, and to misunderstand what it is in its essential constitution. Art is always related to real life, but it is never the same thing as real life: 'the difference between art and the event is always absolute', as T. S. Eliot expressed it.[8] In so far as the authors of these tales are dealing with psychological states (and they may very well be operating at other levels as well), the relation of the double to these states is quite simple: it is what Eliot, again, called the 'objective correlative'.

For the purposes of the story Coppelius, to take the present example, exists, and the critic has no power to make him disappear. He is able to stand for and embody elements in Nathaniel's psyche only by virtue of his real existence in terms of the fable. That this is psychologically convincing is owing to the truth enunciated by Lothario, that psychic forces attach themselves to objects existing outside the psyche in the objective world. But this again is not to say that the device works purely naturalistically; on the contrary, it clearly makes use of the supernatural, and introduces circumstances that cannot be explained solely in realistic terms. Indeed, we shall see towards the end of this study that when a phantom double is clearly ascribed by the author to mental delusion and functions as nothing more than a symptom of madness, then the device of the double is in a state of decadence.

The unhappy Nathaniel is unable to stand sufficiently outside himself to perceive the pertinence of the advice given him by his lover and his friend. Completely mastered by his obsession, he believes that Coppelius is an evil force which has taken possession of him in his childhood and which will wreck his and Clara's love. Blinded by the sand flung in his eyes by the sandman, he fails to understand, just as does Brockden Brown's Clithero, that the conviction of being a victim of fate will be a self-fulfilling prophecy. Clara, in vain, restates her argument: 'Yes, Nathaniel, you are right; Coppelius is an evil, inimical force, he can do terrible things, he is like a demonic power that has stepped visibly into life – but only so long as you fail to banish him from your mind. As long as you believe in him he continues to exist and act – his power is only your belief in him' (p. 103).

It is at this point that Nathaniel begins to be fascinated by the remotely beautiful figure of the daughter of his teacher, Professor Spalanzani: Olympia, a gorgeous and perfectly proportioned beauty, whose eyes, however, have something 'fixed and staring' and even 'sightless' about them. There is a good reason for this, for Olympia is in reality an automaton, created by Spalanzani with the aid of Coppola.

The automaton was a popular phenomenon in eighteenth-century Europe and one that filled Hoffmann with horror, representing as it did the insolent attempt by human reason and the human will to usurp the prerogatives of nature. In a letter he contemplated the possibility of a human person dancing with an automaton, and asked with fascinated repulsion, 'Could you witness such a scene even for a minute without shuddering?'[9] Nathaniel's devotion to a puppet symbolises his voluntary deliverance of himself into the hands of dark forces which then make of *him* a puppet. 'The machine is the bizarre, perverse *Doppelgänger* of true life', as Ronald Taylor observes, and Nathaniel's captivation by a machine therefore denotes his fundamental dissociation from reality, his inability to free himself from the preoccupations and fixations of childhood.

He writes a poem which dramatises his inner condition, in which Coppelius causes Clara's eyes to spring out 'like blood-red sparks, singeing and burning on Nathaniel's breast'. Clara's voice calls to him that Coppelius has deceived him, that she still has her eyes and what burned in his breast 'were glowing-hot drops of your own heart's blood'; but when he looks into her eyes he sees death gazing at him mildly out of them (p. 105). He reads his poem to Clara and when she fails to appreciate it he reviles her, in a classic projection, as a 'lifeless cursed automaton'. A violent quarrel with Lothario follows, and a duel is averted only by Clara's passionate intervention. All three are reconciled, and for a time Nathaniel, complacently assuming that he has successfully resisted the power of darkness, regains his stability and peace of mind.

Hoffmann now shows the subtlety and complexity of his handling of the theme by introducing into the reader's mind a doubt about the validity of Clara's perspective, a slight suggestion that Nathaniel may indeed, as he himself believes, be played upon by fate or by an inimical objective power. He returns to his lodgings to find that the house has been burned down, and that his possessions have been removed by friends and transported to a room they have taken for him elsewhere. This room happens to be immediately opposite the house of Professor Spalanzani, and indeed his window looks directly across to the room in which the beautiful but statuesque Olympia is accustomed to sit. One day he receives a further visit from the repellent barometer dealer Coppola; Nathaniel makes a determined effort to resist his childish fears, though he is thoroughly unnerved when Coppola brings out dozens of pairs of spectacles which cause the whole table to 'sparkle and glitter in an uncanny fashion', like 'a thousand eyes' whose 'flaming glances leaped more and more wildly together and directed their blood-red beams into Nathaniel's breast'. He pulls himself together, however, and assures himself that Coppola is 'certainly not the revenant and *Doppelgänger* of the accursed Coppelius' (p. 110).

Whereas before he has been led astray by lack of self-knowledge into blind credulity, he is now betrayed into over-confidence. We may certainly feel that the cards are indeed heavily stacked against Nathaniel, for by heeding Clara's warning he is now led to a step that is to prove fatal: he purchases from Coppola a pocket-telescope, and looking through it is immediately lost in contemplation of Olympia's 'heavenly beauty'. Hearing the laughter of the departing dealer he concludes that he has been tricked into buying the telescope 'at much too high a price – much too high a price!' A death-sigh echoes through the room, which may or may not come from himself; it is odd, he feels, that 'the foolish idea that I might have bought the glass from Coppola at too high a price still fills me with such strange trepidation. I can see no reason for it at all' (p. 111). His blindness thus still persists, though now it operates not by enslaving him to a delusory danger but by obscuring his perception of a real one.

Fed by what he sees through the fatal telescope, Nathaniel's infatuation with Olympia masters him completely and effaces the image of Clara from his mind. He dances all night with the automaton at a ball, blinding himself to her dead eyes, her stiff posture and movements and the lifelessness of her demeanour. He declares his love to her, sits with her day after day and pours his heart out to her, and though her conversation is limited to 'Ah, ah!' he interprets her silence as profundity and spiritual exaltation. He believes that she understands him, that there is a sympathy and 'psychical affinity' between them; thus he makes manifest his egotism and self-love, which seeks in the other nothing but a passive receptivity to himself. His delusion is swept away only when, about to propose to Olympia, he witnesses a violent quarrel between Spalanzani and the dreadful Coppelius, or Coppola, over their joint creation, which ends with the latter running off with Nathaniel's love over his shoulder, revealed as a lifeless, and now eyeless, doll. Spalanzani in his rage hurls the eyes – 'purloined from you' – at the student's chest in a nightmarish re-enactment of the latter's poem-vision. Nathaniel at once goes mad, attempts to strange the professor and is taken to the madhouse 'raging in hideous frenzy' (p. 121).

The tale now nears its fatal climax. Spalanzani has to leave the town, Coppelius disappears once more, Nathaniel recovers from his madness and wants to marry Clara. Happiness seems assured until, standing with Clara at the top of a tall tower, Nathaniel takes out his telescope and, turning it towards Clara, sees instead the puppet Olympia. At once he succumbs anew to madness and tries to throw his beloved off the tower; Lothario in the nick of time rescues her from the 'raging madman'. As he raves a crowd gathers below, and 'among them there towered gigantically the advocate Coppelius' (p. 124). Seeing him, Nathaniel leaps off the tower to his death, and the dreadful Coppelius disappears for the last time into the crowd. We are told that Clara subsequently finds with another the domestic happiness 'which the inwardly riven Nathaniel could never have given her' (p. 125).

In this penetrating and dramatically arresting story Hoffmann develops, as we have seen other writers do, a dialectic which hinges on our understanding of the idea of fate. It is beyond dispute that it is Nathaniel's vain, inward-looking and self-regarding nature that lays him open to the wiles of Coppelius. It is the blindness of the student which makes possible the power over him of 'the sandman' who embodies an inimical psychic or spiritual force. Yet is this very blindness fated for Nathaniel? At times it seems as if he is as much a puppet in the hands of fate as the automaton to which he is so devoted, and this gives added point to the repeated cry of his madness: 'Spin, puppet, spin!' It is suggested that Coppola has stolen his eyes to provide those of Olympia; symbolically, he has been blinded by a power over which, whether it is seen as being within or outside himself, he has no effectual control; yet, as was suggested above, this loss of control has resulted from his earlier collusion.

We are back with the questions with which Marlowe grappled in *Dr Faustus*: does Faustus 'deserve' to be damned? Is he unable to repent because he *believes* that he is irredeemable, or because he is predestined to damnation? Is the Devil permitted to put such doubts or delusions in his mind? Does he have the power *not* to succumb to them? Can we resort, with St Augustine, only to the utter inscrutability of the Divine will? These problems will continue to recur in examples of the use of the double in fiction, for they are problems which it is the business of this Janus-like device to dramatise. We need not expect clear-cut answers; but in Hoffmann's major contribution to the genre, which we shall now consider, we shall meet a protagonist who does, in the last resort, repent.

## THE DEVIL'S ELIXIRS

*The Devil's Elixirs* was Hoffmann's first novel. Its aim, as he described it in a letter, was 'to reveal, through the strange, perverted life of a man who from his birth had been tossed to and fro by the forces of Heaven and Hell, those mysterious relationships between the human mind and the higher values enshrined in Nature, values whose meaning we glimpse in those rare moments of insight which we choose to call the products of Chance.'[10]

Demonstrably influenced by Lewis's *The Monk*, to which in places it refers directly, it deals, like its predecessor, with a mind riven by conflict between good and evil, and like it, too, concerns the fall through pride and lust of a Capuchin friar who has previously been popularly venerated almost as a saint for his piety and eloquence. Its outcome, however, is quite opposite to that of *The Monk*, and one could hazard a guess that it might have been written with a view to suggesting a different understanding of temptation, fate and the possibility of repentance and redemption from that adopted by Lewis and others who had dealt with these themes. It is no mere *roman à thèse*, however, but a gripping and often lurid romance exhibiting many features of the Gothic novel and the tale of terror, but far exceeding most of them in the quality of its psychological insight.

The complications and convolutions of the plot are extraordinarily intricate, and many of them must be omitted in this account. Nevertheless the almost impenetrable tangles of relationships, the studied parallels, the wildly improbable repetitions of history and inexplicable coincidences are far from being without their purpose. They are all reflections of the notion of hereditary guilt and the part which it may play in individual destiny, and they reveal the novel as yet another variation played on the Augustinian themes of original sin, its hereditary transmission, the place of predetermination and individual free will within the system of salvation, and the issue of whether in the face of the forces of evil repentance is truly attainable and redemption available for the sinner. Until the very end it remains uncertain whether the monk, Medardus, will finally overcome the pertinaciously renewed assaults and temptations of the Devil. The conflict is dramatised in terms of the interlocked destinies of Medardus and the identical double who is his dark second self and also his half-brother.

The counterpoint between free will and necessity, between hereditary guilt and individual responsibility, is early emphasised in the memoirs of Brother Medardus. The infant Franz, or Francisco, spends his early years with his mother in the paradisal environment of the monastery of the Holy Linden, where he learns that his father had been led by Satan to commit a deadly and heinous sin. His soul seems destined to be a battleground between good and evil. An old pilgrim visits the Holy Linden and brings with him a 'marvellous child' whose influence is intended to kindle the flame of love in his heart; we are led to understand that this pilgrim is Joseph and the child Christ, and that Francisco's destiny is to expiate the sins of his father by dedication to the life of the Church.

'Your son is richly gifted,' the old pilgrim tells his mother, 'but the sin of his father still festers within him' (p. 5). At the Holy Linden he is surrounded by the work of a mysterious archaic painter with whose spirit his fate is to be entwined. After a few years they move to a Cistercian convent where the Abbess has known his father. She loves the boy greatly and he in his turn reveres her 'like a saint'; a diamond crucifix on her breast leaves its mark permanently on his neck, denoting his dedication to a sanctified life. His religious vocation takes its course, and he enters the novitiate of the Capuchin monastery at 'B.' as Brother Medardus.

It is not long before Medardus begins to show a strong propensity for the sin of pride. Uneasy with women, he regards his attraction to a young girl as a 'vicious attack of the Devil' and takes a 'guilty pride' in what he regards as his easy victory through ascetic discipline. 'What are you so happy about, Brother?' asks Brother

Cyrillus, the first of a series of good influences who embody the
reminders of his conscience. Cyrillus is the supervisor of the
chamber where the monastery's relics are kept, and Medardus
becomes his assistant. Thus he is introduced to the relic of the
'Devil's elixirs', left by St Anthony, with whose famous and
victorious struggles against demons and their temptations he
comes to identify.

The life of St Anthony is the prototype of that of Medardus. Like
the story of the father of monasticism, his history is to be that of a
prolonged combat with diabolic forces, but the nature of his
particular temptation is involved with spiritual blindness, the lack
of self-awareness which leads him to mistake the real occasions of
the demonic assaults. His self-identification with St Anthony is
therefore peculiarly ironical: when he sees himself as heroically
resisting temptation he is in fact succumbing to rampant spiritual
pride, and he interprets the agents of his salvation as emissaries
of the Devil. Yet in the long run he *is* destined to overcome the
powers of evil, so at a deeper level the parallel with St Anthony
will finally be verified.

As soon as he sees the relic Medardus experiences a prideful
impulse in which he sees himself as a great orator and preacher: 'I
. . . imagined the shining halo of inspiration around my proudly
held head and my outstretched arms' (p. 25). His ambition is
fulfilled, and like Ambrosio in *The Monk* he wins the admiration of
the populace to the degree that he is worshipped almost as a saint.
He succumbs to overweening pride and misinterprets to his own
credit the spiritual influences which are working for his salvation:
'The idea then began to grow in my head that I was one of the
Lord's Elect. . . . I now realised that the old pilgrim in the Holy
Linden had been Joseph, and the marvellous boy the Child Jesus
himself, who had seen in me a saint on earth' (p. 26).

The agent of temptation in this book is not a human individual
or a supernatural personage but the relic of the Devil's elixir. It is
the sight, and later the drinking of the elixir, which evokes the
sins of pride and lust in Medardus and drives him ever deeper
into the toils of sin, crime and depravity. Much later, however, he
comes clearly to see that the elixir would have had no power over
him had there not already been within him a potentiality for sin:
'Like water teeming with foul odours it gave strength to the seed
of evil latent within me, so that it multiplied beyond all knowledge'
(p. 273). Fate and personal responsibility are inextricably linked in

his downfall. Moreover he constantly ignores the advice of those who seek to warn him of his spiritual danger. Prior Leonardus, his spiritual mentor, is quick to observe his burgeoning pride and to rebuke him for it, but he allows him to preach on St Anthony's Day.

During the course of his oration Medardus sees among the crowd a tall, gaunt figure: 'His face was deathly pale, but as his great black eyes stared at me a dagger seemed to pierce my heart. . . . Something resembling bitter scorn and hatred lay on his high, furrowed brow and his drawn lips . . . *it was the mysterious painter from the Holy Linden*' (p. 28). Medardus grows frantic under his gaze and shouts hysterically, 'I AM ST. ANTHONY!'

No one else has seen the dreadful figure, and Medardus identifies him with the Devil in the form of the devout painter, come to wage war against a saint. His possession of the terrible eyes might tempt us to the same conclusion, but in this case their lustre is that of the accusing conscience, and the influence of the painter is Divine in origin. It will transpire that he is the apparition of the ancestor whose long-past sin is the fount and origin of the manifold crimes and outrages which have disgraced his house in every succeeding generation. As such he is a figure of Adam, the first father, the fount of original sin and the source of its hereditary transmission. Now assured of final redemption, the Painter has it as his commission to bring to an end the long chain of sin which he has initiated within his house, and it is to this end that he continually watches over Medardus and seeks, through his contempt and accusing hostility, to recall him to the path of virtue.

Torn and crushed by the apparition, Medardus loses his oratorical power, but having experienced pleasant and revivifying sensations on merely smelling the elixir, he decides to drink from it, and as a result regains all that he has lost. On St Bernard's Day he preaches at the Cistercian convent before the Abbess and his mother. To his consternation, the Abbess sends him a letter in which she ruthlessly castigates the 'proud pomp' of his language: 'Hypocritically you have affected emotions that are not in your heart. . . . The demon of deceit has entered you and will destroy you if you do not search your heart and renounce sin' (p. 36). Medardus, however, is far too infatuated by self-conceit to heed her advice.

By a progression which has now become familiar, the fundamental sin of pride prepares the ground for the onslaught of further temptations, of which the most important is, of course, lust. A mysterious woman comes to Medardus in the confessional and declares her love for him. She is identical to the St Rosalia of the altar painting to which he is so devoted, and immediately the infatuated monk gives way to obsession: 'I wanted to get out into the world and not rest until I had found her and bought her for the price of my soul's salvation' (p. 39). With this end in view Medardus plans to flee the monastery, but fortuitously Prior Leonardus sends him on a mission to Rome, a protracted journey towards redemption. He sets off into the world taking with him the remainder of the Devil's elixir.

The moral reversal characteristic of these cases has inexorably advanced, and the moment has come for the dark and hitherto repressed second self thus released to be externalised in the form of a double. Medardus comes upon a young man in military uniform sleeping precariously on the edge of a ravine (the spot turns out to be 'the Devil's Seat'), and by his own account inadvertently startles him so that he falls into the abyss – though there may be a suspicion that the monk actually pushes him over. This act symbolically initiates Medardus's descent into overt and active evil. Out of the abysmal depths within himself there arises his hideous *Doppelgänger*, stained with blood and infected with madness. Until Medardus has finally worked out his own salvation this horrible reflection will dog his footsteps.

Medardus quickly discovers that he has become the 'double' of this Count Victor, who as it happens has been planning an amorous escapade, disguised as a monk, at the palace of the Baron, at which Medardus now arrives. The two are identical in looks, and this is not coincidence, for it will eventually transpire that they are half-brothers (an extraordinary family resemblance, amounting to almost complete identity of appearance, is characteristic of most of the descendants of the Painter's family through successive generations). Henceforth the fate of Medardus and that of his fearful double (who, unknown to the monk, survives his fall and climbs out of the ravine in a state of madness), are intertwined in an elaborate maze of uncertain and shifting and mistaken identity, each seeing himself in the other and both finally pawns in the hands of an inscrutable destiny.

At the Baron's palace Medardus, in his assumed role as the disguised Count Victor, becomes involved in the fate of the Baron's family: his demonic wife Euphemia, and his children by his first marriage, Hermogenes and Aurelia. All will turn out to be members of the Painter's blighted house. Hermogenes is a kind of secondary double antagonistic to Medardus: suffering from a form of melancholic madness and nursing an obsessive desire to become a monk, he labours under the influence of a 'terrible secret'.

Euphemia, whose advances Hermogenes had at first repulsed and who has revenged herself on him by marrying his father, and subsequently seducing the son, sees in him a 'mysterious spiritual force' of madmen, by which hidden thoughts are pierced and expressed, 'so that the dreadful voice of a second self sends an unearthly shudder through us' (p. 68). Count Victor, Medardus's primary double, will also prove to be a madman. Euphemia herself is a kind of female *übermensch* who despises convention, delights in the exercise of sexual power and regards human beings as puppets to be manipulated for her own pleasure. Medardus, whom she believes to be her lover, Count Victor, plunges into an affair with her, but his heart is elsewhere, for Aurelia is none other than the woman who came to him in the confessional, the incarnation of his wonderful vision of St Rosalia. In his passion for Aurelia is enacted the struggle between fleshly lust and Divine, redemptive love. When the latter ultimately triumphs and the nature of his love is transformed, Medardus's destiny will be fulfilled.

Medardus, believed by some to be Count Victor and known to others as himself, is now caught in the toils of duality: 'I am what I seem to be, yet do not seem to be what I am; even to myself I am an insoluble riddle, for my personality has been torn apart' (p. 58). He believes that in some mysterious way he really is Victor as well as himself, and this belief expresses the dominance of his secondary personality, the evil and monstrous shadow-self summoned up by pride: 'Something superhuman had entered into me, lifting me to an eminence from which everything assumed a different perspective, a different character' (p. 69). Frustrated in his attempts to seduce Aurelia, finding Euphemia repulsive, and accused by Hermogenes of being inspired by Satan, Medardus is driven inexorably towards violence. He now believes himself emancipated from every moral restraint by his possession of a superhuman spirit.

Medardus poisons Euphemia with the cup she has intended for himself; intent on the rape of Aurelia, he is confronted by Hermogenes and stabs him twice with a fatal stiletto which will mysteriously come to hand at repeated crises in his history. As he escapes he cries out, 'You mad fools, will you tempt the providence that passes judgment on guilty sinners?' There is a surprise in store for him, however: 'But – O horrid sight! – before me stood the bloody figure of Victor. It was he, not I, who had spoken' (p. 80). The appearance of his double will recurrently confront him, from outside himself, with a horrible embodiment of the evil impulses which he has sublimated into the mission of an avenging angel.

The spiritual forces working for the redemption of Medardus continually cross his path. Having discarded his monk's habit (which will be assumed by his double), he arrives at a city where the first person he meets is a droll and paradoxical barber, Pietro Belcampo, who is quick to recognise the monk's self-division in the way he moves: 'two different natures were in conflict with each other'. (pp. 89–90). The barber is a quaint guardian angel to Medardus, offering him ambiguous but penetrating advice in a curious, half-mocking but humorous style. He himself personifies the theme of duality, for as 'Peter Schönfeld' he has a German as well as an Italian identity. Just as the loathsome Coppelius of 'The Sandman' has an *alter ego* in the repulsive barometer dealer Giuseppe Coppola, so Schönfeld doubles as Pietro Belcampo, whom he calls his 'real self'. But he is also a further double of Medardus himself. His role is ambiguous; as Ronald Taylor has remarked, in Belcampo 'protective irony is raised to the power of grotesque insanity', and he, too, stands in need of redemption.[11] At the time of Medardus's death he will enter the Capuchin monastery as a lay-brother.

Medardus infiltrates literary circles in the city, where he is confronted by the mysterious Painter, who publicly accuses him of the murder of Count Victor and the crimes at the Baron's palace. 'You yourself are Satan!' shouts Medardus, and attacks the Painter, who throws him to the ground. Medardus escapes, rescued by Belcampo, who asserts that the Painter is 'a contemptible ghost . . . since he is a mere thought, it must be possible to kill him with a thought' (pp. 102, 104). This is the same advice as Clara gave Nathaniel in respect of Coppelius; yet the Painter is no 'mere thought', but a spectral embodiment of real spiritual forces.

Medardus now roves through the countryside like a nomad. At a gamekeeper's cottage he has a new and fearful confrontation with his double. He dreams that he meets himself in Capuchin garb and that this double challenges him to fight on the roof. 'You are not me, you are the Devil!' Medardus screams; but on waking he finds that his gruesome dream is coming true, for there before him is a Capuchin friar, resembling Hermogenes, who drinks some of the Devil's elixir and runs off laughing raucously. He now finds it increasingly hard to distinguish dream from reality. The double reappears, is caught and locked up by the gamekeeper and his sons until he renounces Satan.

On hearing the gamekeeper's story of this mad monk, a history which seems to be his very own, the real Medardus feels himself 'sunk to the level of a miserable plaything of that sinister power which held me in its chains, for I who believed myself free could only move about within the cage in which I was helplessly imprisoned' (pp. 122–3). Here we are confronted by the central paradox of *The Devil's Elixirs*. Medardus is indeed the plaything of dark powers, but, like Nathaniel, he is a puppet only because, and so long as, he *believes* himself to be so. But is his collusion with darkness itself inescapable? It will become clear that not only his fall but also his ultimate redemption – though it clearly comes about by the free exercise of his independent will – is, if not preordained, at least *foreknown*.

It can be seen that the status of Medardus's double is left intentionally ambiguous and multilayered by Hoffmann's complicated ingenuity. The narrative base is the confusion of identity with the mad Count Victor, who has donned the monk's garb. His assumption of his brother's identity at the level of detail revealed by the gamekeeper's story cannot, however, be susceptible of naturalistic explanation, for the two were unknown to each other until their fatal meeting at the Devil's Seat. It appears at times as if some of the double's appearances to Medardus are hallucinatory, and we have seen how his dreams and visions mysteriously interpenetrate with his counterpart's physical presence. Beyond this, however, there is a supernatural element, for the double repeatedly materialises at moments of crisis and temptation for Medardus and in extraordinary circumstances, several times bearing the sinister knife which is linked with the crimes of the Painter's family. We have to conclude that both Medardus and Count Victor are subject to the manipulative wiles of a demonic power which seeks to enslave them to its own purposes. The blend of naturalistic, psychological and supernatural elements in the treatment of the double is subtly varied and makes considerable demands on the attention and alertness of the reader.

Medardus himself begins to fear that he is under demonic

influence: 'My soul was divided within itself, and I was in the grip of a paralysing fear.' Throwing away the now empty elixir bottle, he makes his first very tentative move towards resisting the evil within him. The mad monk has taken off. But Medardus has a long journey yet ahead of him before his hope of throwing off his evil fate will be fulfilled.

He now arrives at a cultured, quiet town where, under the disguise of 'Herr Leonard', he obtains the favour of the Prince. The Princess bears a remarkable resemblance to the Abbess of the Cistercian convent, and she is her turn finds in his face a reminder of past sorrows. When he asks the court physician why the Princess appears to dislike him, he is shown a small portrait bearing an astonishing likeness to himself. This portrait, the work of a mysterious painter who was at court in past days, revives the memory of a 'terrible incident which befell the court several years back'; it portrays the Prince's former favourite, Francesco.

The physician relates to the friar this tangled tale of lust, jealousy and murder, involving the Prince and his brother the Duke, the Princess and her sister, and an Italian princess. The black sunken eyes of the Painter have been fixed admonishingly on Francesco just as they have on Medardus, and the latter now gains a horrid insight into his familial inheritance of guilt. The illegitimate son born to Francesco by the Italian princess (married to the Duke), is Count Victor; the Princess's sister, formerly in love with Francesco, is the Abbess. 'All was now plain to me: Francesco was my father, and it was he who had murdered the Duke with the same knife with which I had stabbed Hermogenes' (p. 162). Fast on the heels of this revelation comes a fresh intervention of Fate: a new maid-of-honour appears in the entourage, and this is Aurelia.

At once the powers of evil are again active in Medardus, suggesting to him that he is 'the master of fate'. Maddened by lust for Aurelia, he is convinced that he and she are linked by 'an inscrutable destiny' and that 'what had sometimes appeared to me a sinful crime was only the fulfilment of an irrevocable decree' (p. 168). But Aurelia has recognised him as the murderer of her brother, and he is arrested and imprisoned. In his captivity he hears his name called from the depths below his cell in what seems his own voice, with hideous laughing, groaning and wailing: 'Me-dar-dus! . . . Bro-ther! Bro-ther!' The evidence brought against him at his trial seems damning, and he is identified by Brother Cyrillus. Back in his cell, the disturbance from below begins again, eventually a flagstone crumbles and an arm appears holding a knife. A naked figure emerges 'like a grotesque spectre, leering and cackling like a madman. The full light of the lamp fell on his face and I recognised – *myself*' (p. 187). He faints, and on waking finds a knife in his pocket. It is the knife that his 'ghostly double' has handed up to him, the same with which he murdered Hermogenes. He now perceives that he has been deluded in his vainglorious beliefs and that he must atone for his deeds.

The Painter appears to him in his cell in the form of a Dominican friar, and explains his salvific role. Medardus must achieve his own salvation through the work he has been called to do. The next day he is unexpectedly set free, the mad monk having been captured and having confessed to being the real Medardus. Now once more taken to be Herr Leonard, a Polish nobleman, he is free to pursue his love for Aurelia, who surrenders to him in 'utter innocence'. Medardus, however, is rent by conflicting emotions; once more he gives way to lust and cruelty, his love vanishes, and he becomes 'filled with the idea that her downfall might form the brilliant climax of my life' (p. 212).

Aurelia, too, is fearfully ambiguous in her emotions. In her attraction to him, which recapitulates earlier events in the tortured history of their family, she too is fulfilling the laws of their destiny. She seeks to persuade herself that her lover, 'Herr Leonard', is quite distinct from the wicked Medardus, but his 'flashing eyes' perpetually renew her terrors.

The wedding day comes; above the altar is a picture of the martyrdom of St Rosalia, dressed just as the bride is dressed now. But then Medardus sees his 'gruesome double' being led to execution in a cart: Aurelia tries to drag her bridegroom from the window, but 'The demons of hell raged within me, and I seized her in fury' (p. 226). Shouting that he is Medardus, her brother's murderer, he stabs at her and, as he believes, kills her. Rushing downstairs he seizes the mad monk, stabs out at his pursuers in all directions and escapes into the forest. He loses consciousness, and when he recovers his senses, his double jumps on his back and forces him to carry him, as the Old Man of the Sea did to Sinbad the Sailor. A grotesque struggle and pursuit ensues, with the double clinging on to Medardus pertinaciously in a graphic symbolisation of their identity and inseparability: 'Hee, hee, hee! Hee, hee, hee! Little Brother! I . . . am . . . al-ways . . . with you, will . . . not . . . not . . . leave you . . .' (pp. 227–8).

This is the climax of Medardus's suffering, and from this point the powers of good begin gradually to gain over those of evil. Hoffmann depicts the process of repentance and regeneration as no single, decisive, once-for-all event but as a painful, chequered progress full of setbacks and backslidings. Until the last page of the book the final salvation of the monk's soul remains in doubt. His developing self-knowledge is linked to the gradual unfolding of the guilty family history which denotes his binding by the cords of destiny, and he comes slowly to understand the part he must play in the drama of its redemption. It is difficult not to see in all this an allegory of original sin, its hereditary transmission and the conquest of that sin through repentance in Christ; but, as Taylor has pointed out, such an orthodox viewpoint is to be found nowhere else in Hoffmann, and the Catholic ethic 'is not to be transferred elsewhere'.[12]

Medardus awakes from a long unconsciousness and finds himself in a simple, lofty room dressed as a Capuchin: 'my character seemed split into a thousand parts.' He is in a madhouse in Italy, where he has been brought by the barber Schönfeld, who has rescued him, clothed him in his own habit abandoned by the mad monk, and brought him here: 'I myself am that Folly that is always pursuing you in order to assist your power of reason. And whether you realise it or not, you will only find salvation in Folly, for your much-vaunted reason is an utterly worthless thing and cannot sustain itself' (p. 234). This suggests the Pauline praise of folly, of the foolishness of Christ, as the deepest kind of understanding.[13] But Medardus shows little gratitude to the 'horrible little clown'. When he has recovered sufficiently to leave, he sets out for Rome.

Proceeding as a mendicant, he is allowed to stay at a Capuchin monastery, where the prior treats him kindly, and persuades him to confess, which he does fully. A terrible penance follows, Medardus so torturing himself that he is considered a 'saint', and this terrifies him with the thought of his former pride. The prior is reassuring, however. 'A destiny which you could not elude gave Satan power over you', he tells him, yet 'you were given the strength to resist Satan boldly and conquer him' (p. 248). He tells Medardus that Aurelia is alive: it was his own arm that he stabbed. He reveals also that the Painter (the reality of whose physical presence he doubts) is a frequent visitor to the monastery, and has left a story to which he adds a few lines on each of his visits.

This is the story of the Painter himself and his sinful house.

'When diagrammed,' as Kenneth Negus has noticed, 'the family tree resembles the rampant growth of a parasitic plant as described by Hoffmann himself in the foreword.'[14] The Painter's own guilt had its roots in vanity and pride, swollen through drinking the Devil's elixir, and the struggle in his soul between pious inspiration and wicked lust was focused on his portrait of St Rosalia. He had modelled her face on that of Venus, whom he then summoned to life as a woman who was actually in alliance with the Devil. From this union sprang the fated line. But the Painter prayed to St Rosalia and was directed to the Holy Linden, where he expiated his sins by works of devotion. Saved from eternal damnation by the saint's intercession, he was permitted to suffer the torments of damnation on earth until his sinful line should have perished for ever. This history is echoed in that of Medardus's father, Franz or Francesco, who similarly ended his life in repentance at the Holy Linden where Medardus was born; and Medardus it is who must finally expiate the familial curse.

The friar has now reached Rome, where, because of the fervour of his public devotion, he begins to be regarded as a saint, and is summoned to account for himself to the Pope. The conversation which ensues between them on the subject of hereditary sin, and guilt for that sin, may be regarded as the theological heart of the novel. 'This then would be the original sin,' says the Pope, 'an eternal ineradicable curse on a guilty house, for which no sacrifice could atone.' Medardus replies that there can be no true sin if the sinner cannot but sin as a result of his heritage. 'Indeed there can,' the Pope replies. 'The spirit of God has created a giant, capable of subduing the wild beast within us. This giant is called Self-Knowledge and from its struggle with the beast emerges Freedom of the Spirit. The giant's victory is virtue, the beast's victory, Sin' (p. 273). We have seen that failure in self-knowledge is repeatedly the fatal weakness in those spiritually and psychologically divided characters who spawn a double as their second self, the weakness which issues in moral blindness and makes repentance impossible. Medardus, however, will, painfully and with Divine aid, overcome this weakness.

This he will do through confronting further, graduated temptations. The crudest is that of obtaining prestige and influence in Rome; the most subtle the hope of the glorious death of a martyr. Medardus prays to be delivered from the powers of Hell, and is rewarded by a healing and redemptive vision of Christ. He leaves

Rome, understanding that in his desire to escape his calling he had unconsciously taken the most direct road to the goal set before him by Prior Leonardus.

At last the penitent monk arrives home at the Capuchin monastery at B. The tangled history of the Painter's family (which includes all the important characters with whose fate that of Medardus has been intertwined) is gradually untied. Medardus's double has appeared at the monastery, and, regaining his senses for a time, admits to being not Medardus but Count Victor. His experience now appears as an exact mirror-inage of that of Medardus: 'when I searched my heart, it seemed that my secret thoughts were emerging in human shape as horrible forms of my own self'. In his madness, he has come to confound himself with this 'second self' and to attribute to himself Medardus's crimes. His encounters with the latter have seemed to him to be struggles between his own mind and body; his personality, it appeared to him, 'had split into two mutually antagonistic parts' (pp. 304–5).

Medardus now finally puts an end to the confusion of identity by disclosing the whole truth to the prior. Victor, explains Leonardus, was 'the mere plaything of that sinister force which intervened in your life, distracting your gaze from your true goal' (p. 306).

The final trial of Medardus is yet to come. On the morrow, Prior Leonardus tells him, Aurelia is to take the veil and receive the name of Rosalia. At once the familiar chaos of conflicting emotions threatens to overpower him. Leonardus, aware of his inner conflict, makes Medardus sit beside him at the investiture and urges him to resist the evil demon which assaults him. After a terrible struggle, in which the tortured monk even begins to fumble for the fatal knife, the forces of good take over as Aurelia repeats her vows, and Medardus emerges victorious from the conflict. But, just as Aurelia is about to receive the robe, a wild figure in a tattered Capuchin habit rushes in with clenched fists, and shouting 'She is my bride!' plunges a knife in her breast and escapes. '*It was my double.*'

A terrible ambiguity thus casts a shadow over the repentance of Medardus. His higher will has indeed been victorious over the dark impulses of his lower nature, yet the very wickedness which he had contemplated is performed, as it were vicariously and on his behalf, by the double who has been the embodiment of that evil second self. This has finally detached itself from him and 'got away', escaped into outer darkness. The degree to which this evil has emerged from within himself remains uncertain; Medardus is in no doubt that it was his own pride and lust which gave the Devil his opportunity, for when Aurelia came to him in the confessional he surrendered himself 'body and soul into the hands of evil'; yet it appears to him that 'Satan had fettered me to a monster whose body I was to inhabit with my mind and whose spirit was to enter my own spirit' (p. 317).

In spite of this element of dubiety which Hoffmann retains in effecting the resolution of his lurid metaphysical drama, there is no suggestion that Medardus's repentance is not entirely genuine: his higher, Christian will has gained the victory over his lower nature, even if that lower nature has not thereby been annihilated. The dying Aurelia begs for reconciliation, taking upon herself some of the guilt for having kindled in his mind the flame of lust. Ordained to redeem the sins of their forebears, they misunderstood their love and were tempted to 'interpret the Sacred after the manner of the Profane' (p. 314). Medardus now experiences the bliss of the higher love and takes his place among the brethren. Yet he still prays that in the hour of death the powers of Hell may not overcome him and hurl him 'into the pit of everlasting damnation' (p. 320).

An appendix by Father Spiridon, the Librarian, gives an account of the death of Medardus on the first anniversary of the murder of Sister Rosalia. A horrible voice, he tells the reader, attested the continued ghostly existence of the monk's dark self: 'Come with me, Brother Medardus, and we will look for your betrothed.' But this sinister influence was banished by a peal of bells, the scent of roses and the appearance of the Painter, come to announce the hour of fulfilment. Medardus passes away in the prior's arms, and during the requiem mass a bouquet of roses is attached to the portrait of Sister Rosalia by a beggar. This beggar is received into the monastery as a lay-brother: he is the barber Peter Schönfeld, Medardus's ironical guardian angel. Medardus, Father Spiridon informs us, 'died a truly pious man' (p. 323).

It has been necessary, while omitting many of the less essential details, to give some impression of the exceptionally dense texture and complicated plotting of Hoffmann's novel, for it is devised, with extraordinary ingenuity, in order to provide metaphors for the way in which the individual soul is entangled, by its innate sinful condition, in an almost impenetrable and binding skein of obscure cause and effect. The familial guilt in which Medardus is unwittingly involved, his own individual propensity to sin, the lures of the Devil, and the existence of the dark second self which those temptations prompt to emerge and which embodies itself in a physical double, are elements which interpenetrate each other and sometimes appear as different aspects of a single phenomenon. The nexus of theological problems which we pointed to in the first chapter of this book – original sin, its hereditary transmission and relation to individual sin – is elaborated in the breathless adventures and bloody crises of *The Devil's Elixirs* with remarkable thoroughness and penetration. It is in the nature of these questions that no unambiguous 'answers' emerge, but Hoffmann does affirm emphatically the real possibility of repentance and redemption for even so black a sinner as Brother Medardus.

Within this context the device of the supernatural, or semisupernatural, double acquires a new complexity and depth. Count Victor is a real person in whose familial likeness to his half-brother the confusion of identity is rooted. At the same time he is experienced by the protagonist as the horrible detached embodiment of the dark side of his nature, and prepares him for self-knowledge by repeatedly confronting him with the repulsive reality of the evil impulses which he has sublimated as self-aggrandising delusions. As such he has hallucinatory meetings with Medardus as well as physical confrontations. And at yet another level, the double is the tool of the demonic powers which assail Medardus, and which are enabled to present their victim with his image or his physical presence in a mysterious manner at crucial points in his spiritual and psychological history. Hoffmann's innovating contribution to the development of the double theme, especially in *The Devil's Elixirs* and 'The Sandman', is grounded in his acute percipience of the tortuous byways of the human heart.

# 5

# James Hogg

*The Devil's Elixirs* appeared in an abridged English translation in 1824. The translator was R. P. Gillies, who moved in the same Edinburgh literary circles as James Hogg, 'the Ettrick Shepherd', whose *Private Memoirs and Confessions of a Justified Sinner* was also published in that year. John Carey was the first critic to notice the probable relation between the two dualistic fictions.[1] Apart from the pervasive thematic similarities, there are striking parallels in matters of detail. There seem to be strong verbal echoes of the description of the Painter's apparently baleful haunting of Medardus in the relationship between Robert Wringhim and his demonic double, Gil-Martin; as Medardus pushes Count Victor off the Devil's Seat, so the Sinner makes an attempt on his brother's life on the edge of a precipice on Arthur's Seat in Edinburgh; like Medardus, Wringhim finds that a diabolical dagger has been insinuated into his possession by supernatural means. Beyond this, there is a more organic resemblance at the level of language, in the rhetoric of self-aggrandisement that is employed in the respective memoirs of the two protagonists.

Yet the world of discourse which we find reflected in Hogg's masterpiece is utterly different from the Catholic religious background of Hoffmann's work. It is the world of the Scottish Calvinist sects, of antinomian controversy, and if continental dualism plays a part in the genesis of the *Justified Sinner*, there is a no less crucial contribution in the influence of such a work as *The Confession of Nicol Muschet of Boghall* (reprinted in 1818), the account of the actual murder, prompted by devilish suggestion, of his wife by a Scottish religious fanatic believing himself emancipated from the moral law by free grace and mercy. It has also been shown that Hogg would have been fully aware of controversy over antinomianism – the doctrine that salvation depends not on faith but on justification by grace, and that those so justified are not bound by the moral law – involving the minister of his own parish of Ettrick in the early years of the eighteenth century, the era in which Robert Wringhim's career of justified sinning took its disastrous course.[2]

Hogg's work is, in fact, wholly original and *sui generis*. It draws on the duality or diversity of the man himself, a shepherd more or less illiterate until late adolescence who taught himself to read with the Bible as his textbook, aspired to poetry and found himself ambiguously accepted or tolerated in Enlightenment Edinburgh, lionised in London but often treated as a buffoon by the sophisticates at home. He even had an *alter ego* foisted on him in the form of 'The Shepherd', John Wilson's depiction of him in the 'Noctes Ambrosianae' in *Blackwood's Magazine*, which he rightly regarded as a distorted and offensive parody. He remained something of a puzzle even to early-twentieth-century critics, and it is only comparatively recently that the quite groundless suggestion that the *Justified Sinner* might have been partly written by his friend J. G. Lockhart (who had, after all, been to Oxford) has been finally laid to rest. Yet Hogg's extraordinary novel was no flash in the pan. He wrote a great deal of accomplished poetry, and was a brilliant parodist, as witness the biblical parody of the 'Chaldee Manuscript' in *Blackwood's* (Hogg's work on this contaminated, however, by Wilson's and Lockhart's alterations), and his pastiches of English Romantic poets (notably of Wordsworth in 'The Flying Tailor'), which show a highly developed literary sensibility.

A quite separate but no less important element in Hogg's writing is his inheritance from Border folk tradition. His mother was a notable tradition-bearer with a wealth of tales and supernatural anecdotes at her command, and many of Hogg's stories – 'Mr Adamson of Laverhope', 'Mary Burnet', 'The Brownie of the Black Haggs', 'The Cameronian Preacher's Tale' – as well as his compulsively readable historical extravaganza *The Three Perils of Man*, are richly informed with this material. Traditional folklore concerned with the 'Deil' represents an important element in the structure of the *Justified Sinner*, especially towards the end of the book.

There is, however, an even more salient contribution from the native Scots tradition, and that is the use of the Scots tongue as a counterpoint to the exalted English of the Sinner's religious utterance (and that of his 'reverend father'): a reductive idiom which, by its qualities of sturdy common sense informed by a perceptive and sceptical humour, cuts down to size the inflated rhetoric which cloaks hypocrisy and spiritual pride. Hogg was a consummate master of conversational Scots, and equally certain in his parodic mastery of the formal English of Calvinist religious discourse, which he exploited with immense subtlety in the theological exchanges and tendentious declamations that constitute the intellectual backdrop of the novel's action.

This English–Scots counterpoint is part of a quite intricate system of checks and balances which pervade the dualistic schema of Hogg's novel. Of these the most fundamental is the dual-viewpoint structure whereby Robert Wringhim's memoirs, comprising rather less than two-thirds of the whole, are prefaced by an 'Editor's Narrative' which presents many of the events of the fanatic's life in a subtly different light, and rounded off by an editorial postscript of a few pages which serves to shroud his history in further dubiety. In *The Devil's Elixirs* there is a rudimentary editorial presence in a preface, an explanatory note which aims at clarifying the Painter's manuscript, and in Father Spiridon's Appendix, but these elements are structurally unimportant. Hogg, however, uses the popular editorial device to provide the basic dialectical framework of his fictional argument.

There are two doublings in the *Justified Sinner*: that between Robert Wringhim and his half-brother, George Colwan, and the central one between Wringhim and his demonic tempter, Gil-Martin. These are interrelated, for Gil-Martin has the 'chameleon art' of taking on the likeness of another, and while he first appears as Robert's identical double, he later more and more frequently assumes the guise of Wringhim's now murdered brother.

The Editor's Narrative relates the parentage of the two dissimilar brothers. George Colwan, laird of Dalcastle and Balgrennan, an easy-going, sensual character 'with a very limited proportion of the fear of God in his heart', marries in middle life a young lady from Glasgow who 'was the most severe and gloomy of all bigots to the principles of the Reformation'.[3] Not surprisingly the marriage is not a success. Declaring her husband to be a limb of Antichrist, Lady Dalcastle insists on a separate establishment within the mansion-house and the laird takes a mistress, Miss (or Mrs) Logan. For spiritual consolation the laird's lady calls upon the Reverend Mr Wringhim from Glasgow, who moves into her 'elevated sanctuary', and much humorous play is made with the dissecting of the minutiae of Calvinist doctrine to which they are devoted. The heart of their discourse is the tenet, enunciated by Wringhim, which will be central to young Robert's destiny: 'To the wicked, all things are wicked; but to the just, all things are just and right' (p. 39).

The lady in due course gives birth to a son, George, the fruit of her early congress with her husband; the laird acknowledges him and brings him up himself. A year later she presents him with a brother, Robert, of whom the Editor remarks, 'A brother he certainly was in the eye of the law, and it is more than probable that he was so in reality. But the laird thought otherwise' (p. 43). References to Robert's paternity remain uncommitted throughout the novel, but the overall balance leans heavily towards the laird's opinion. The boy is raised by his mother and Mr Wringhim and baptised by the name of Robert Wringhim; later he drops the surname Colwan altogether, though without explicitly acknowledging his illegitimacy – something which, as Douglas Gifford has pointed out, was regarded by Hogg as morally suspect.[4] We thus have two opposed and contrasting family groups which exist in ambiguous and inverted relationship – one brother rejected by his real but unnatural mother and raised by a loving adopted mother, the other rejected by his supposed father (later described as 'unnatural') and raised by his probable natural father who is in another sense unnatural.

The brothers are probably thus, like Medardus and Count Victor, in the equivocal relationship of half-brotherhood, which denotes both likeness or relatedness and opposition. Their characters indicate that, as doubles, they come into the category of complementary opposites, the divided halves of a sundered whole. Robert is stern and gloomy, though of 'ungovernable passions'; he is also intellectually precocious, 'fond of writing essays on controverted points of theology, for which he got prizes, and great praise from his mother and guardian'. George, on the other hand, 'was much behind him in scholastic acquirements, but greatly his superior in personal prowess, form, feature and all that constitutes gentility in the deportment and appearance' (p. 44). Robert is encouraged to regard both the laird and his brother with 'utter abhorrence', and, the Wringhims having moved to Glasgow, the brothers do not meet until both are fully grown. It is necessary here to summarise the editorial account of their subsequent relations, in order to understand the subversion of their fate by the powers of evil.

Their first confrontation is in Edinburgh, at a tennis match. We are told how Robert provocatively and obdurately impedes his elder brother in his play, repeating his conduct on subsequent occasions: 'the same devilish-looking youth attended him as constantly as his shadow . . . and ever and anon his deep and malignant eye met those of his elder brother with a glance so fierce that it sometimes startled him' (p. 46). Robert's demonic credentials are thus established; but he also suggests the shadow-side, the undeveloped or unacknowledged night-side of George's open, sunny, but somewhat complacent personality. The provocation, described by Hogg with great dramatic flair as well as much black humour, issues in a minor assault by George on Wringhim and a row which results in the brief imprisonment of the latter. There follows a party scuffle between Whigs and High Church youths, George and his friends being involved on the prelatic side. The elder Wringhim in effect now curses George by singing a malevolent hymn in which God is petitioned to give Satan leave to stand 'at his right hand'. The significance of this will shortly become clear.

George incurs the hostility of the populace and has to seclude himself; but he is more fearfully pursued by 'a fiend of more malignant aspect . . . in the form of his brother', who ever and anon darts at him 'looks . . . that chilled his very soul . . . piercing to the bosom's deepest core'. A supernatural element appears to attend these hauntings, for 'this unaccountable being knew all his motions, and every intention of his heart, as it were intuitively' (p. 58). He appears beside George in places where it is impossible that he could have known him to be by natural means, always in the same position relative to himself – at his right hand, in fact – dogging him 'as regularly as the shadow is cast from the substance' and continuously unnerving him with glances 'too appalling to be withstood' (p. 59). The complex irony of this haunting will only become fully apparent when we read Wringhim's account of the same incidents. From George's perspective, 'The attendance of that brother was now become like the attendance of a demon on some devoted being that had sold himself to destruction' (p. 60).

George generously resolves to be reconciled with his brother should it prove possible, and thereafter the visitations cease for a time. One day, in a benign and blessed frame of mind, he takes a walk up Arthur's Seat, the imposing volcanic mountain that dominates the city of Edinburgh. It is a morning on which a dense early mist is being gradually dispersed by the powerful rays of the sun, producing the dazzling effect of a 'sublunary rainbow'. Seated on the pinnacle of a rocky precipice near the summit of the hill, George is surprised by a terrifying apparition: delineated in the cloud he sees the dreadful face of his brother, 'dilated to twenty times the natural size', gazing on him with a terrible look in which 'murderous malice' is strangely compounded with 'fear and trembling' (p. 63). Hogg here makes use of the natural phenomenon sometimes known as the 'spectre of the Brocken', by which a magnified human image can be projected in atmospheric conditions such as he describes.

George takes the vision to be that of a haunting demon in his brother's form; seeing it advance menacingly towards him as if about to spring on him, he flees precipitately in the opposite direction and runs headlong into the real Robert Wringhim. A bloody scuffle follows between the brothers, in which Robert acquits himself ignominiously, and pondering on the extraordinary incident, George speculates 'that he was haunted by some evil genius in the shape of his brother, as well as by that dark and mysterious wretch himself' (p. 66). This supposition will later be shown to be well-founded.

The quarrel between the brothers now approaches its fatal climax. George is, at the instigation of the elder Wringhim, apprehended on a charge of assault and battery and attempted fratricide, but is at length acquitted, and young Wringhim bound over to keep the peace. George, about to leave Edinburgh, holds a farewell dinner-party at the Black Bull tavern, during the course of which he quarrels with a friend named Drummond. Drummond departs in anger, but a short time later 'a young gentleman, in appearance like him who had lately left the house', appears at the door and asks for young Dalcastle. George goes out, and the following morning is discovered slain nearby, on a washing-green at the side of the North Loch. Drummond, ill-advisedly concealed by his relations, is found guilty of the murder in his absence and escapes abroad. Old Colwan dies of grief within a few weeks of his son, and Robert Wringhim, 'as the lawful son of the late laird, born in wedlock, and under his father's roof', succeeds to his estates. At his investiture he is observed to indulge 'more freely in the bottle than he had ever been seen to do before' (p. 75).

Mrs Logan is deeply suspicious that it was the Wringhims who were responsible for the young laird's destruction. Through a train of circumstances which we need not enter into here, she eventually succeeds in learning the story of one Bell Calvert, an unfortunate lady fallen in the world (and, like Robert, the victim of an 'artful and consummate fiend'), who has been a chance witness of the death of young Colwan. She has seen two men, one dressed in black and the other, like Drummond, in tartans, at the same time as she has witnessed Drummond's departure from the tavern. All three have been simultaneously within her vision, the man in tartans being identical to Drummond, so that she had the impression that she 'looked upon some spirit, or demon, in his likeness' (p. 90). Soon she hears this figure urging on the man in black to some deed which he describes as 'God's work'; he gives her a 'sly nod'.

Having concealed the youth in black in a dark close, the figure summons Dalcastle from the tavern and challenges him to fight. Flitting from George's thrusts 'like a shadow', he manoeuvres him up to the mouth of the dark entry, and calls out, 'Ah, hell has it! My friend, my friend!' At this signal the man in black rushes from concealment and pierces Dalcastle twice in the back with his rapier. 'Oh, dog of hell, it is you who have done this!' cries out the dying man (p. 94). Bell's description of the man in black leaves Mrs Logan in no doubt that he is Robert Wringhim.

The two ladies determine to travel to Dalcastle to gather evidence. They see Wringhim walking with 'another young man', and Bell immediately recognises Robert as the murderer; but Mrs Logan faints away with shock at another recognition: the second man is the double of the murdered George. The following day the dames conceal themselves in a thicket and hear the companions debating predestination. The elect youth, incited by his associate to confront the ladies, is then abandoned to their fury, and they leave him bound hand and foot.

The women return to Edinburgh where they discuss their experiences. Mrs Calvert likens Wringhim to a demon in flesh and blood, hideous in the 'depth and malignity of his eye', while Mrs Logan sees him as 'puffed up with spiritual pride'. She is more struck, however, by the 'extraordinary being' who accompanies him, and his uncanny likeness to George: 'I think he imitates him in everything, for some purpose or some effect on his sinful associate'. She cannot avoid the impression 'that they are one and the same being, or that the one was a prototype of the other' (p. 104). From this we begin to obtain some idea of the complexity of the interrelationship of these three figures.

Mrs Logan and Bell Calvert report all they discover to the Lord Justice-Clerk, and on the basis of their evidence and that of another witness of George Colwan's murder (a former associate of Mrs Calvert) the authorities decide to arrest Wringhim and bring him to trial. But at Dalcastle all is found to be in confusion and disarray, and the laird's mother (whom the ladies had heard Gil-Martin inciting her son to murder) missing. Officers are despatched to 'apprehend the monster', but he has disappeared for ever. Here the Editor's Narrative comes to an end.

Thus far we have been dealing with an account which is purportedly impartial, based on 'history, justiciary records, and tradition' (p. 106). It would be a mistake, however, to assume that the counterpoint between this version of events and that about to be furnished by the Sinner's memoirs is a simple one of objective and subjective, trustworthy and suspect. Douglas Gifford and John Carey have clearly shown that in terms of hard evidence, the editorial narrative is in its own way just as suspect and limited as the Sinner's prejudiced version of events. Between the lines of the editorial account we can decipher a distinctly ambivalent message. Hogg, it must be remembered, was himself an orthodox Calvinist, though certainly of a moderate persuasion. That one of his purposes was to satirise antinomian extremism is not in doubt, but he would certainly not have shared the religious position of the Colwans and their party.

At the level of the sympathetic portrayal of character, the Colwans do not have it all their own way. For all the humorous appeal of his down-to-earth contrast with his spouse and the Reverend Wringhim, the old laird is a coarse sensualist, whom Mrs Calvert has known 'never for any good' (p. 79). Young George, while bluff, hearty and good-natured, is also rather shallow and self-satisfied. On the other hand Robert Wringhim, though clearly the primary object of Hogg's satire as a deluded victim of the monstrous growth of his own spiritual pride, is not portrayed entirely without sympathy. This is apparent not only in the perceptive inwardness with which his character is developed in his own memoirs, but also in a certain biting zest with which his behaviour is described even in the editorial section.

This partial counterweight to the general tendency of the novel's moral argument should not be over-emphasised; in part it may simply reflect the possibility that Hogg, like Milton in the opinion of Blake, was to some degree 'of the Devil's party without knowing it'.[5] However there is another more important reason for suggesting that we should recognise an element of subjectivity in the editor's account. When it deals with the relations between the two brothers, it does so essentially from George's point of view. The editor is conventionally omniscient, but if we were to ask the question,

Where did the editor obtain this information?, we would have to reply that much of it could have come only from George. George, of course, is quite unaware of the existence of his brother's double; and as we have already seen, his brother's double is also his own double (or more strictly his revenant, since he appears in his guise only after George's death). When he describes his haunting by Robert, George is actually, it will transpire, describing his haunting by Gil-Martin. However trustworthy a witness we may assume him to be, his version of events is prejudiced by the fact that he himself, just as much as his brother, is a plaything in the hands of a power which neither of them is able to comprehend. Both unknowingly give the Devil his opportunity through their own weaknesses, in George's case rash combativeness and youthful debauchery.

Everything connected with the activities of the mysterious Gil-Martin will be found to be ambiguous and double-edged. He is like a bridge between the two brothers, since he can take the form of either, but he is also something like an extension of their relation to each other. To the degree that they are complementary opposites, divided halves of the same whole, Robert may be said to represent the unacknowledged dark side of George's psyche. But even more clearly, Gil-Martin is the projected embodiment of Wringhim's dissociated second self. Beyond that he is, more unequivocally than any double or tempter figure we have yet encountered, the Devil. He is the evil within Wringhim, but also the evil which seduces him from without. Both brothers are ultimately his victims, and betray that lack of awareness that first allows him to control them and then blinds them to the reality of what is happening. Let us see, then, how Gil-Martin comes to Robert Wringhim.

The pattern is the one we can now recognise as classical, that of spiritual pride and inflation leading to moral depravity. Robert, by his own account, grows up a monster of personal and spiritual conceit. The insolent frankness of his style, which is in some respects disarming, is really the mark of the unassailability of his vanity. He thus reports quite openly that his father's earthy servant, John Barnet, regarded him as a 'conceited gowk', and admits to having been 'particularly prone to lying' (pp. 111, 118). This has obvious implications for the reliability of his narrative, as well as laying him open to the attentions of the Father of Lies; but most of his deliberate distortions are at the level of simple vanity, as when he represents his own part in the scuffle with his brother on Arthur's Seat in a heroic light, and readily accepts Gil-Martin's later assurance that he killed George in face-to-face combat. He openly acknowledges his envious malice in his dealings with others: he succeeds in securing the dismissal of the irreverent John Barnet, and similarly manages to remove from the scene his school rival M'Gill, whose superiority over himself he attributes to dealings with the Devil. (It is possible that M'Gill's name may be intended to chime with that of Gil-Martin, who first introduces himself simply as 'Gil'.)

At the same time, a kind of sympathy for Robert that is not intended by himself is encouraged in the reader's mind by his account of his upbringing, for he is undoubtedly in part the victim of his nightmarish religious environment. The terror tactics of his 'reverend father' early instil into his soul a profound horror at the possibility of his being among the reprobate, and, while conscious of the overwhelming pressure of his sins, he believes himself denied 'the grace of repentance'. In this frame of mind he wilfully represses his sexual instincts, bringing himself to 'despise, if not abhor, the beauty of women', to the extent that even his mother taxes him as an 'unnatural wretch' (p. 123). It is small wonder that he grows up acutely aware of the 'opposing principles in the soul of man' (p. 113).

When Mr Wringhim finally gives Robert the glad tidings of the assurance of his justification, it is clear that his first reaction is one of immense relief, of release from constant anxiety: 'I wept for joy to be thus assured of my freedom from all sin, and of the impossibility of my ever again falling away from my new state.' But this emotion is almost instantaneously transformed into the crudest kind of spiritual pride: 'An exaltation of spirit lifted me, as it were, far above the earth and the sinful creatures crawling on its surface; and I deemed myself an eagle among the children of men, and looking down with pity and contempt on the grovelling creatures below' (p. 125).

It is at this moment of psychological crisis that the double makes his entry: 'I beheld a young man of a mysterious appearance coming towards me.' Wringhim tries at first to shun him, but he casts himself in his way; the deluded youth feels the influence of a power like 'the force of enchantment', and strange sensations thrill through his frame. As they approach each other, 'What was my astonishment on perceiving that he was the same being as myself!' Wringhim takes him for his guardian angel, but his double, reading his throughts, explains, 'You think I am your brother . . . or that I am your second self. I am indeed your brother, not according to the flesh, but in my belief in the same truths, and my assurance in the same mode of redemption' (p. 126).

Gil-Martin, as he is to name himself (a name probably associated with 'Gil-Moules', a traditional Border folk name for the Devil[6]), is thus, psychologically speaking, a concrete figure for a separated fragment of Robert's personality, born of his inflation and dissociation and the repression of his natural desires. His intent is to confirm Wringhim in the purpose which he had long before entertained, of freeing the world from the 'noxious burden' of the wicked, and to carry his own antinomian beliefs 'to extremes'. But Hogg has chosen to embody this sub-personality in the figure of the traditional demonic tempter (who of course always has his interior aspect), and at the spiritual level Gil-Martin is, quite straightforwardly, the Devil. There seems no reason to doubt that Hogg actually believed in the Devil in the sense of an objectively existing spiritual entity capable of taking on physical form. For the purposes of the fable that is certainly what Gil-Martin is; Wringhim himself comes reluctantly to suspect this truth, though he always pushes the idea away from him again; no one else in the story remains long in doubt of it.

The justified sinner is early aware of his companion that 'by setting his features to the mould of other people, he entered at once into their conceptions and feelings' (p. 127). Gil-Martin explains the nature of this 'chameleon art', a preternatural extension of the natural mimetic faculty and 'a gift of the God that made me': by contemplating a person's face minutely he is able to assume its likeness, and along with that likeness he attains gradually to 'the possession of their most secret thoughts' (p. 132). At one level this capacity signifies the means by which Gil-Martin enters into someone's personality and takes possession of his soul; but at another it can be simply a very convenient supernatural trick, as when he assumes the form of Drummond in order to incriminate him in the murder of George Colwan.

What Wringhim never remarks upon, strangely enough, is that Gil-Martin has actually *no* form that is simply his own. The two likenesses which he most habitually assumes are those of Robert and George. In the early stages of their association he is simply Robert's double, but after the murder of George, when the companions are together, Gil-Martin appears to have the form of the slain brother, both in Robert's eyes and in those of other witnesses. The meaning of this is somewhat obscure. In part it may signify a constant reminder by Wringhim's conscience of his crime of fratricide, but this is not much emphasised. It is more probable that it indicates that the division of his personality is intimately connected with his relation to his brother, that their fates are inseparably linked, and that Gil-Martin is both the emblem of that link and an extension of each of them.

Gil-Martin's ability to reproduce himself as Wringhim is used to most sinister ends. During the period after the tennis-match confrontation with George, Robert is seized by a 'strange distemper' which he attributes to bewitchment by Mrs Logan, and is confined to bed for many days. It is during this time that George is haunted by the constant presence of his brother in a manner that seems to him quite inexplicable. 'I generally conceived myself to be two people', the memoirs tell us. 'When I lay in bed, I dreamed there were two of us in it; when I sat up I always beheld another person, and always in the same position from the place where I sat or stood, which was about three paces off towards my left side.' This positioning corresponds exactly to George's experience. Yet this is not a simple doubling by his 'second self': 'The most perverse part of it was that I rarely conceived *myself* to be any of the two persons. I thought for the most part that my companion was one of them, and my brother the other' (p. 157). His authentic personality has thus split into two halves represented by his two doubles.

This is indeed an enchantment, though Mrs Logan is not its source. Much later in the narrative, a woman accuses Wringhim of seducing her daughter. At this time he believes that he has been at Dalcastle only a month, but it appears that the period has really been four months, and the lady claims that he has been in a state of inebriety all this time. He confesses that he has several times had cause to suspect that 'I have a second self; or that there is some other being who appears in my likeness' (p. 177). He continues to lose time – an experience entirely consonant with actual schizophrenic pathology – and finds his experience of a second self 'an anomaly not to be accounted for by any philosophy of mine' (p. 180). Later still, Wringhim is accused of the murder of his mother and the young lady he has seduced. Gil-Martin insists that he did commit both crimes, 'in your own person, and with your own hands'. The unfortunate man can only conclude that he has 'two souls, which take possession of my bodily frame by turns, the one being all unconscious of what the other performs' (p. 189).

It never does become clear whether these crimes have been committed by Wringhim himself or by Gil-Martin in his likeness. Hogg's point in maintaining this ambiguity is precisely to suggest that a point has been reached in Wringhim's spiritual and psychological descent at which the distinction is no longer of importance. At first he acts as his tempter's assistant, then as his collaborator, and finally they become more or less identified. Wringhim's servant, Penpunt, phrases it sagaciously: 'They say that the deil's often seen gaun sidie for sidie w'ye, whiles in ae shape, an' whiles in another. An' they say that he whiles takes your ain shape, or else enters into you, and then you turn a deil yoursel.' Robert is constrained to admit that 'the insinuation was so like what I felt myself that I was greatly awed and confounded' (p. 193).

The dramatic tension of the tale is located in Wringhim's hopeless struggle to maintain in his own mind his distinctness from Gil-Martin. It is on this issue that his salvation will depend: whether or not he will become totally identified with his aberrant second self. In his resistance to the extreme antinomian conclusions asserted by Gil-Martin, and to their practical implications, is projected the internal struggle between, on the one hand, the fearful and bloody impulses that have been set loose by his unrestrained pride, and on the other, the feeble but persistent activity of his conscience. It is the Devil's part to insist on the indissolubility of the link between them, to confirm the Sinner in his infatuated blindness, and to inure him to the idea that he is bound to his diabolical associate by Fate.

Even at the beginning of the association, Wringhim is uneasily aware that the sophistical arguments of this 'unaccountable being' have diverted him from the actual worship of God. The transformation wrought in him by the first encounter makes his reverend parents wonder – until convinced of the rectitude of his religious principles – whether his companion might not be 'an agent of the devil' (p. 129). Gil-Martin, however, asserts the infallibility of the Elect with constantly renewed eloquence and passion, appealing equally to Wringhim's vanity and to his established desire to 'cut sinners off with the sword'. He is ordained, his tempter assures him, 'to perform some great act for the cause of Jesus and His Church' (p. 134). Gil-Martin drops several strong but sly hints (for he is always strictly and literally honest) as to his true identity, but Wringhim, given to understand that he is a prince or potentate of

some kind, prefers to suppose that he is the Czar Peter of Russia
rather than the Prince of Darkness. When warned by Mr Blanchard,
a moderate clergyman, that 'your creed and his carry damnation
on the very front of it', he is almost persuaded to drop Gil-Martin,
but finds himself unable to do so. 'He was constant to me as my
shadow, and by degrees he acquired such an ascendancy over me
that I was never happy out of his company, nor greatly so in it'
(p. 139).

Gil-Martin is able to influence the unconscious workings of
Wringhim's soul, and he begins to dream of a great triumph in
which 'the overthrow and death of Mr. Blanchard was the first
step by which I attained the eminent position I occupied' (p. 141).
He sees a vision of golden weapons let down to him in a cloud
with their points towards him, and this inflames his zeal until he
is 'as one beside himself'. Urged on to the outrage by his infernal
associate, he seems to hear the 'sweet voice' of conscience warning
him to beware, but Gil-Martin intentionally misses his shot at
Blanchard and leaves it to Wringhim to do the deed himself.

Douglas Gifford has forcefully argued that at the crucial moment
of moral decision Wringhim never acts under direct duress. It is of
the greatest importance in Hogg's scheme, and also in accordance
with the traditional rules governing the Devil's activities, that he
is never ultimately deprived of free will: 'The Devil is allowed to
possess him as a result of sin, but not at the point where Robert
chooses to commit the sin.'[7] The promptings of conscience are
much stronger when he makes the attempt on the life of his brother
on Arthur's Seat. He has been provided by Gil-Martin with a small
dagger (a piece of equipment doubtless borrowed from *The Devil's
Elixirs*), but before he can use it is visited by 'sinful doubtings' on
the infallibility of the Elect. In the mist he perceives 'a lady robed
in white' and hears 'a still small voice' condemning his purpose;
but Gil-Martin intervenes to nullify the influence of the good angel
(p. 160). He still has qualms, however, and his wavering and
fluctuation cause the attempt to miscarry.

At each stage of his descent into depravity and wickedness,
Wringhim offers some resistance, but this is never strong enough
to overcome the eloquence and the wiles of Gil-Martin. The
argument between them revolves always on justification and the
absolute infallibility of the Elect, and Wringhim's fears of falling
from his 'upright state' provoke Gil-Martin to fury. At last the
taunts and contempt of his 'illustrious friend' persuade Wringhim

to the murder of his brother, and from this point nothing can loosen the stranglehold in which he is held, 'like one round whose body a deadly snake is twisted' (p. 190). Driven even to the satisfaction of a lust that had seemed to him foreign to his nature, he becomes sick of his existence: 'I began to have secret terrors that the great enemy of man's salvation was exercising powers over me that might eventually lead to my ruin' (p. 165). Such is his wilful blindness, however, that he does not link this infernal power with the person of Gil-Martin, and remains reluctant to admit to himself that the latter's presence has become irksome and insupportable to him. Their identity has become literally inescapable: 'we were incorporated together – identified with one another, as it were, and the power was not in me to separate myself from him' (p. 166).

Gil-Martin constantly drives home the identical message. Sometimes he leaves Wringhim for a while, but always he returns, with that voice which now seems like 'the sounds of the pit, wheezed through a grated cranny', to fill Robert's heart with despair: 'sooner cause the shadow to relinquish the substance, than separate me from your side. Our beings are amalgamated, as it were, and consociated in one, and never shall I depart from this country until I carry you in triumph with me' (p. 171). It is because of this incorporation, the way in which Gil-Martin, as Devil, has become interiorised in Wringhim's soul, that he cannot apprehend his true nature. He can, in fact, be seen in either of two ways with equal validity: as the evil within projected as an external figure, or the evil without interiorised as part of the self. Once Wringhim looks at his illustrious companion's foot to see if it is cloven into two hoofs: 'It was the foot of a gentleman in every respect, but the form of his counsels was somewhat equivocal, and, if not double, they were amazingly crooked' (p. 185).

After the discovery of the bodies of Mrs Colwan and the girl he is said to have murdered (a detail in which the memoirs differ significantly from the Editor's Narrative, in which the former cannot be found dead or alive, and the latter is never even mentioned), Wringhim becomes a hunted outcast, driven from pillar to post, pursued by the 'ruined and debased potentate' and descending gradually into delirium and madness. One incident symbolises his plight with horrible vividness. A weaver locks him for the night in the room where his looms are kept, and in the dark he becomes entangled in their web of endless confusion.

Hanging upside down by his feet, he is thrashed and taunted by the weaver: 'Are you fawn inna little hell, instead o' the big muckle ane?' 'I wanted to be at the light', he explains pathetically, but he is now caught fast and 'utterly powerless' (p. 209).

Just thus, seeking, as he believed, the light, did he become entangled in the Devil's web, and now he is powerless to extricate himself. 'I am wedded to you so closely', Gil-Martin assures him, 'that I feel as if I were the same person. Our essences are one, our bodies and spirits being united, so that I am drawn towards you as by magnetism, and wherever you are, there must my presence be with you' (p. 207). For a moment there comes the flicker of a possibility of repentance, when, afflicted with despair and loathing of his tormentor, he curses the time when they met; but then he remembers that this was the time when he was assured of his final election and confirmation by an eternal decree, recalls his curse and repents instead of his 'rashness'. Thus he confirms himself in the spiritual pride which has been his undoing; but as the hour approaches when he must fulfil the pact he has made with Gil-Martin that they shall die together, and he must commit the ultimate sin of suicide to which it has all along been the Devil's aim to drive him, his assurance of salvation deserts him: 'But, ah! who is yon that I see approaching furiously, his stern face blackened with horrid despair! My hour is at hand. Almighty God, what is this that I am about to do! The hour of repentance is past, and now my fate is inevitable' (p. 230).

The resumption of the editorial framework at the end of the novel, in an episode which describes the exhumation of the Sinner's corpse by the editor and Hogg's friends Lockhart and Laidlaw at the prompting of a letter written by Hogg himself to *Blackwood's*, serves to cloak the mysterious events of the narrative in further dubiety by questioning their objective veracity. In suggesting that the author was a religious maniac who 'wrote and wrote about a deluded creature, till he arrived at that height of madness that he believed himself to be the very object whom he had all along been describing', it rounds off this classic fiction of the double by proposing a further shadowy duality (p. 242). But it leaves the Sinner himself held still in the vice of his own doctrine, by which the impossibility of his repentance is unanswerable: for if he was truly one of the Elect then remorse was needless (which, as we have seen, in his heart of hearts he does not believe); and if he was not, then it could have been of no avail.

Six years after the appearance of the *Justified Sinner* Hogg returned to the theme of the double in the story 'Strange Letter of a Lunatic' (1830).[8] This wittily conceived tale in many respects astonishingly anticipates the story of Dostoevsky's Mr Golyadkin, though there can be no question of influence. Its main interest, however, lies in the light which, in its much simpler structure, it sheds on the *Justified Sinner*, and especially on the question of whether there are *alternative* explanations of the status of Gil-Martin.

Douglas Gifford analyses the novel in terms of two possible readings, psychological and demonological, and claims that 'these rational and supernatural explanations exist in ambiguity together'.[9] His analysis is a highly perceptive one, but this way of putting it loses sight of an essential point. Rather than allowing two mutually exclusive possibilities an ambiguous but peaceful coexistence, Hogg wants us, I believe, to see these different ways of reading Wringhim's experience as separate but mutually supportive aspects of a single truth; and the short story lends credibility to this assumption.

Like the novel, 'Strange Letter of a Lunatic' has a dualistic structure. The lunatic's letter, addressed to Hogg, is followed by a short letter from a third party which brings apparently objective evidence to bear on the subjective account. The letter of the lunatic relates how the narrator, walking very early one morning on the Castle Hill in Edinburgh, notices an old man who appears anxious to introduce himself but refrains from doing so until he is beckoned. He then offers a pinch of snuff from a gold box, and to his intense delight it is accepted. 'The devil I am sure is in that body', the narrator observes, and, of course, he is right. The old man has followed the diabolic rules in waiting to be invited in, and the acceptance of the snuff is a miniature compact with the Devil.

That evening, at a tavern, the lunatic sees 'another me sitting at the end of the table'. This identical double, yet another 'unaccountable fellow' in a long line, claims to be James Beatman, younger, of Drumloning, and the original finds himself in a protracted struggle to maintain his identity in the face of the usurper, to establish 'which of us was the *right* James Beatman'. At first the double seems benevolent enough, for he has a habit of settling his senior's bills for him; but the latter is not impressed. He finds himself pursued on a journey north by his rival, who always has a 'sly leer' on his face. They drink together on board a boat sailing up the Forth to Alloa (like Wringhim in the latter stages of his possession, Beatman is certainly fond of the bottle), and afterwards he is accused of molesting a young lady, and briefly imprisoned.

On finding himself still dogged by this shadow on reaching the Highlands, where he is to shoot with a Mr Walker, he confronts his double as an imposter: 'A most unaccountable and impalpable being, who has taken a fancy to personate me, and to cross and confound me in every relation in life.' He receives no satisfaction, of course, and finding himself in the terrible dilemma of being, in his own eyes, entirely sane, but having 'become, as it were, two bodies, with only one soul between them', determines on decisive measures. In this state he dreams of the old man with the snuff-box telling him that 'I was now himself, and that he had transformed his own nature and spirit into my shape and form.' His confusion is terribly compounded when, anticipating his own protests, his double appears again and demands that he cease from impersonating him: 'you are either a rank counterfeit, or, what I rather begin to suspect, the devil in my likeness.'

The upshot is that Beatman and his double meet in a duel; Beatman falls wounded, 'but which of the I's it was that fell I never knew till this day, nor ever can'. He recovers consciousness in a lunatic asylum, where the keeper tells him that he has drunk himself out of his wits. But, as the lunatic protests to Hogg, his derangement, to which he readily admits, was 'solely caused by my wound, and by having been turned into two men, acting on various and distinct principles, yet still conscious of an idio-syncrasy'.

Hogg now intervenes editorially, saying that he would have regarded the letter 'altogether as the dream of a lunatic, had it not been for two circumstances'. These are the fact that Beatman was undoubtedly left behind at Stirling on his journey although Mr Walker believed himself to have picked him up in his gig; and the reality of the duel and his wound. He then presents Walker's letter, in which the correspondent limits himself strictly to facts, as his thoughts on the matter 'will not conform to human reason'. Neither he nor his friend Mr Watten ever saw more than one person, but he confirms the anomaly of Beatman's 'second' arrival in a carriage on the night on which his 'hallucinations' commenced. As to the duel, two shots were heard though only one person was seen to go to the scene; two pistols were found discharged, and the position of the wound was such that it could not have been self-inflicted: 'it must either have been fired at him while in a stooping posture, or from the air straight above him'.

Hogg's wording in the short passage linking the two letters is careful. He does not deny that Beatman is a lunatic: the question is whether there is more to it than that, whether his narrative is 'altogether the dream of a lunatic'. The suggestion is that the presence of the Devil is real; Beatman is possessed, and his lunacy *is* his possession. This is, after all, the traditional view of the nature of madness, having its roots in the New Testament and even further back than that. It is the metaphor on which Dostoevsky based his novel *The Devils* or *The Possessed*, with its motto from the parable of the Gadarene swine. In Hogg's story, as in many stories of the double, someone goes mad because he is possessed by the Devil, because the Devil is *in him*; and the Devil is able to be in him because he has been granted admittance.

# 6

# Edgar Allan Poe

In America, Gothic Romanticism was received in a spirit which reflected both the distance that separated the consciousness of the New World from the cultural history of Europe, and the fascination which that half-possessed inheritance exerted upon the American soul. Harry Levin has argued, in *The Power of Blackness*, that the overt ideals of nineteenth-century American society, the belief in material progress and human perfectibility, the 'bland perfection' of Americans' daylight selves, were offset by a compensating visitation of darkness and insecurity in the night-side of the nation's collective psyche. Creative minds were drawn to this neglected or repressed dark component: 'Where the voice of the majority is by definition affirmative, the spirit of independence is likeliest to manifest itself by employing the negative.'[1] That negative is most memorably voiced in the melancholy reiteration of Edgar Allan Poe's hauntingly insistent Raven: 'Nevermore.'

Charles Brockden Brown employed a pervasive imagery of light and dark which marked off his conscious commitment to Enlightenment values, to dispersing the lurking shadows of mystery and superstition, from his intuitive insights into the power of the irrational and the unconscious within the human soul; a cleavage symbolised in his frontier settings, where a fragile civilisation resting upon European culture and values exists in close proximity to the wilderness and the savage, which impinge upon it and threaten to overwhelm it in a catastrophic inrush of the primitive. In Poe, the dichotomy of black and white is even more strongly emphasised, and reflects a not dissimilarly ambivalent relation to the scientific and materialist vision of the nature of man. Gothic romance spoke eloquently to the historical situation of mid-nineteenth-century America, but in the work of Poe that voice is echoed back in a different tone whose accents bespeak a deep longing to establish the materiality of the very soul itself. Poe's spiritual world has even an architectural quality – which he referred, interestingly enough, to the example of Beckford's *Vathek*.

Poe's early work is profoundly imbued with the influence of the

German *Schauerroman* as mediated through *Blackwood's Magazine*; yet in the preface to his first collection of stories, *Tales of the Grotesque and Arabesque* (1840), he protested against criticisms of '"Germanism" and gloom' in his fiction, and dissociated himself from the 'pseudo-horror' of the cruder terror-tales: 'If in many of my productions terror has been the thesis, I maintain that terror is not of Germany, but of the soul'. But 'Germanism' was not always meretricious, and the example of Hoffmann left pervasive and undeniable traces on the creativity of Poe.[2] The climate of their worlds, however was subtly different. It was Dostoevsky who, in a preface to a Russian translation of Poe, first pointed out his materialist quality; referring to Hoffmann's idealism, he remarks, 'Poe's fantasticalness as compared with that, seems strangely "material", if such expression may be allowed.'[3] Hoffmann and Poe are alike, though, in the deep-rooted duality of their consciousness, and their cultural divergence covers an underlying temperamental affinity, which is partially manifested in a predilection for the tale as a medium of creative expression.

The narrator of 'The Murders in the Rue Morgue' says of his friend, the amateur sleuth Dupin, 'I often dwelt meditatively on the old philosophy of the Bi-Part Soul, and amused myself with a fancy of a double Dupin – the creative and the resolvent.'[4] We may well suppose that these complementary facets reflect a corresponding duality in the person of Dupin's creator. Certainly the protagonist with whom Poe himself is associated by the clearest autobiographical signposts is William Wilson, the eponymous hero of his classic tale of the double. There are two obsessive themes which repeatedly elicit images of duality in Poe's fiction: that of survival after death, and that of the avenging conscience.

In 'Eureka' Poe went so far as to deny the reality of the spiritual world: 'God is material.' The 'other' was intensely real to him, but he sought to assimilate it to the physical and the material. The survival after death which he longs for is therefore some form of *physical* continuance. This is the animating principle of the imaginative tale 'Ligeia' (1838), one of several in which metempsychosis is a leading idea.[5] The narrator's one and only love is the prodigiously beautiful, learned and accomplished Lady Ligeia. Her defining characteristics are the intensity of her passion and the power of her will, her 'gigantic volition'. He associates her character with a supposed quotation from Joseph Glanvill which serves as the tale's motto: 'And the will therein lieth, which dieth not. Who knoweth the mysteries of the will, with its vigor? For God is but a great will pervading all things by nature of its intentness. Man doth not yield him to the angels, nor to death utterly, save only through the weakness of his feeble will.'

When Ligeia falls mortally sick, she long resists death with all the superhuman force of her will, and finally she dies with the words of Glanvill on her lips. The narrator's mourning is measureless and unappeased, but under the influence of opium, as he tells us, 'in a moment of alienation, I led from the altar as my bride – as the successor of the unforgotten Ligeia — the fair-haired and blue-eyed Lady Rowena Trevanion, of Tremaine'. The new bride is the diametric opposite of the raven-locked and black-eyed Ligeia; as Levin has noted, this polarity undoubtedly refers to that between Rowena and Rebecca in Scott's *Ivanhoe*, but the relationship between the two brides may also owe something to the parasitic possession of the heroine of Coleridge's 'Christabel' by the Lady Geraldine, who is the daughter of Lord Roland de Vaux of Tryermaine.

History repeats itself: Rowena in her turn sickens and wastes away in the ebony bed of the sinister sepulchral bedchamber adorned by the morbid fancy of her unloving husband. A few nights before her death he seems to see a few drops of a ruby-red liquid mysteriously drop into her goblet of revivifying wine. She deteriorates and apparently dies; but throughout a long and hideous night of vigil, the narrator, wrapt in visions of Ligeia, watches as Rowena's corpse is repeatedly reanimated, and as often slips back into an icier and seemingly more final death. But at last the shrouded figure rises from the bed, totters towards him, and unloosening the cerements that confine her head, reveals not the blue eyes and fair hair of Rowena, but the raven tresses and the wild, black eyes of his lost love.

In order to achieve a physical rebirth which defies and defeats the confining tomb, Ligeia has taken possession of the form of her complementary opposite and reanimated it with her spirit and her will, until her rival is obliged to yield to her even her material being. A not dissimilar process occurs in 'The Oval Portrait', in which the portrait, the art-double of the beautiful maiden it portrays, steals her life: her painter husband, exclaiming on completing his work, 'This is indeed *Life* itself!', turns to find that his wife is dead. (The idea corresponds closely to that of Hoffmann's 'Die Jesuiterkirche in G.'.) Another way in which Poe envisaged the possibility of cheating death was the indefinite suspension of final dissolution in mesmeric trance. The narrator in 'The Facts in the Case of M. Valdemar' (1845) performs this experiment on a man in the final stages of consumption.[6] After manifesting all the clinical symptoms of death, M. Valdemar speaks; or rather, words issue from his mouth as from a vast distance or from a subterranean cavern, announcing that he has been sleeping and is now dead. He remains for many months in a state of suspended animation, but when awakened from his trance almost instantly dissolves into 'a nearly liquid mass of loathsome – of detestable putridity'.

This story does not make use of the concept of a double, but a closely related tale relies on the associated idea of the revenant, and combines the notions of mesmerism and metempsychosis in a manner which almost certainly derives from Hoffmann's 'Der Magnetiseur'. 'A Tale of the Ragged Mountains' tells the story of Mr Augustus Bedloe, a gentleman of ambiguous age – he *seems* young but sometimes gives the impression that he might be a hundred years old – and extraordinary appearance.[7] His expression is melancholic and normally he makes a bloodless and corpse-like impression, but at moments of excitement his eyes – cat-like as those of Hoffmann's loathsome Coppelius – become lustrous 'to a degree inconceivable'. His condition is attributed to chronic neuralgia, for which he is treated by a Dr Templeton, a convert of Mesmer; between these two 'there had grown up, little by little, a very distinct and strongly marked *rapport*, or magnetic relation'. Bedloe will enter a magnetic trance almost instantaneously at Templeton's suggestion.

Bedloe's sensitive and excitable temperament and vivid imagination have been enhanced by morphine. One misty autumn day he sets off for a walk in the Ragged Mountains south-west of Charlottesville. Entering a secluded glen, he mysteriously finds himself in a tropical and savage landscape and sees an 'Eastern-looking city' spread out below him, which in his subsequent account of his experience he describes in great detail. He is certain that he is not dreaming. Descending into the city, he becomes physically and emotionally involved in a battle raging between a native crowd and a small, hard-pressed band of British-led soldiers, whom he joins. In the course of this desperate struggle he is struck in the right temple by a poisoned arrow, and dies. After some minutes, during which he experiences feelings of nonentity and death, he feels something like an electric shock pass through his consciousness; his soul separates itself from his body and flits buoyantly back to the ravine where his 'vision' commenced. Again he experiences a 'shock as of a galvanic battery' and finds himself his original self once more.

On hearing this extraordinary story, Templeton shows him a miniature dating from 1780, depicting a friend of his own, Mr Oldeb, whom he had known in Calcutta in his youth. It was Bedloe's 'miraculous similarity' to Oldeb, and the 'not altogether horrorless curiosity' that this aroused, which had first induced Templeton to seek his acquaintance; his vision has been induced by the doctor's mesmeric suggestion, for at the very same moment Templeton was detailing the events described in a notebook at home. Bedloe had described Benares, and the events of the insurrection of Cheyte Sing in 1780 in which Oldeb lost his life, killed by a poisoned Bengalee arrow. A week after this conversation Bedloe himself dies, as a result of a poisonous 'sangsue', mistaken for a leech, being applied to his temple - the site of Oldeb's fatal wound. In the newspaper obituary which reports Bedloe's death the final 'e' is omitted by a typographical error so that his name is rendered as 'Bedlo', which, as the narrator rather needlessly points out, is Oldeb reversed.

This story of metempsychosis has no great psychological interest, but it illustrates graphically the contribution which the idea of the magnetic trance was still making in the mid-nineteenth century to the literature of duality, in providing images of the double life and in giving access to an interior world in which secondary personalities might be supposed to be discoverable.

The idea of the other self externalised as accusing or reproachful conscience is adumbrated in 'The Tell-Tale Heart'. The extreme nervousness of the narrator (as with so many of Poe's characters, his denials of madness serve only to persuade the reader to an opposite conclusion) has resulted in prodigious acuity of hearing. As he skulks awaiting his moment to murder the old man whom he loathes for his 'Evil Eye', he believes that he hears the heart of his victim beating in terror. The deed done and the evidence concealed, he receives with complacency a visit from the police: but the horrible sound of the beating heart – perhaps his own, perhaps a phantom conjured up by his disturbed imagination, but certainly unheard by any but himself – returns to betray him into confessing his guilt.

The reproaches of conscience are far more concretely embodied in 'The Black Cat' (1843).[8] The narrator, by nature a homely animal lover, experiences a change in his character under the influence of the 'Fiend Intemperance' and becomes the tormentor of his formerly beloved companion, the huge black cat, Pluto. Pluto is an ambivalent figure: his pitch-blackness evokes the half-serious notion in the narrator's wife that he is, like all black cats, a witch in disguise, and it also reflects the encroaching darkness in his master's heart; yet he is portrayed as loving and unoffending. In a fit of demonic fury the man cuts out one of Pluto's eyes; and later, possessed by the unaccountable 'spirit of PERVERSENESS', hangs the cat from a tree. The passage in which Poe analyses this perverse spirit reveals an acuteness of insight into the psychology of mental extremity which foreshadows Dostoevsky.

This atrocity is described as 'a deadly sin that would so jeopardise my immortal soul as to place it – if such a thing were possible – even beyond the reach of the infinite mercy of the Most Merciful and Most Terrible God'. That same night the narrator's house is burned down and the image of the hanged cat is found imprinted on a surviving wall. A rationalistic explanation is offered for this phenomenon, but at the same time its extraordinariness is strongly emphasised, so that the possibility of a supernatural causation is left open: 'Although I thus readily accounted to my reason, if not altogether to my conscience, for the startling fact just detailed, it did not the less fail to make a deep impression on my fancy.' Pluto now spawns a double: another black cat attaches itself to the killer in a tavern and, though at first he welcomes it out of 'a half-sentiment that seemed, but was not, remorse', he soon comes to feel its presence as a permanent reproach and to look upon it with 'unutterable loathing'.

This new cat is the image of its predecessor in every particular (even to being one-eyed) save one, that on its breast it has a patch of white, at first indefinite in shape, but soon – to the guilty eyes of its master, at least – taking the form of a horrible representation of the gallows. The avenging cat now lures him on to a final crime. Perpetually haunting his footsteps as he moves about his dwelling, it drives him towards madness. The 'feeble remnant of the good' within him succumbs to the darkness of evil; he is filled with 'hatred of all things and of all mankind' and abandons himself to ungovernable fits of fury. When the cat causes him to trip on the stairs and his wife deflects the blow he aims at it, he turns on her in demonic frenzy and cleaves her skull with an axe.

Poe now reverts to the formula of 'The Tell-Tale Heart'. The murderer walls up the corpse in a niche of the cellar; the cat, to his immense relief, has disappeared, and untroubled by remorse, he sleeps soundly. The police arrive to search the premises but find nothing; so mad is his self-confidence that in a 'phrenzy of bravado' he boasts of the solidity of the house and raps heavily on the very portion of brick-work behind which the body is concealed. From within the tomb there echoes back to him the cry of the cat which he has inadvertently (and inexplicably) walked in with his wife's body: a scream 'utterly anomalous and inhuman – a howl – a wailing shriek, half of horror and half of triumph, such as might have arisen only out of hell, conjointly from the throats of the damned in their agony and of the demons that exult in the damnation'.

'The Black Cat' is, in the compelling psychological inwardness of its horror and the ambiguous relation of its realistic and supernatural elements, perhaps the most Hoffmannesque of Poe's tales. The power which the avenging cat exercises over the guilty conscience of the narrator, the control which he allows it to wield over his freedom of choice as between good and evil, is very reminiscent of the dominance of the detestable Coppelius over the imagination of Nathaniel. And just as the inexplicable appearances of Coppelius and his repulsive *Doppelgänger* Coppola suggest Nathaniel's binding by fate, so does that advent of the second, all-but-identical one-eyed cat suggest the intervention of forces that cannot be accounted for in terms of the tale's overtly rationalistic perspective.

The figure of the black cat is a striking and unusual embodiment of the externalised conscience. 'William Wilson' (1839), Poe's earlier essay on this theme, is more centrally in the tradition of the identical supernatural double. Karl Miller has indicated the sources from which Poe derived the idea of the good double to which he here assigns the role of admonitory conscience.[9] Robert Wringhim's confessions were written by one still blinded by spiritual pride, and those of Medardus, although transcribed when he was repentant, speak from the viewpoint of his former deluded and inflated self. William Wilson, on the other hand, is not a whited sepulchre; he has never been under any illusions as to his own moral turpitude, and there is thus no need for any tempter figure or embodiment of an unacknowledged dark self. The device of the double is therefore released to carry the personification of his subordinate better nature.

William Wilson is a pseudonym, his own name being one of 'unparalleled infamy'. He writes as an outcast with a cloud between his hopes and heaven, and like so many protagonists in the literature of the double, claims that in the story of his downfall there is an element of 'fatality'. Possessing the excitable and imaginative hereditary temperament so frequently encountered in Poe's characters, he grows up 'self-willed, addicted to the wildest caprices, and a prey to the most ungovernable passions'.[10] Unrestrained by any discipline imposed by his weak parents, he is left entirely to the guidance of his own will and accustomed to get his own way in everything. He recalls his happy schooldays in an old-world and atmospheric English village, at a school housed in a building which is a 'palace of enchantment', its 'incomprehensible subdivisions' suggesting the tortuous byways of the unconscious mind.

Wilson acquires an ascendancy over all his contemporaries save one, his double and namesake. The latter competes with him in everything, and alone refuses 'implicit belief in my assertions, and submission to my will'. Their relationship is very similar to that of M'Gill and Wringhim: 'I secretly felt that I feared him, and could not help thinking the equality which he maintained so easily with myself, a proof of his true superiority; since not to be overcome cost me a perpetual struggle' (p. 163). In contrast with Wilson's ambitious and competitive pride, his namesake is relaxed and whimsical in his opposition, which he combines with an inappropriate and unwelcome *'affectionateness of manner'*. In an unconscious projection the narrator attributes this to his 'consummate self-conceit'. The completeness of their identity only gradually becomes apparent to Wilson: they entered school on the same date, have the same date of birth (sharing their birthday, 19 January, with Poe himself), are of the same height and almost identical in appearance; the senior boys assume them to be brothers. In spite of their rivalry and quarrels they are congenial in temperament and 'the most inseparable of companions'.

Wilson's feelings towards his friend and double are very mixed, and their rivalry is mainly at the level of banter and practical joking, partly because the second William Wilson lacks any Achilles' heel other than a curious vocal weakness precluding him 'from raising his voice *above a very low whisper*' (p. 165). The vain Wilson hates his 'common name', and his rival for sharing it, and therefore, by the 'detestable coincidence', causing its frequent repetition. He grows increasingly vexed at their points of resemblance, 'moral or physical'. Curiously, although both Wilsons are acutely aware of their similarity, others seem not to notice it.

This odd circumstance is introduced to emphasise the subjective element in the status of the double, that he is really a projection of the narrator's secondary self; but it shows Poe up against a recurrent difficulty associated with the device of the supernatural double. In so far as the second self is incarnated as an objective double existing in the physical world, this embodiment must be observable by other people. An identical double is such an extraordinary occurrence that it must be expected to provoke comment and astonishment; but to emphasise that would be to focus on something which would detract from the opposite but necessary stress on underlining the personal, subjective aspect. This is a problem that cannot really be satisfactorily confronted, and writers employing the device are obliged simply to side-step it as adroitly as they can.

The second Wilson is aware of how galling their resemblance is to the original, and with the object of provoking him he develops a habit of making a perfect imitation of the narrator as to manner and voice: *'and his singular whisper, it grew the very echo of my own'* (p. 166). In its perfect gradation, assuming the spirit rather than the letter of the original, this mimetic trick closely resembles the 'chameleon art' of Gil-Martin in the *Justified Sinner*. The double's mocking and sarcastic attitude to his prototype is also very like Gil-Martin's to Wringhim, but whereas the latter denotes the exultation of power and control as well as contempt for the gullibility of the victim, the second Wilson's sarcasm has a significance of warning, more like the threatening glances of the Painter directed at Medardus. His 'frequent officious interference with my will' is associated with the hinted or insinuated advice which Wilson receives with 'growing repugnance'. He recognises that his double's 'moral sense . . . was far keener than my own', and acknowledges that he would have done well to have taken heed of those 'meaning whispers', which the reader is now beginning to recognise as the voice of conscience (p. 167).

Wilson's increasing hatred of his double is associated with an incoherent sense, whose significance he cannot grasp, of his having been associated with his earliest infancy, a 'belief of my having been acquainted with the being who stood before me, at some epoch very long ago – some point of the past even infinitely remote' (p. 167). It is becoming clearer that this copy of himself is the troubling incarnation of a repressed part of his nature. One night he visits his namesake's bedroom to play a malicious practical joke. Observing him asleep, an iciness of feeling overwhelms him: was it possible 'that *what I now saw* was the result, merely, of the habitual practice of this sarcastic imitation?' (p. 168). Though it is not explicitly stated, Wilson has had a gruesome, though fleeting, insight that his double is himself. In the wake of this chilling experience he leaves the academy for ever.

At Eton, he feels scepticism at his own earlier 'credulity', and giving way entirely to his vicious propensities, plunges into a 'vortex of thoughtless folly'. A night of debauchery and vice is interrupted by news of a person wishing to speak to him. He sees a youth of his own height and dressed similarly to himself, who strides up to him and whispers the words 'William Wilson!' in his ear. The tone of 'solemn admonition', the key of the familiar whispered syllables, strike his soul with 'the shock of a galvanic battery' (p. 170). The simple repetititon of his name thus symbolically reminds him that he is being false to his true self. The effect is evanescent, however. He realises who his visitor is, but fails to understand his purpose; proceeding from Eton to Oxford, he progresses from debauchery to crime, and becomes not only a colossus of vice but a professional gambler and cheat. After a gambling party he has arranged in order to dupe a weak-minded nobleman of his fortune, the stranger reappears, and in the same chilling whisper exposes his villainy. 'Humbled to the dust' and feeling 'all the horrors of the damned', Wilson is obliged to leave Oxford (pp. 174, 175).

This experience is constantly duplicated as Wilson travels over Europe, leading a depraved and worthless life: again and again his double (always, however, with his face hidden) comes between him and the fulfilment of his ambition, frustrating schemes which 'if fully carried out might have resulted in bitter mischief'. We are again reminded of Wringhim, pursued by Gil-Martin: 'From his inscrutable tyranny did I at length flee, panic-stricken, as from a pestilence; and to the very ends of the earth *I fled in vain*' (p. 175). Still Wilson is blind to the purpose of this shadowing, and bitterly resentful of the curtailment of his freedom of action. Hitherto he has succumbed supinely, out of awe and terror, but now, his courage boosted by drink, he determines to resist. With this, an opposite effect occurs to that experienced by Andersen's scholar in relation to his usurping shadow: 'And was it only fancy that induced me to believe that, with the increase of my firmness, that of my tormentor underwent a proportional diminution?' (p. 176).

Wilson has resolved to kill the voice of conscience. The final confrontation takes place at a masquerade at Rome: engaged on an adulterous errand, he feels a hand on his shoulder and the familiar whisper in his ear. He turns on his identically clothed and masked tormentor: 'you *shall not* dog me unto death!' They fight with rapiers; Wilson overcomes his double and stabs him repeatedly. Averting his attention for an instant when someone tries to enter the room, he turns back to see what at first he takes to be a mirror – his own image, pale and bloody, totters towards him, the face, figure and clothing 'even in the most absolute identity, *mine own!*' His now maskless double speaks out, too late for Wilson, not with the still, small whisper of conscience but in a clear voice which Wilson fancies could be his own: 'You have conquered, and I yield. Yet, henceforward art thou also dead – dead to the World, to Heaven and to hope! In me didst thou exist – and in my death, see by this image, which is thine own, how utterly thou hast murdered thyself' (p. 178).

At the beginning of the tale, Wilson had emphasised the element of fatality in the history of his downfall. Once again we see how hard it is for these anti-heroes of duality to resist the force of evil destiny in their lives. Ambrosio, Falkland, Clithero, Wieland, Nathaniel, obsessed by the idea of an inscrutable fate against whose operations they are ultimately powerless, react to this consciousness in ways which ensure that their predictions will be self-fulfilling. Wringhim, feebly resisting temptation, succumbs to his demonic double and is damned; William Wilson overcomes his beneficent double and is also damned. Only Medardus, certainly no less hardly pressed by the influences of sinful inheritance and a hostile destiny, finally succeeds in turning aside this evil fate and embracing the good; and he is enabled to do so only because he firmly believes in the real and effectual possibility of repentance.

# 7

# The Russian Double

## GOGOL, AND DOSTOEVSKY'S *THE DOUBLE*

The age of Hoffmann and Hogg might be called the 'high noon' of the double in Western Europe; in the middle years of the century, as we saw in Chapter 2, the theme fell somewhat into abeyance as a serious literary preoccupation, to experience a new resurgence in the last years of the century, a fresh access of vitality which was related to a revival of the Gothic mode and to new scientific developments which cast a beguiling light on matters of duality and psychic division. In Russia, however, the hiatus was bridged, for the influence of Hoffmann and the 'Russian Hoffmannists' bore new fruit in the 1840s in the early work of Dostoevsky, who throughout his career continued pertinaciously to revert to the preoccupation with duality and self-division which had so fascinated him in his youth. In his last book, *The Brothers Karamazov*, the double proper was to surface again as a crucial dramatic motif.

By far the most influential Russian prose writer of the 1830s and early 1840s was Gogol. The inimitable mixture of social satire, fantastic humour and aberrant psychology which characterises his writing was a rich spawning-ground of dualistic obsession, and in some of his stories he verges on adopting the device of the double to carry these preoccupations. In his most famous story 'The Overcoat' (1842), the prized coat of the wretched clerk Akaky Akakievich becomes his 'companion', a kind of extension of his self, and hence a rudimentary double. In 'The Nose' (1836), Gogol had created a gruesome and evocative image of dissociation: Collegiate Assessor Kovalyov, an aspiring social climber, wakes up one morning to find that his nose has vanished, and when he later sees it in uniform and confronts it, it claims, 'I am a person in my own right!'[1]

Charles E. Passage has seen this story as a 'bitter parody' of Hoffmann, a *'reductio ad absurdum'* of the habits of the writer whom Gogol had at first so unreservedly admired: the loss of Kovalyov's nose is absurdly analogous to Spikher's loss of his mirror-image in

'Die Abenteuer der Sylvesternacht', and its adventures are a burlesque of Hoffmann's *Doppelgänger* themes.[2] The nose travels all over St Petersburg in the guise of a State Councillor, cutting a figure to which Kovalyov cannot attain; there are satirical references to the popularity of magnetism in the capital at that date. Eventually, the nose returns to the Collegiate Assessor's face as mysteriously as it had parted from it. Still earlier, in the farcical tale 'The Story of the Quarrel between Ivan Ivanovich and Ivan Nikiforovich' (1834), Gogol had used to great comic effect the motif of complementary opposites. The two absurd characters are 'friends the like of whom the world had never seen', of whom it was said that 'the devil himself tied Ivan Nikiforovich and Ivan Ivanovich together with a rope' (p. 51); but they become mortal enemies when, in the course of a crazy altercation, one of them calls the other a goose.

These essays on the theme of the double are fairly vestigial; the importance of Gogol in the present context lies in the immense influence which he exercised on Dostoevsky, who was to become one of the great masters of the double. Gogol's characters are typically viewed from without, sometimes, as in the case of Akaky Akakievich, with real compassion, but always with the detached, microscopic eye of a scientist examining a specimen. The reader is encouraged to deduce, as it were, the obscure movements of their souls from the very exact information which Gogol provides about their externals.

Dostoevsky, by nature a writer of passionate psychological inwardness, is also deeply interested in the clues provided by behaviour and appearance to the inner psychology of his characters. His early work inhabits the world of Gogol, the world of seedy, depressed, tyrannised government clerks and minor civil servants looked down upon as insects by the lofty superiors to whose altitude they hopelessly aspire. But from the start Dostoevsky was instinctively involved with the great passions of the human soul, though not, in his pre-Siberian days, from any consciously developed or deeply committed position. In his attempts to harness the style and tone of Gogol to the demands of a more emotional and inward-directed art he turned to the tale of terror, and drew on what he had imbided from the example of writers such as Mrs Radcliffe, Eugene Sue and, above all, Hoffmann.

Yet if *The Double* (1846) was born of a marriage between Hoffmann and Gogol, Dostoevsky himself was very much more than just the midwife. His distinctive tone of voice and way of seeing things is already unmistakably present in this, his second novel. Greatly shaken in his high hopes for the book, and his confidence in its excellence, by the quite hostile response it provoked after the rapturous reception of *Poor Folk* by Belinsky and his circle, Dostoevsky continued to believe that the idea itself was first-rate and seminal, and that there were elements in it that were of great and permanent value. During the 1860s he planned to recast it in a radically new form to do the concept greater justice and to reflect his new ideological preoccupations; but this was never done. The revision which he undertook in 1866, resulting in the version with which we are familiar, was much less far-reaching: he cut out the original mock-heroic framework, simplified the plot, and strengthened the ending by making Golyadkin's ultimate fate more explicit. As Joseph Frank observes, 'Golyadkin is the ancestor of all Dostoevsky's great split personalities, who are always confronted with their doubles or quasi-doubles (whether in the form of other "real" characters, or as hallucinations) in the memorable scenes of the great novels.'[3]

Dostoevsky's story introduces to the literature of the double the element of humour, which had earlier, if present at all, been merely marginal or incidental. The humorous tone derives from Gogol, though its particular *timbre* is already very much Dostoevsky's own: according to Passage, the idea for *The Double* had its origin in an attempt to amalgamate the spirit of Gogol's 'Diary of a Madman' with the framework of Hoffmann's 'Sylvesternacht', whence the important role of the mirror-image in *The Double*.[4] It is a very funny book, combining the mock-heroic, the absurd, sometimes almost the grotesque, with an inspired inwardness which imparts to the comic vision an underlying realism. The horror of the tale is entirely internalised: its hero, Mr Golyadkin, does nothing outwardly wicked or outrageous, yet his humiliated soul is fertile in monstrous growths.

Dostoevsky's perception of his protagonist's weakness and vanity is relentless, and the narrative tone may seem cruel in its detachment, the mocking, parodic distance of its viewpoint, yet his power of entering imaginatively into the minute obscurities, hesitances and dubieties of the psyche involves a counterbalancing sympathy and understanding. The novel is also more 'psychological' in a modern scientific sense than anything we have yet encountered: we are now closer to the world of the neurosis, the complex and the case history. With Dostoevsky, though, psychology is never divorced from the moral consciousness. Mr Golyadkin does go mad, but his madness has its roots not only in the restrictions, frustrations and oppressions of his social situation, but in vanity, ambition, envy and wounded pride. Dostoevsky's *feuilleton* for the novel says that Golyadkin 'goes mad out of *ambition*, while at the same time despising ambition and even suffering from the fact that he happens to suffer from such nonsense as ambition'.[5]

On the morning on which we first make the acquaintance of Mr Golyadkin, his first action on rising from his bed is to look in the mirror, and we are told that he is 'evidently quite satisfied with all that he saw there'.[6] The world is smiling on him, and he responds with a 'complacent smile'. The first emotion he exhibits on contact with another human being, his servant, Petrushka, is 'righteous indignation'; riding in a carriage he assumes a 'sedate and decorous air' when he thinks he is being looked at. It is quickly apparent that Mr Golyadkin's dominant characteristics are extreme self-consciousness, morbid suspiciousness and complacent vanity. When the head of the section of his Department passes in a droshky, he is utterly overcome with confusion, with 'indescribable anguish', for Mr Golyadkin does not usually ride in a carriage. Shall he acknowledge their acquaintance? he asks himself. 'Or shall I pretend it's not me but somebody else strikingly like me, and look as if nothing's the matter?' He raises his hat to Andrey Philippovich, but at the same time whispers to himself, 'It's quite all right; this is not me at all, Andrey Philippovich, it's not me at all, not me, and that's all about it' (p. 132). The psychic dissociation has already begun, and his flight from himself will become complete with the appearance of the double whom, by these words, he in a sense conjures up.

Mr Golyadkin's consciousness is riven by inner conflict and he swings constantly from arrogance and self-assertion to utter self-doubt, collapse of confidence and self-depreciation. He has two mechanisms of defence to which he recurrently resorts: 'a terrible challenging stare . . . a stare calculated to reduce all his enemies to dust' (p. 132), and an inner voice which, however sorry his plight, seeks to reassure him that in spite of everything he is really 'all right'. He believes that he has been invited to a very important dinner party, but on the way he feels suddenly impelled to visit his physician, Dr Rutenspitz, an impressive elderly gentleman 'with an expressive glittering eye' (p. 133). The description of Golyadkin's excruciating indecision and self-consciousness at the start of their interview – and even his paranoia – cannot fail to remind one of Dostoevsky's own sufferings in this respect during his tormented youth – for the novelist's crippling social gaucherie and sense of persecution apparently disappeared during his Siberian exile.[7]

The hero protects himself with his 'annihilating' stare, however, a stare which 'fully conveyed Mr Golyadkin's independence, that is, it stated clearly that Mr Golyadkin didn't care, that he was his own master, like anybody else, and his life was his own' (p. 134). Dr Rutenspitz recommends 'something to take you out of yourself' and, getting to the heart of the matter, 'in a certain sense, a change in your character' (p. 135). Golyadkin responds with a confused, incoherent tirade which bears all the marks of envy, social resentment and incipient paranoia. He is, he tells the doctor, 'proud to be not a great man but a little man. I am not an intriguer – and I am proud of that too'. Ironically, in view of the fate that is soon to befall him, he claims not to like 'petty two-faced people . . . I only put on a mask at a masked ball, I don't wear one in public every day.' The source of Mr Golyadkin's troubles is securely outside himself: unexpectedly bursting into tears (a touch which arouses the reader's reluctant compassion), he confides to the doctor, 'I have enemies, Christian Ivanovich, I have enemies; I have bitter enemies who have sworn to ruin me' (p. 139).

Golyadkin's sense of a conspiracy against him centres on the promotion to the rank of Assessor of one Vladimir Semyonovich, an admirer of Clara Olsufyevna, who is the object of his own ambitious affections. Clara is the daughter of the distinguished Olsufi Ivanovich Berendeyev, a retired State Councillor and 'at one time Mr. Golyadkin's patron', to whom all in his office look up as to a god, and 'who had been deprived of the use of his legs by his long service' (p. 153). A dinner party followed by a ball is being held to celebrate Clara's birthday, but to his utter horror our hero is refused admission. After extraordinary fluctuations of mood and intention, however, Golyadkin determines to assert himself and gate-crash the party (or at least, somehow to insinuate himself into it), for, as he had told some young clerks earlier in the day, 'You all know me, gentlemen, but up to now you have only known one side of me' (p. 147).

Mr Golyadkin's enterprise issues in a nightmare of humiliation. After lurking for three hours in the passage from the back entrance to the flat amid trash and lumber, half-hidden behind a screen and awaiting the 'right moment' for his entry, he at last steps inside and mingles with the crowd. He makes a ludicrous speech of congratulation to Clara Olsufyevna, is rebuked by Andrey Philippovich, and after 'hopelessly striving at all costs to find a centre and a social status among the bewildered crowd' and finally attempting to dance with Clara, he is manhandled out of the building. Utterly crushed, he starts to run home in a driving blizzard, scarcely knowing what he is doing. 'Mr Golyadkin', we are told, 'looked as if he was trying to hide from himself, as if he wanted to run away from himself . . . to annihilate himself, to cease to be, to return to the dust' (p. 166). Occasionally he stops in bemusement, then runs madly on 'as though trying to escape from pursuit or an even more terrible disaster' (p. 167). Trying to escape from himself, he is about to encounter himself face to face.

At his very lowest moment of despair, 'beside himself' in fact, leaning on the parapet of the embankment above the Fontanka, it suddenly seems to him as if someone were standing beside him, someone who had even said something 'about a matter touching him nearly'. But there is no one there. Soon he hears the sound of a cannon and thinks to himself, 'Listen! isn't that a flood warning? – Evidently the water is rising very fast' (p. 168). He is about to be psychically overwhelmed. No sooner has he thought this than a figure approaches him, and the idea comes to him: 'perhaps this passer-by is – *he*, himself, perhaps he is here, and, what makes matters worse, he is not here for nothing'. The stranger passes him, disappears, passes him once more from the same direction. Mr Golyadkin knows him very well, but 'not for the greatest treasure in the world would he have been willing to name him' (p. 170).

Mr Golyadkin Junior, as he will come to be called, is the most completely identical double of all those we shall encounter in this study, with the exceptions of the second James Beatman and the second William Wilson. He has no basis in any character distinct from his original, as is the case with Medardus's double, Count Victor. He is not a manifestation of the Devil, like Gil-Martin, and has no power to take on any form but that of Mr Golyadkin; he is not even, like Wilson's double, a personification of conscience. He is simply the second Mr Golyadkin, absolutely similar in every respect to the first, except that he does what the first wants to do but cannot do. He embodies the truth that the forces which destroy the hero come from within himself, yet have their own autonomy and are beyond his control.

There are perhaps stronger grounds than in the case of any other of our examples to suppose the double to be purely a figment of the protagonist's diseased imagination, since the novel is written in a mode of psychological realism rather than supernatural romance; but it is part of the craftiness of its design that while the reader may at times be tempted to this conclusion, it is never possible finally to accede to it – there are simply too many incidents in the book which depend upon the objective existence of Golyadkin Junior. Again, there can be no doubt that by the end of the story Golyadkin is mad; but is his double a symptom of his madness, or its cause – or, in some obscure way, both?

Golyadkin fears this encounter, this 'evil thing' that is about to befall him, but at the same time he desires it. As he runs along, a mongrel dog follows at his heels, shadowing him, and at the same time 'some far-off long-forgotten idea' hammers away in his head, refusing to leave him alone. He sees the stranger ahead of him, now going in the same direction as himself, and follows him to his own house, up the stairs and into his own flat; then, with horror in his heart he at last allows himself to recognise the figure sitting on his bed and nodding at him familiarly: 'Mr. Golyadkin's nocturnal acquaintance was none other than himself, Mr. Golyadkin himself, another Mr. Golyadkin, but exactly the same as himself – in short, in every respect what is called his double' (p. 173). The knowing tone indicates a fresh approach to the familiar theme. In Dostoevsky's *Double* there is an element of pastiche, and while the treatment is wholly convincing psychologically, he will also exploit in an innovatory way the humorous potential of the material.

On waking the next morning, Golyadkin explains this extraordinary development to himself in a paranoid manner: he 'had known for a very long time that something was being prepared, that there was *somebody else* in reserve' (p. 173). He decides, for the time being, to 'submit', an attitude which will become habitual. When, after much vacillation, he arrives at the office, he finds to his shame and horror that his double is there too, and has been put in the seat opposite him. To his fright, nobody shows any sign of surprise at this shameful and scandalous 'farce', so that Golyadkin begins to doubt his own identity. His double, on the other hand, sits 'staidly and peacefully'. It is only when it is explicitly pointed out to him that Anton Antonovich, Golyadkin's superior, sees the miraculousness of the likeness, and then, after encouragingly mentioning that his aunt had seen her double just before she died, suggests that the occurrence is God's will and that to murmur against it would be sinful. The hero's passivity is thus enjoined upon him by the authority he worships and fears.

The second Mr Golyadkin, like the shadow in Hans Christian Andersen's fable, is a usurping double. Though, as Chizhevsky acutely remarks, the 'place' from which his double squeezes him is almost completely illusory to begin with,[8] as the successful embodiment of his original's hopeless aspirations he takes from the latter even the little that he has. 'For my part,' he tells the hero, 'I felt attracted to you at first sight'; and Golyadkin's first instinct is to appease him. Though feeling that 'It's putting my head into a noose of my own accord', he invites him in, listens to his double's long trivial history, and, when the latter asks for his friendship and protection, feels conciliated.

He discovers that they share the same name and patronymic – Iakov Petrovich – and come from the same province. They get drunk together and No. 1 asks No. 2 to stay the night; but in the morning the double has gone. Thereafter he treats his benefactor with increasing carelessness and insolence, exhibits the most odious officiousness, starts usurping his office functions and takes credit for Golyadkin Senior's work. The latter finds the situation impossible, but when he tries to confront his rival, the usurper, in full view of the clerks, pinches and tickles his cheek and prods him in the paunch. This is the other side of himself that Mr Golyadkin had earlier promised the clerks they would soon see.

Golyadkin vows revenge, but his resolution is always nullified by vacillation and indecision. His determination is rendered in biblical and mock-heroic terms: he will take a 'certain step' which will 'crush the serpent and bring low the horn of pride' (p. 206). Golyadkin Junior, however, is of course a projection of Golyadkin's Senior's own pride, and there are moments when he half admits it, and even attributes the whole mix-up to the Devil in the most traditional way: 'My God! What a hell-broth the Devil's concocted here! As for him, he's such a base and ignoble wretch, so mischievous and wanton, so frivolous and sycophantic and grovelling, such a Golyadkin! . . . And he'll supplant a man, supplant him – take his place as if he was nothing but an old rag, and never stop to think that a man's not an old rag' (p. 212). There are moments of high farce, as when Golyadkin goes into a restaurant and, having eaten one savoury patty, is charged for eleven; he starts to protest, but the veil is lifted from his eyes when he sees his double with the last piece of the tenth patty in his hand and about to enter his mouth. The original suffers a 'paroxysm of wounded pride'.

Under the influence of this emotion he writes to Mr Golyadkin Junior, linking his appearance to 'discourteous and unseemly treatment at the hands of enemies of mine' (p. 215). He has now found a new phrase with which to defend himself mentally from the violation which is occurring: 'I'm in the right.' In this way he continues to thrust responsibility from himself and project the origin of his woes upon external enemies and upon Fate. But his decisive and heroically conceived resolutions are perpetually nullified by the reality of his passivity and pusillanimity: his violent swings of mood toss him from assertion to abjection. Immediately regretting having written the letter, he castigates himself: 'Fool that I was, I let my pride run away with me! My pride drove me to it! That's what pride does for you, that's your proper pride, wretch that you are!' (p. 220). Even the servant, Petrushka, now experiences revulsion at his doubleness, and reproaches him in a speech which ironically echoes or parodies Golyadkin's complacent tirade to Dr Rutenspitz on people who wear 'masks': 'Good people live honestly,' says Petrushka, 'good people live without any faking, and they never come double' (p. 222).

All kinds of immoral and unseemly behaviour begin to be attributed to Mr Golyadkin. As was the case with Robert Wringhim and Gil-Martin, it never becomes altogether clear whether these actions have indeed been committed by the original, perhaps in a disordered state of mind, or whether, as he believes, they are the work of his double and represent a malicious campaign of character assassination on the part of the latter. The narrative voice, while utterly detached and ironical in its attitude towards Mr Golyadkin, limits itself progressively to describing events as they appear to the unfortunate Titular Councillor, whose consciousness is increasingly chaotic and distorted by projection. As his own mental condition deteriorates he protests that his double deserves the 'lunatic asylum'. He begins to have tortured dreams in which are mingled rebuffs, slights, his own mean tricks, and the arrogation of his life by his rival. The latter has Golyadkin's own character but succeeds where he fails and shows up his qualities as spurious. Thus he is the expression of both the fears and the conscience of the real and 'altogether rightful Mr Golyadkin'. In his dreams this mirror-image exhibiting himself to himself is hideously replicated, so that a long line of identical Golyadkins stretches back 'in a long file like a string of geese and scurrying after Mr Golyadkin, so that there was no escaping from perfect counterfeits of himself' (p. 232). 'Either you or I', Senior writes to Junior, 'but both of us together is impossible!' (p. 232).

Mr Golyadkin Junior has become immensely popular and important, and he behaves in reality just as he has in the dream. When Senior, who in some moods still seeks conciliation with his 'deadly enemy', attempts to shake his hand, that wretch snatches his hand away, shakes it in the air 'as though he had dirtied it in something extremely nasty', spits, and ostentatiously wipes his fingers with his handkerchief (p. 242). This is going a little too far, and the office clerks are momentarily disapproving, but the double once more turns the tables with an offensive jest. Further woes are at once heaped on Golyadkin's shoulders as Anton Antonovich accuses him of 'unbecoming conduct' towards Clara Olsufyevna and a German woman with whom he used to lodge (an element much more fully developed in the earlier version of the novel), and of 'slandering another person', that is, the second Mr Golyadkin. A confrontation with the double in a coffee house, during which Golyadkin's conversation consists mostly of high-flown but ludicrous inanities, ends when the usurper's behaviour becomes intolerably offensive. However Golyadkin manages to force his way into the latter's droshky, and when he is finally jolted off into the snow he finds himself in Olsufi Ivanovich's yard: his rival disappears into the house.

As Dostoevsky's tale moves towards its climax, his fable approaches more closely the model of the demonic double motif, with Mr Golyadkin Junior taking the part of the Mephistophilean tempter and Dr Rutenspitz that of Lucifer. As Golyadkin's psyche disintegrates, hallucination and reality become increasingly indistinguishable, and he descends into a delirium analogous to those of Medardus and Wringhim during the climactic days of their possession. After falling off the droshky, he finds in his pocket a letter delivered to him by the porter that morning; written by Clara, it is addressed to *one* of the Golyadkins, castigates the other as an intriguing scoundrel who has engineered her destruction, declares her love for the other, and invites him to elope with her. Whether this letter has any real existence is open to doubt, for later Mr

Golyadkin cannot find it and wonders whether it has been purloined by his 'undeserving twin'.

The hero is thrown into utter confusion by the letter, and meanwhile his identity is crumbling and his life collapsing about his ears. In a tavern, he suddenly imagines that he is being poisoned; returning home, he is handed a letter from Andrey Philippovich instructing him to hand over all the business in his hands to Ivan Semyonovich. Even Petrushka is about to leave his service. He prepares for his parodic elopement, though terrified at the very thought of it: 'Here's a man on the way to destruction, a man is losing his identity, and he can hardly control himself – and you talk to him about a wedding!' (p. 265). Desperately determined to maintain his individuality and distinctness from his double, he goes to His Excellency's house to denounce the usurper; the latter is present, along with Dr Rutenspitz, whom, however, the crazed Golyadkin fails to recognise. After a fruitless and humiliating interview he is propelled towards the door and seen off the premises by his obnoxious rival.

Mr Golyadkin's hideous experience on the occasion of the first party at Olsufi Ivanovich's is now duplicated in an exaggerated form. He arrives with a carriage and awaits his lover for two hours in the courtyard in the bitter cold, beside a pile of logs. As he waits he talks out his torments, addressing himself mentally to Clara; he is more or less raving, but occasional flashes of distorted sense from time to time light up the confused darkness of his mind. He pays off the cabman and dashes off cheerfully: then immediately returns to the yard. All at once he realises that the entire company within is staring down at him from the windows. His double comes down the steps, and in spite of his protests the hero, 'feeling as though he was being roasted over a slow fire', is dragged up and into the drawing-room by this 'notorious detrimental' (pp. 280–1).

He is led up to the chair of Olsufi Ivanovich, and it now seems to him as if there were sympathetic tears in the eyes of all around him – 'Or perhaps Mr Golyadkin only imagined all this because he himself had broken down and could distinctly feel the scalding tears running down his cold cheeks' (p. 282). In the structure of this episode, as Passage has noted, 'Dostoevsky is at pains to parallel a scene of heavenly justice pronounced upon a sinner.'[9] Golyadkin tries to speak, but can only point to his heart. The crowd follow him about with curiosity and a certain enigmatic sympathy. Then he is led up to Mr Golyadkin Junior, who holds out his hand; Mr Golyadkin takes it, and they embrace, but even at the very moment of this 'Judas-kiss', he detects his double in a perfidious grimace and a conspiratorial wink to the crowd. In horror, he imagines 'that an endless string of Golyadkins all exactly alike were bursting in through the doors of the room; but it was too late. . . . The resounding treacherous kiss had been given, and . . .' (p. 284).

The scene that follows is one more variation on Faustus's carrying-off to hell by the avenging demons. Dr Rutenspitz appears, now grown terrible and unspeakably threatening, and is announced by Mr Golyadkin's twin, in whose face there shines 'an unseemly and sinister joy'. Dostoevsky could never have read Hogg, but there is a striking parallel with the gloating triumph of Gil-Martin as Wringhim goes to his doom. Golyadkin is led down to a closed carriage and the door opened by his double, and as he drives off with the doctor he is pursued in farewell by 'the piercing frantic yells of his enemies'. Mr Golyadkin Junior runs after the carriage, jumping up and blowing kisses. For a time the hero loses consciousness, then awakes to a new horror: 'two fiery eyes were watching him in the darkness, and they shone with malignant hellish joy. This was not Chistian Ivanovich! Who was it?' For Mr Golyadkin, at least, Rutenspitz has become the Devil, and in truth the doctor is carrying him off to eternal torment. The latter's final words, which make it clear that their destination is an asylum, ring out in his ears 'like the stern and terrible sentence of a judge' (pp. 286–7).

Dostevsky's masterly treatment of the theme of the double in this early novel thus combines a more clinically searching and carefully elaborated psychological realism than anything attempted by his predecessors (enhanced by a wonderful exploitation of the previously untapped comic potentiality of the motif), with the retention of essential traditional elements. The place of supernatural and fantastic causation in earlier double romances is here entirely supplied by the subjective and hallucinatory emanations of the protagonist's psyche (a development initiated by Hoffmann and Hogg, but in their work still ambiguously intertwined with the supernatural); but the independent existence of the double is safeguarded by a narrative structure which requires our acceptance of his objective presence, at least at some points in the story.

In later writers, as we shall see, this subjective–objective balance will be lost, largely due to changes in sensibility connected with scientific and psychological advance and altered attitudes to religious belief, changes which make it more difficult to render convincing such an interpenetration of the moral–spiritual and the physical worlds. Tales of the double then tend to divide off, on the one hand into pure moral allegory, which depends once more on the frankly fantastic, or on a scientism that is really glorified magic; and on the other into a merely clinical interpretation which lacks any spiritual dimension.

It is Dostoevsky's strength that his innovating development and extension of the psychological–realistic strand is securely based on traditional moral foundations. This is underlined by the pointed diablerie of the closing scenes, but the source of Golyadkin's troubles in his exclusive preoccupation with self is reverted to throughout the novel. He is not just an unfortunate victim of mental disorder, nor yet simply of social injustice, though that element is undoubtedly contributory. In spite of his being partly at the mercy of his social circumstances, of the autocratic, hierarchically repressive Russian society of his day, his character is relentlessly depicted by Dostoevsky as that of a man in whom vanity, pride, paltry ambition and envy have been allowed to develop monstrously and unchecked. The psychic disintegration which overtakes him is thus the fruit of what is traditionally called sin, and particularly of a variety of the sin of pride, which we have repeatedly observed to be the precondition for the appearance of a double.

Mr Golyadkin himself mutely acknowledges the connection between his mental collpase and his transgressions when, in the penultimate sentence of the book, he perceives the doctor as judge. Because *The Double* is a comic novel, this view may at first sight appear to be overstated, but the analogy of Dostoevsky's later work may persuade us otherwise. In his last novel he resorts once again to the device of the double to express one of the most important thematic ingredients of his narrative, and here, as in *The Double*, the appearance of the second self is associated with mental breakdown, this time quite explicitly arising from the dark, evil side of the subject's psyche, and specifically from the sin of pride.

Joseph Frank has expressed the view that Dostoevsky's final dissatisfaction with the form of his novel refers to its 'uncertain oscillation between the psychic and the supernatural', the fear that the objective aspect of Golyadkin's double was too troubling and mysterious for the reader. Feeling this as a weakness, Dostoevsky makes sure that this ambivalence in the status of the double does not recur in his later work: 'his doubles will either be clear-cut hallucinations, or what may be called "quasi-doubles" – characters who exist in their own right, but reflect some internal aspect of another character in a strengthened form'.[10] This supposition is highly plausible, but it may well be that adverse criticism had caused Dostoevsky to question a procedure which his original artistic instinct had assured him could be both valid and effective. The ambivalence referred to is an inherent characteristic of the supernatural double, and to realise that it can constitute its essential strength, indeed its *raison d'être*, we need look no further than Hoffmann's Coppelius or the *Justified Sinner*. In *The Double* it is partly this ambiguity which makes possible an analysis that is, as Chizhevsky puts it, both 'realistically' and 'transcendentally psychological', a successful interpenetration of naturalistic and fantastic modes.[11] But Dostoevsky did move in the direction Frank indicates, and the results certainly cannot be any cause for regret.

## THE LATER DOSTOEVSKY

The split personality and the divided will are such pervasive and important themes in the work of Dostoevsky that a full treatment of them would be almost equivalent to a comprehensive study of the novelist's *oeuvre*. During his years in the prison-camp and his subsequent exile in Siberia, Dostoevsky's attitudes underwent a profound transformation. The social-psychological frame of reference of his early work is transcended by a moral and metaphysical world-view in which suffering becomes the precondition for spiritual advance and understanding, the Russian people appear as the central symbol of his hope for the salvation of society, and their orthodox faith, centred on the Russian conception of Christ, is seen as the road to individual redemption and freedom.

In 1854, shortly after his release from *katorga*, Dostoevsky formed a project, never carried out, of translating C. G. Carus's notable work, *Psyche, zur Entwicklungsgeschichte der Seele*, which had been published in 1846, the same year as *The Double*. Carus, a highly distinguished physiologist and a man of very wide culture, inherited the psychological tradition of G. H. Schubert, and exercised an influence on the later work of Dostoevsky comparable to that of Schubert on the Romantic generation. While Carus subscribed to the most advanced biological and physiological theories, he remained committed to Schelling's idealist conception of the universe, with which the young Dostoevsky was permeated, and entertained what we would now call a 'holistic' view of nature. The universe, for Carus, had its origin in a Divine Idea, and the human soul was immortal because it shared in the Divine creative principle. 'The law of love' should be the animating principle of human conduct, moral evil is comparable to a state of physical illness, and conscience acts as a regulator to correct moral and psychic imbalance and restore the equilibrium of the soul.[12]

Carus believed that 'The key to the understanding of the essence of the conscious life of the soul lies in the region of the unconscious.'[13] It is not surprising, then, that he has been regarded as an important forerunner of psychoanalysis, but his world-view is much closer to Jung's than to that of Freud. Dostoevsky's distinctive artistic province, the area in which his genius was most characteristically at home, was that of describing the emergence into consciousness of obscure, complex and half-submerged movements of the soul, and here the ideas of Carus provided him with an invaluable theoretical framework to facilitate the articulation of his intuitive insights.

Dostoevsky used a rich variety of approaches to dramatise internal division. Among these is the shadowy doubling of one character by another quite separate one, in whom are evoked and embodied latent or hidden or half-developed elements of the psyche of the first character, or even elements which the novelist has excluded purposely from the character. Many years ago Harry Levin, in his study of Marlowe, likened the dialogues between Faustus and Mephistophilis to 'those cat-and-mouse interrogations, in which Porfiry [the examining magistrate in *Crime and Punishment*] teaches the would-be criminal, Raskolnikov, to accuse and convict himself';[14] that is, he is Raskolnikov's buried conscience, externalised and challenging him in the form of another. The figure of Svidrigailov, in the same novel, reflects in a heightened form the tendencies which have turned Raskolnikov into a murderer, and confronts him with the embodied moral implications of the nihilistic philosophy which has inspired him.

In *The Idiot*, Myshkin and Rogozhin were in Dostoevsky's original conception one single, complex and ambivalent figure, akin to Stavrogin in *The Devils*, a figure who in successive drafts separates off into two opposite, contradictory characters who are also of necessity complementary. George Steiner describes their relationship incisively:

> Rogojin is Muishkin's original sin. To the extent that the Prince is human, and thus heir to the Fall, the two men must remain inseparable companions. They enter the novel together and leave it to a common doom. . . . Their inextricable nearness is a Dostoevskyan parable on the necessary presence of evil at the gates of knowledge. . . . Without darkness, how should we apprehend the nature of light?[15]

Nowhere is their identity more apparent than in the scenes in which Rogozhin mysteriously shadows Myshkin before the latter succumbs to the renewed onset of his epilepsy, the Prince's disturbed state of consciousness lending a phantasmagoric quality to his perception of the appearances of his rival for the love of the possessed Nastasya Philippovna. On his arrival at the station that morning he had seen 'two strange, burning eyes' staring at him out of the crowd, but believes that he has imagined it. Later he goes to see Rogozhin and realises that the eyes were his, though Rogozhin effectively denies it. Myshkin notices a new knife on his table. He and Rogozhin exchange crosses, Myshkin asserts their brotherhood and Rogozhin renounces his claim to Nastasya. But when they part the Prince becomes conscious that he is being followed, and is repeatedly aware of Rogozhin's fiery eyes fixed upon him. He experiences his suspicion of the other as a potential murderer as almost a 'temptation', a 'demon' which has taken possession of him and which he cannot shake off.

He goes to Nastasya's house, but she is not there; he realises that he has gone because he expected to see 'those eyes' there, and indeed he does see them: Rogozhin stands opposite, 'like an accuser and a judge – in full view'.[16] Unbearably ashamed of his suspicions yet aware that they have grown to conviction, Myshkin returns to his hotel and sees Rogozhin lurking inside the gates by the stairs. He follows him up, and is confronted by his rival's two eyes staring at him from a niche. A knife flashes in Rogozhin's hand, as it did in the hand of Medardus, but before he can strike the Prince falls to the ground with the terrible scream of an epileptic fit. It is the scream which saves the Prince, for the attacker is paralysed by its 'unbearable' and 'mystical' horror, the sense that the victim is alienated from himself: 'One gets the impression that it is someone inside the man who is screaming' (p. 268).

These scenes are eerie with the sense of shifting and shared identity. The two characters acknowledge their kinship, the almost mystical cords that bind them together, yet this finds expression in fear on the one hand and murderous antagonism on the other. Myshkin's perception of Rogozhin as accuser and judge strikes the reader as a kind of acknowledgement on the Prince's part of the impossibility of his Christ-like goodness, a recognition that Rogozhin, as his blood-brother, is a separated part of himself which is necessary to his wholeness; it is the lack of his Rogozhin-part which is the focus of his ineffectuality, of the failure to bring into reality the ideal which he represents. It is this, too, which is symbolised in the self-alienation expressed by his epileptic cry.

Versilov, in *A Raw Youth*, is conscious of a mental split which he likens to the presence beside one of his double; consulting a medical book, he finds that this experience is said to be the first sign of a serious mental derangement which may end fatally. Something of the sort is the case with Stavrogin, who in passages excised when *The Devils* appeared in book form, tells Dasha about visitations he has received from a 'demon' who is 'stupid and impudent' and wishes to make himself out to be independent, whereas Stavrogin knows that 'it is I myself divided in different ways and that I speak with myself'.[17] In his 'Confession' he relates to the monk Tikhon how these hallucinations came to him, mostly at night, when he 'saw or felt beside him the presence of some kind of malignant creature, mocking and "rational", in all sorts of guises and in different characters, but it is the same, and it always makes me angry. . . . It is myself, different aspects of myself. Nothing more. You don't think, do you, that because I've just added that – er – phrase I'm still doubtful and not sure that it's me and not in fact the devil.'[18] Tikhon is aware of his perplexity, and tells him that it is 'most probably' an illness, though he confirms that devils most certainly exist. Stavrogin himself then makes a point of asserting that he believes canonically 'in a personal devil, not an allegory'; so the purely hallucinatory status of his demon remains somewhat in doubt.

Stavrogin is the ultimate in protean personalities. Chizhevsky has argued that he does not really live himself, but others live for him and through him, so that he dwells 'among the emanations of his spirit, in a world of phantoms, of "demons"'.[19] Thus

Shatov and Kirilov, themselvs utterly opposing characters in their ideologies and views of life, both live in his shadow, as his disciples, in a sense his creations, acting out the potentialities that lie latent and unrealised in Stavrogin's rich but also finally barren soul. Pyotr Verkhovensky is his 'ape', Fedka the convict his 'little devil'. All look to him for leadership, see in him either an idol and a prophet or else a great criminal; but he cannot carry his spiritual potential into reality because he is 'divided from living reality by his pride, his limitless pesumption, his scornful relation to life, his contempt for his concrete neighbours' – ultimately by his complete lack of love.[20] Fundamentally unrelated, he is unable to act in the real world, he knows 'only negation', and this negation finds its final expression in his suicide. His fruitless spiritual power is known only through his multifarious emanations, his doubles, and in their actions it is seem to be a power mostly for evil.[21]

Stavrogin's hallucinatory double remains a shadowy creation, alluded to but not active in the dramatic structure of *The Devils*. The major characters who function as 'emanations' of his soul, on the other hand, carry the idea of the double into a dimension very far removed from its roots, and one that goes beyond the scope of the present study. In *The Brothers Karamazov* (1880), however, Dostoevsky returns to the theme in a way that is more traditional and delimited, though closely related to the approach developed in the earlier work. Ivan, the most inwardly riven of the brothers, attracts both types of double. In the character of Smerdyakov he is confronted with an embodiment of his half-conscious wicked desires, of everything in himself that is vulgar, inferior and evilly disposed. Like the second Mr Golyadkin, but in a far more sinister way, Smerdyakov acts out what in the primary character are impulses that are not fully formed, which are desired but have not received the full consent of the will. But Ivan also spawns another kind of double: as he succumbs to mental breakdown he projects a hallucinatory embodiment of his intellectual pride, his destructive negativity, and this figure is explicitly identified by Ivan as his Devil.

*The Devils* and *The Brothers Karamazov* were both in origin fragments of a huge projected work to be called *The Life of a Great Sinner*, and it is certain that Ivan's Devil brings to fruition the idea of hallucinatory phantoms emanating from a morbidly divided psyche which is adumbrated in Stavrogin's 'Confession'. The unrealised project was to trace the life history of a would-be saint who struggles to true sainthood by way of the expurgation of demonic pride. In *The Brothers Karamazov* both Ivan and Alyosha fall heir to different attributes of this single character as originally conceived.

*The Brothers Karamazov* treats of three brothers, and also a fourth. C. G. Jung has written a good deal of what he has called 'the dilemma of 3 + 1'. He describes how in alchemy 'There are always four elements, but often three of them are grouped together, with the fourth in a special position.'[22] Similarly the Christian Trinity can become a quaternity by the addition of the Devil (or of the Virgin Mary).[23] This 'uncertainty as to three or four amounts', according to Jung, 'to a wavering between the spiritual and the physical'.[24] Psychologically, in the context of the self, three is a 'defective quaternity', the complement of quaternity being unity. In the *complexio oppositorum* which is the self, the quaternity is contrasted with the 3 + 1 motif, 'and the positive, good, admirable and lovable human being with a daemonic, misbegotten creature who is negative, ugly, despicable and an object of fear'.[25]

In *The Brothers Karamazov*, the first half of this contrast exactly describes the saintly Alyosha, the second half the bastard Smerdyakov. In Jung's psychology of the functions there are three relatively differentiated functions and one undifferentiated, 'inferior' function. In Dostoevsky's novel the 3 + 1 motif is exemplified in the three legitimate Karamazov brothers and the illegitimate fourth, who bears every mark of inferiority – the bastard offspring of Fyodor Karamazov's intercourse with an idiot girl, a 'lackey', epileptic and morally despicable.

Of the three legitimate brothers, Dmitry, the eldest, represents the earthly, the physical, the unrestrainedly sensual. Alyosha, as we have seen, is almost entirely spiritual, the nearly impossible incarnation of a soaring religious ideal. Midway between them stands Ivan, divided between his sensual Karamazov nature and his higher aspirations. It is because he is divided that he attracts to himself a double in the form of Smerdyakov, who is his inferior nature separated off and personified. Smerdyakov is his admirer, his ape and his parody. Ivan's intellectual prowess finds its distorted reflection in the servant's cleverness and animal cunning. One of the first things we are told about Ivan is that very early in his life he began to show 'quite an extraordinarily brilliant aptitude for learning'.[26] Of Alyosha, by contrast, we are told that though he was always one of the best pupils 'he was never singled out as the top boy of the form'. The very first opinion about Ivan expressed by another character is, 'He's proud' (p. 15). Intellectual pride is Ivan's leading characteristic and the root of his inner conflict.

Passage has argued forcefully that the ground-plan of *The Life of a Great Sinner* is based on the structure of *The Devil's Elixirs*, and that *The Brothers Karamazov* inherits this schema.[27] Certainly the relation of Ivan to Smerdyakov echoes that of Medardus to Count Victor, and it is plausible that Ivan's Devil owes something to Peter Schönfeld/Pietro Belcampo. It is true also that Father Zossima's sending of Alyosha into the world can be related to the similar action of Prior Leonardus with respect to Medardus; but Passage is surely on less firm ground when he claims that Alyosha, undergoing a similar temptation, fails and falls. The fact is that Alyosha does not fall, unless to be subject to temptation is in itself to fall, which, of course, it is not.

The argument is based on the assumption that *The Brothers Karamazov* is simply the first part of *The Life of a Great Sinner*, and that Dostoevsky's references to Alyosha as the hero of a future novel indicate that he is the great sinner whose history was to be developed in the manner originally intended. It is far more likely, however, that the primary conception of this character became split into the two separate figures of Ivan and Alyosha, which was precisely the fate of the earlier projected protagonist whose personality came to be divided in *The Idiot* between Myshkin and Rogozhin; and that Dostoevsky decided to develop his theme in terms of a dialectical dramatic encounter between the opposing values represented by these two brothers. If this is the case, spiritual pride inheres solely in Ivan, and indeed all the internal evidence points to such a conclusion.

The activating theme of *The Brothers Karamazov*, that which propels into motion the great metaphysical issues which the novel confronts, is parricide. In the last years of his life Dostoevsky was perhaps reliving and re-enacting his tangled emotions respecting the death of his own father, who was murdered by his serfs when Dostoevsky was seventeen. It is the naïvely outspoken and impetuous Dmitry who first articulates the longing to kill the hateful and hated father (hateful and hated to all but Alyosha): 'Why does such a man live?' he snarls; and old Karamazov cries out to the witnesses of the outburst, 'Listen, listen, monks, to the parricide!' (p. 83). Yet Dmitry, though accused and convicted of murdering his father, is not the parricide. Dmitry wants and threatens to kill his father, but does not do so; Smerdyakov actually does so; but it is Ivan who, desiring it, passively and half-consciously colludes in the murder and thus makes it possible, and at last comes to believe himself the true parricide.

From the time of Ivan's arrival in 'our town' Smerdyakov, his father's cook, shows an admiration for him and a desire to imitate him. His atheistic and reductive arguments, superficial and sometimes illogical but always tortuously cunning, reflect in a horrible distorted fashion the nihilistic blankness at the heart of Ivan's brilliantly articulated and passionately expressed discourses on God, the world and the Devil. Old Karamazov shrewdly divines that the servant's speeches are for Ivan's benefit and mischievously encourages the latter to praise him. Ivan for his part exhibits a fascinated, though often repelled, interest in Smerdyakov, who becomes in a sense his protégé. The servant is repeatedly described as shrivelled and 'eunuch-like'; the idea which we are encouraged to form of him is of one who is unproductive, barren, sterile and malicious. Yet it is just these qualities in him which make Ivan see in him 'First-class material . . . when the time comes' (p. 153). Ivan means the time of revolution; and it is Smerdyakov's essential heartlessness, his empty but envious negativity, which will make him 'first-class material'.

Ivan too has a cold and heartless side to his character. When Dmitry, overwhelmed by fury, resentment and jealousy, rushes into his father's house and attacks him, kicking him viciously on the head, Ivan whispers, 'with a malicious grin, "One reptile will devour another reptile, and serve them both right!"' It is a phrase which will later repeatedly return to haunt him. Alyosha shudders, and Ivan adds, 'I won't of course let him be murdered as I didn't just now' (p. 164). But in the event Ivan does let him be murdered, though the murderer is not Dmitry but Smerdyakov. Ivan is not, however a whited sepulchre, but a man in real conflict. There is a passionate side to his nature, and even an impulsively sensual one. When he talks to Alyosha about his love for children, about their suffering and about how the doctrine of inherited sin is 'incomprehensible to the human heart here on earth', he is speaking with full and passionate conviction (p. 278). He believes it, too, when he says that 'if the devil doesn't exist and, therefore, man has created him, he has created him in his own image and likeness' (p. 279).

There is, however, a deeper reason for Ivan's atheism than his unwillingness to accept a God who permits suffering, and especially the suffering of children, in his world. When he says that he does not want harmony, that 'out of the love I bear to mankind . . . I'd rather remain with my suffering unavenged and my indignation unappeased, *even if I were wrong*', Alyosha realises that there is a profounder rebellion in his heart (p. 287). Essentially he has uttered a *non serviam*, and has revealed his deepest motivation to be his intellectual pride. It is this which underlies his gentle rejection of Christ in his beautifully thought-out and exquisitely modulated 'poem', the legend of the Grand Inquisitor (a set-piece which, incidentally, reveals the Gothic presence in the novel in the setting of the Spanish Inquisition and in 'the light like a fiery spark' that gleams from the sunken eyes of the Grand Inquisitor). Ivan does not shrink from the logical conclusion of his atheism, that in the absence of any moral sanction existing outside man himself, everything is allowed, 'everything is permitted'. Or rather, he does not shrink from it intellectually. Whether or not he will shrink from it in his heart is the great issue of conscience to which the action of the novel tends. How can he live or love, Alyosha asks him, 'with such a hell in your heart and your head?' (p. 309).

It is in the wake of his long conversation with Alyosha that Ivan's attitude to Smerdyakov begins to change from an absorbed interest in his 'originality' to an intense dislike and even hatred. The thought of him at the back of his mind afflicts Ivan with intense depression, and 'something gloomy and loathsome' fills his heart. He notices 'an inordinate vanity and an injured vanity' in the servant, and this is the beginning of his aversion. But what particularly enrages him is Smerdyakov's 'peculiar and revolting familiarity' with himself, as if he were 'in some sort of league with him . . . some secret understanding about something' (pp. 312–13). In spite of Ivan's anger and disgust at his 'eunuch-like, haggard face' he feels himself to be in some way in the servant's power, unable to pass him by.

Ivan has begun to be half-consciously aware of Smerdyakov as a horrible reflection of his own dark side. He also realises that the man is darkly hinting at something, something which he expects Ivan to understand without his making it explicit, and moreover Ivan really knows what it is. In frustrated fury he tries to drag it out of him, but at the same time he colludes with the servant by not himself giving it a name. Smerdyakov, with insinuating insistence, keeps persuading Ivan that he should go to Chermash-

nya, a town at some little distance where his father has some
business which he wishes him to attend to. Ivan divines his
motivation in this too, but again merely appeases his own conscience by his unsuccessful attempts to make Smerdyakov state this
explicitly. He is planning to go to Moscow, anyway. On the night
before his departure, up in his bedroom with 'a feeling of hate . . .
gnawing at his heart', he listens for a long time to his father moving
about downstairs. Although he does not himself 'know' why he is
doing so, subliminally he is aware that he is hoping that Dmitry
will come and murder his father, and later he will come to think
of this as 'the vilest action of all his life' (p. 324).

The following morning, he accedes to his father's repeated plea:
'"You're driving me to that damned Chermashnya yourself, aren't
you?" cried Ivan with a malicious smile' (p. 327). As he gets into
the carriage, 'against his will' he says to Smerdyakov, 'You see I –
I am going to Chermashnya.' Now all that Smerdyakov truly
requires for his purpose is Ivan's absence, where it does not matter.
But to persuade him to go to Chermashnya, rather than Moscow,
has been the mark of his pretence that he desires Ivan's departure
for perfectly honourable reasons, and Ivan knows this, and Smerdyakov knows that he knows. This is their understanding, their
collusion, not fully admitted by Ivan to himself. By telling him that
he is going to Chermashnya, rather than to Moscow (where he in
fact goes), Ivan is symbolically giving Smerdyakov the go-ahead
to murder his father. '"Yes, sir," said Smerdyakov firmly, looking
meaningfully at Ivan, "people are quite right when they say that
it's nice to have a chat with a clever man"' (p. 329).

The theme of moral responsibility has been insistently emphasised throughout the novel. Ivan knows very well that he *did*
collude with Smerdyakov in order to fulfil his desire for his father's
death, yet if he can believe that Smerdyakov is not the actual killer
then he can push further from him the sense of responsibility. He
is too honest, however, to allow the voice of his conscience to be
stilled. Almost masochistically he three times goes to visit the
servant to try to assure himself, one way or the other, of the truth.
During the first two interviews the 'lackey' maintains the fiction
of his own innocence, while mockingly and unrelentingly spelling
out the truth of their collusion. Smerdyakov knew that Ivan wanted
someone to do the killing, that he 'counted' on himself as much
as on Dmitry, and that by announcing his departure for Chermashnya he was saying, 'you can murder my father, I won't stand in

your way'. With rage and shame in his heart, Ivan is compelled to
admit to himself that all of this is true (pp. 714, 720–3).

Everything now hinges, for Ivan, on whether it is Smerdyakov
or Dmitry who is the real killer: 'If Smerdyakov and not Dmitry
murdered father, I'd be as guilty as he, for I put him up to it'
(p. 725). In this state of mind he comes actually to hate Dmitry
*because he had killed his father'*, thus deflecting on to his brother his
hatred of himself. He pays a third visit to Smerdyakov. This time,
after playing cat-and-mouse with him for a little, Smerdyakov tells
him the full truth: 'You murdered him. You are the chief murderer.
I was only your accomplice, your loyal page, and I done it because
you told me to' (p. 732). Although he has really known it all along,
Ivan is transfixed with horror. Suddenly he thinks Smerdyakov 'a
dream, a phantom sitting before me'; for he has another double
who is really a phantom, and he sees that both speak the same
language and that both are really himself. But the servant answers
him that the only 'other one' who is with them is God, or
Providence, which he won't find by looking.

Smerdyakov pulls from his stocking the money taken from the
murdered Karamazov, and Ivan can no longer push away the
truth. His father has been killed with his help, because he silently
gave his approval, and he is the 'rightful murderer'. Worse, he
has been the killer's teacher. Smerdyakov did not really want the
money at all; his idea of starting a new life in Moscow was only a
dream, a whim; the real reason was that 'everything is permitted',
and this, Smerdyakov tells Ivan, 'you did teach me, sir . . . for if
there's no everlasting God, there's no such thing as virtue, and
there's no need of it at all'. But this is not the end: Ivan's debased
double has yet more salt to rub in his wounds. Ivan will not give
evidence against Smerdyakov, he tells him, because he is too
proud, too fond of respect, of beautiful women, of money, of peace
and comfort. He is more like Mr Karamazov than any of his other
children: 'You've got the same soul as he, you have, sir.' Ivan is
amazed at the man's insight – he had thought he was a fool. 'It's
because you're so proud that you thought I was a fool. Take the
money, sir' (p. 743).

Ivan and Smerdyakov have met for the last time. Ivan's further
instruction in self-knowledge will be acquired in his confrontation
with his second, phantasmal double. We have already learned that
he receives visits from a hallucinatory second self. When Alyosha
sought to assure him that he was not the murderer, Ivan at once

believed that his brother must have been in the room when 'he' came, that it was 'he' who had told Alyosha of Ivan's thoughts. Now the reader is to make the acquaintance of this visitor, who as it were 'takes over' from Smerdyakov, raising Ivan's quarrel with himself to a higher level of consciousness.

We must be clear, however, that the 'Devil', as Ivan thinks of him and as he characterises himself, is entirely a hallucination. The narrator emphasises that his appearances are pathological, symptomatic of the severe nervous breakdown to which Ivan is soon to succumb. The cup which he hurls at his double is still intact on the table when Alyosha enters the room. Ivan knows this; the question which torments him is whether the apparition is a mere emanation of his psyche and nothing more, or *corresponds* to a non-physical but real entity in the spiritual world. He is an embodiment of the evil within Ivan; but is he also an embodiment of an evil that exists *in itself*, and independent of any individual? The question is not answered, but on it hinges the dialectic of Ivan's argument with his double.

The visitor comes in the guise of a sponger, 'a well-bred gentleman who was rather hard-up . . . ready to assume any amiable expression that occasion should demand' (p. 747). Ivan is clear enough about the relationship between them: '*it is I*, I myself who am talking and not you!' To begin with he denies his reality with fury: 'You're the embodiment of myself, but only of one side of me – of my thoughts and feelings, but only the most vile and stupid.' He addresses him as a 'flunkey', the epithet with which he has frequently insulted Smerdyakov, and regards him, too, as 'stupid and vulgar'. Yet he knows that he is insulting himself, for the phantom is only himself with a different face, one who put his own thoughts into words (pp. 749–50).

The Devil propounds his own position. He is a fallen angel who sometimes assumes a human form, 'and yet I'm only your nightmare and nothing more' (p. 752). But this is only his 'special method' of convincing Ivan of his reality. When the latter protests again that his visitant is not an independent entity but 'I and nothing more', the Devil makes the essential point: 'Well, if you like, I have the same philosophy as you. That would be fair' (p. 756). In his unwelcome guest's flippant, sceptical, nihilistic rationalism Ivan is forced to see, more unavoidably than in the distorting mirror of Smerdyakov's tortured logic, the moral emptiness on which his own more high-flown and poetic arguments are really founded. Confronted by this reflection, Ivan changes his ground: he still does not believe in the Devil's real existence, but he would like to, for otherwise he must acknowledge this horror as existing only in himself, and consequently must accept responsibility for it.

The Devil now has Ivan at his mercy. 'Leave me, please, you are hammering on my brain like an excruciating nightmare', the sick man pleads, in words which echo the experience of Mr Golyadkin when confronted by *his* double. The visitor, however, is relentless. He tells Ivan that he is hurt in his aesthetic feelings and, more importantly, in his pride: 'how could such a vulgar devil come to visit such a great man?' (p. 761). Ivan is in torment: all that is 'stupid' in him, all that he believes he has rejected and flung out 'like carrion' is being thrown back in his face. He is deeply and furiously ashamed: 'Why should my soul have begotten such a flunkey as you?' he cries in anguish as he recognises the Smerdyakov in himself. The Devil now rams his message home: Ivan has seen that in order to overturn society all that must be done is to destroy 'the idea of God in mankind'. Then man will become divinised and the man-god will appear, and then 'everything is permitted'. Dostoevsky here offers his deepest critique of the philosophy of Nietzsche, which he hated and feared so much because he was in many ways so close to it himself and recognised its attraction. So the Devil leaves his cruellest thrust to the last: 'All this is very charming; only, if you want to lead a life of crime, what do you want the sanction of truth for?' (pp. 763–4).

This is too much for Ivan and he hurls his cup at his visitor. And here, with the sense of timing of which he is such a master, Dostoevsky switches his attack from the realm of philosophical argument to that of dramatic enactment. Alyosha arrives with a piece of news, and the Devil vanishes. Smerdyakov, the Judas within Ivan, has hanged himself. Ivan seems to know it: 'it was *he* who told me that'. For Smerdyakov had not sought the sanction of truth in order to lead a life of crime. His crime has been committed in the true spirit of the philosophy of his teacher, Ivan, taken to the conclusion from which Ivan shrank.

He has commited the murder for no real reason, but only because 'everything is permitted'. At their last interview, before they parted, Smerdyakov asked Ivan to let him look at the money once more and stared at it for ten seconds, as if to say, 'Was it for this? He knew that it was not for this; and, unable to live with his own nullity, his own lack of meaning, he hanged himself. The life and death of Smerdyakov constitute perhaps the most powerful expression in literature of Augustine's theology of evil, that evil is not a thing in itself, but only the privation of the good. At the centre of Smerdyakov is nullity, non-entity, and Ivan has been forced to see that he, too, has the seed of this negativity, this evil, in his heart.

Ivan has one more struggle of conscience to endure. He has told Alyosha that the Devil is himself, 'All that is base, rotten and contemptible in me!' He is also 'stupid', but 'cunning, cunning like an animal' (p. 768). 'Still, he told me a great deal about myself that was true', he adds, and one of the things is that he intends to give evidence at the trial out of pride: he wishes to perform a great act of virtue without believing in virtue, so his true motivation must be the desire to be praised for his generous feelings.

He is now in a terrible dilemma: his first double, Smerdyakov, has assured him that he will *not* tell the truth because of his pride, and now his second, the Devil, has told him that he *will* do so, also out of pride. Alyosha understands his torment. Ivan does not yet believe in God or the truth, yet they have gained a hold on his heart. He will give evidence, because in spite of everything his conscience is still deep-seated and alive; and he will do so knowing that he will not be believed, because Smerdyakov is dead. So he must either acknowledge to himself that he does believe, must 'rise up in the light of truth', or he must 'perish in hate' because he has served the truth in which he does not believe (p. 771).

Ivan tells the truth at the trial, but he does so in hatred. He leaves the witness-box without having spoken up, but then returns and says his piece with casual directness, in the process rather strikingly anticipating one of Freud's more deathless insights: 'It was he and not my brother who murdered my father. He murdered him, and I told him to do it. Who doesn't wish his father dead?' (p. 807). His struggle of conscience, 'the agony of a proud decision', has been too much for him to withstand, and he breaks down in the courtroom in madness and delirium. Whether he is destined to rise up again from hell, Dostoevsky does not tell us.

In the story of Ivan the theme of the double reaches the apogee of its development, giving access to recesses of the soul and subtleties of inner division never before opened up and laid bare, and charting what Ralph Tymms has well described as 'the emergence of half-formed emotional reactions into the conscious mind'.[28] Using successively the devices of the external, independent shadow-figure and the hallucinatory projection to embody the dark and deformed second self, Dostoevsky brings to his psychological–realist approach a passionate inwardness which allows him to depict the terrors of the soul with a sharpness and vividness beyond the reach of even the greatest of his Gothic-inspired predecessors. But Dostoevsky's psychology is never merely clinical or diagnostic; he knows that *psyche* means soul, and that madness is born of the conflicts of the soul, of its quarrel with its own evil tendencies. This synthesis is about to be lost, and in the writers we shall now examine the allegorical and the psychological under-standings of the double will begin to draw apart.

# 8

# The Double in Decline

## R. L. STEVENSON

The representative figure in the history of the literary double in the last two decades of the nineteenth century is Robert Louis Stevenson. A writer of romances *par excellence*, he was, as Edwin M. Eigner has fascinatingly demonstrated, deeply imbued with the traditions of both the principal lines of Romantic fiction, that of the entertainment and the sensational romance, and that of the visionary or idealistic novel (though these are not, it must be said, always so clearly distinguishable from one another as Eigner seems sometimes to suggest).[1] No aspect of Romantic fiction attracted Stevenson so much, or was so germane to the concerns natural to his temperament, as the pervasive duality that was common to both traditions.

A fellow-countryman of James Hogg, Stevenson shared his Presbyterian theological heritage and his sense of the sharply overdefined opposition between good and evil which this entailed (a consciousness now complicated by the respectabilities and hypocrisies of Victorian Edinburgh). He was, in addition, a profound admirer of Hoffmann, and regarded Dostoevsky as the greatest of contemporary novelists; thus Stevenson fell heir to the richest psychological insights of the imaginative exploration of mental and moral duality. He was also, however, deeply interested in the new discoveries of scientific psychology, and his most dualistic creations were, according to his wife, inspired by the work of the French psychologists; towards the end of his life he carried on a correspondence with F. W. H. Myers, one of the most respected figures in the contemporary psychological world.[2] In Stevenson's imaginative work we can see the attempt to integrate these two kinds of understanding, and its only partial success. The Romantic and scientific psychologies are beginning to pull apart, and the tradition of the double as exploited by Hoffmann, Hogg, Poe and Dostoevsky will become a victim of this development.

Stevenson's leaning towards duality seems to have been with

him almost since the cradle. From the very beginning of his career he wrote books and stories which in greater or lesser degree dramatise complementarity and opposition, division in the will and the double life. He was greatly attracted to paradoxical and divided characters, such as François Villon. He continually reverted to these topics in his essays and discursive prose and referred to them in letters. Such preoccupations, certainly native to his temperament, found a focus and received stimulation in childhood through the story of the notorious Edinburgh cabinet-maker, Deacon Brodie, respectable citizen by day and professional thief by night (and thus a figure having much in common with Hoffmann's Cardillac), whose divided personality and existence led him all the way to the gallows.[3]

Some of Stevenson's earliest stories make unimportant use of the double, the wraith and the split personality for sensationalist purposes, but his first serious essay on such a theme was the play *Deacon Brodie, or the Double Life* (1878, revised in 1884), on which he collaborated with W. E. Henley. Brodie calls the evil side of his divided nature 'my maniac brother who has slipped his chain', and in this conception it is not hard to discern the germ of Stevenson's central investigation of duality, *The Strange Case of Dr Jekyll and Mr Hyde*.

Before we examine Stevenson's contributions to the literature of the double proper, we should refer to *The Master of Ballantrae* (1889), a romance which takes as its subject two brothers of opposite character, rivals in love, who become mortal enemies. The wrong done to the initially stable, reliable and unimaginative younger brother by and because of the impetuous, proud, daring and 'Satanic' elder, becomes the former's obsession which destroys him from within. James Durie, the Master, is presented as a figure of almost unalloyed evil, though not without his attractive qualities. Henry, on the other hand, is no paragon of virtue, but an ordinary individual whose darker attributes are activated by the circumstances which lead him to become consumed by hatred of his brother. As this process develops, Henry comes to see James as possessed of a diabolic immortality and to believe in their inseparable identity. Their relation is described by him in terms which cannot fail to bring to mind that between Gil-Martin and Robert Wringhim: 'He is not mortal. He is bound upon my back to all eternity – to all God's eternity! . . . Wherever I am, there will he be.'[4]

After Henry's first attempt to kill James in a duel, his character quickly degenerates and begins to acquire the evil qualities of his brother's, very much as, in *Caleb Williams*, Falkland takes on the character of the murdered Tyrrel, originally his complementary opposite. James then appears as the embodiment of the evil latent in Henry's nature, as well as the force which provokes it and draws it out. The younger brother becomes possessed by his determination to rid himself of the figure who is thus his accuser as well as his persecutor, and when he finally succeeds in murdering him it is his belief in their inseparability, in the immortality of James, which proves fatal to himself. When he sees the body of his brother apparently reanimating after death and the eyes flickering open, he drops dead from shock. But the Master does not survive, and the brothers, in life bound together in opposition, are thus strangely and symbolically united in death.

Stevenson's first attempt on the true double motif is the story 'Markheim' (1885), in which, as in Poe's 'William Wilson', the double figures as a projection of the protagonist's conscience. The story is undoubtedly related to *Crime and Punishment*, which Stevenson greatly admired, and probably also to *The Brothers Karamazov*; and the ambition of the theme is perhaps too much for its diminutive scale. The early pages of the story are marvellously atmospheric. On Christmas Day Markheim enters an antique shop, or pawnshop, with evil intent. The shop is full of ticking clocks, marking the passing of time which is for Markheim a reminder of ill-spent years. When the dealer suggests a mirror as a Christmas present for his lady, he rejects it with horror as a 'hand-conscience'.[5] He pretends to want to be friendly – 'Why should we wear this mask?' – but no sooner has he said this than he stabs the dealer with a 'long skewer-like dagger'. The room is full of shadows; all at once all the clocks in the shop strike three in their different voices; and in dozens of ornate mirrors Markheim sees 'his face repeated and repeated, as it were an army of spies' (p. 93).

It is not surprising that in these surroundings the murderer begins to wonder whether he is alone. He becomes conscious of some presence which at times seems 'a shadow of himself'. Yet looking at the body he is unmoved and feels no remorse – he has thrust his conscience outside himself. He has no fear of God in his heart, only a fear that the laws of nature will betray him, or 'some wilful illegality of nature' which might be called 'the hands of God reached forth against sin' (p. 98). But now his conscience returns to haunt him, animistically, from without: 'The sense that he was not alone grew upon him to the point of madness. On every side he was haunted and begirt by presences' (p. 97). These vague phantoms are about to take a more definite shape. Markheim is upstairs in the drawing-room, going through the keys. A footstep mounts the stairs, and the door opens; a face looks in, and smiles 'as if in friendly recognition'.

From the moment of the double's entry, the story loses its impetus and becomes an argument. A vast novel such as *The Brothers Karamazov* can carry within it such discursive episodes without losing its structural coherence or its dramatic tension, but a story of less than twenty pages is thrown severely out of balance by a protracted debate between a man and his personified conscience who materialises very much as a *deus ex machina*. The real point of the tale lies in its surprise ending, a feature of short-story writing which was coming into popularity around this time with no very good results for the future of the genre. Markheim's visitor is very like Ivan's Devil, a thing which seems to bear a likeness to himself but is 'not of the earth and not of God', yet at the same time appears commonplace and everyday. Markheim takes him for the Devil, and his visitor goes along with him, not only playing the Devil's advocate but using the Devil's arguments to lead Markheim unawares towards an opposite conclusion. This is a cruder version of the approach of Ivan's Devil.

The visitor warns Markheim that the maid will return early, thus putting him under further pressure from his old enemy, time. Markheim starts to justify himself, that is, to champion his submerged but true self: 'My life is but a travesty and slander on myself. I have lived to belie my nature.' He cannot be judged by his acts; he has been dragged down by the 'giants of circumstance'. Evil, he claims, is hateful to him: 'Can you not see within me the clear writing of conscience. . . . Can you not read me for a thing that surely must be common as humanity – the unwilling sinner?' (p. 101). But this reminder of St Paul cuts no ice with the other, who is interested only in the outcome. He offers to tell him where to find the money, but Markheim refuses to take anything at his hands: 'I will do nothing to commit myself to evil.' The double pours contempt on this 'truckling peace with God', but Markheim is firm: this crime will be his last; through the riches it brings he will become an agent of good and live at peace. But his better self, with something of the incontrovertible air of a modern newspaper astrologer, gives him the bad news: he will lose the money on the Stock Exchange.

Still Markheim is determined in the face of this blow that his worst part will not triumph. 'Evil and good run strong in me, haling me in both ways . . . good, also, is a spring of acts.' The *soi-disant* Devil, however, seeks to deny him this comfort and to bind him by the old predestinarian argument that he is powerless except for evil: 'Downward, downward lies your way; nor can anything but death avail to stop you' (p. 104). Markheim is grateful: 'I thank you for these lessons from my soul; my eyes are opened, and I behold myself for what I am' (p. 105). They hear the servant enter; the visitor tells him that he must let her in and then get rid of her. But Markheim has a trump card up his sleeve to counter Augustinian theology: if he is condemned to evil acts, then he can cease from action. 'My love of good is damned to barrenness; it may, and let it be! But I still have my hatred of evil; and from that, to your galling disappointment, you shall see that I can draw both energy and courage' (p. 106). At this the features of his visitor brighten and soften in a 'tender triumph' and he fades away. Markheim gives himself up to the police.

There is an embarrassing air of contrivance about the whole dialogue. Apart from the structural weakness which it imparts to the story as a whole, it carries within it a conceptual flaw: having projected his conscience outside himself as an *advocatus diaboli*, Markheim still seems able to draw on it from within himself and give form to its promptings in a coherent argument, even if one which, in the detestation of evil which it expresses, seems to come very oddly from one who has plunged a knife into an old man a few minutes previously. If his conscience is already so developed and articulate, why should it have to conduct a Socratic argument with itself? The philosophical validity of its clinching argument is, besides, highly suspect: he admits that he is capable only of evil acts but argues that he can 'cease from action'; to give himself up to the police is, however, an action, and, we must suppose, a good action.

Stevenson's next and major exercise in the double struck, however, on an image so vivid and arresting, and of such dramatic force, that its title has provided the most popular proverbial shorthand for the divided personality. *The Strange Case of Dr Jekyll and Mr Hyde* (1886) is a pure allegory, and this is at once its strength and its weakness. Stevenson was aware that it was its allegorical quality which made the story what it was, and his destruction of the first version, on the basis of his wife's criticism, appears to have sprung from a recognition that the trial run had not sufficiently played to that strength. The tale fastens on a single moral insight, of no great originality in itself and not elaborated with any marked psychological profundity, but embodied in an image so telling and unforgettable and of such a powerful visual quality that in spite of the technical difficulties involved there have been many attempts to dramatise and to film the story.

The weakness, of course, lies in the means chosen for the transformation from Dr Jekyll to Mr Hyde. A commentator writing early this century hits exactly on the difficulty Stevenson faced here. Referring to the novelist's hold on the actual and the matter-of-fact, he points out, 'In *Jekyll and Hyde* there is the powder and the licquor which positively smell of the chemist's shop. Had it been possible by any means to get rid of these, and by some mystic spell to accomplish the transformation, the story would have gained a safer foothold in the spectral world. Yet, on the other hand, any such device would have taken it out of the actual life of modern men, and its hold on that was more important for its real purpose than the mere point of artistry.'[6]

The trouble is, however, that the story's crude scientism no longer gives it any such hold, that it appears to the modern reader to be indeed nothing more than a 'mystic spell', and in that respect the device renders the story very dated. The problem for a late-nineteenth-century writer such as Stevenson attempting a version of the supernatural double was that the loss of confident belief in any spiritual reality outside the human psyche had robbed him of a concrete figure through which to articulate the psychological–spiritual nuances to which he aspired to give form. We will encounter the same problem with Wilde's *The Picture of Dorian Gray*. The pseudo-science of *Jekyll and Hyde*, though it was integral to the vision from which Stevenson's allegory arose, now seems quite unreal, little more than a lurid latter-day necromancy. There could not be a greater contrast with Dostoevsky's firm grip on the reality of the spiritual world. Dostoevsky could plumb the depths of unbelief as well as the abyss of belief, but the intensity with which he experienced both made it possible for him to bridge with dramatic conviction the gulf between the spiritual and the material.

The structure of *Jekyll and Hyde* has something in common with that of Hogg's *Justified Sinner*, in that both consist of a factual, external narrative of the events, followed by the intimate confession of the protagonist. 'Henry Jekyll's Full Statement of the Case', however, represents a much smaller proportion of the whole than does Robert Wringhim's Confession. The main narrative is essentially a mystery of detection, a pursuit, an uncovering of strange events: 'If he be Mr Hyde . . . I shall be Mr. Seek', as Mr. Utterson the lawyer says.[7] The principal sleuths are themselves a double pair: Utterson, an unsociable but tolerant man who admits to 'Cain's heresy' – 'I let my brother go to the devil in his own way' (p. 29) – and his distant kinsman, Richard Enfield. We are told that the two, although they appear to have absolutely nothing in common, are the closest of friends and place the greatest value on their Sunday walks together. The other important figure is Dr Lanyon, a former friend of Jekyll's who has become alienated from him because he has perceived that Jekyll was going 'wrong in mind', devoted to 'Such unscientific balderdash [as] would have estranged Damon and Pythias' (p. 36). We can perhaps detect in Lanyon's stricture a reflection of Stevenson's uneasy consciousness of the very dubious status of the hero's 'science'.

Enfield's first encounter with the horrible Mr Hyde comes when he observes him trample over the body of a child who has accidentally run into him in the street. The man immediately appears to him like Satan, and when it is discovered that Hyde is a protégé of Jekyll's, Utterson, having now also made Hyde's acquaintance, muses, 'O my poor Henry Jekyll, if ever I read Satan's signature upon a face, it is on that of your new friend' (p. 40). It is interesting, however, that the marks of Satan are different from those he impressed on the features of his Gothic emissaries. Those earlier embodiments of evil were usually characterised in terms of lofty pride, Promethean audacity, mocking contempt, baleful malevolence – the qualities most galvanically expressed by the 'terrible eyes'. Mr Hyde's marks of the Devil, however, are essentially those of inferiority. We have already seen the principle of evil, in the person of Smerdyakov, developed in terms of moral inferiority; in Hyde this defectiveness is given a full physical expression.

There is something animal, 'scarcely human', about Hyde. He hisses like a snake and snarls like a beast. Perhaps there is an ironical allusion to this in the unattractive name 'Jekyll', which has an uncomfortable way of bringing 'jackal' to the mind. Hyde is an underground creature, 'troglodytic', arising gnome-like from the lowest levels of the soul. He is small, stunted, dark in complexion. Though he is not outwardly deformed he gives 'a strong feeling of deformity', 'a haunting sense of unexpressed deformity' (pp. 34, 50). There is something 'abnormal and mis-begotten' in his very essence, and Dr Lanyon comments on the 'odd, subjective disturbance caused by his neighbourhood'. He is the natural and instinctive enemy of innocence and goodness; the first victim of his 'ape-like' fury is a child, and his principal crime is the unmotivated murder of Sir Danvers Carew, an old man with a look of 'such an innocent and old-world kindness of disposition, yet with something high too, as of a well-grounded self-content' (p. 46). Like Claggart's persecution of Billy Budd in Melville's tale, Hyde's malice is directed against all that is good precisely and solely because it is good, because the good is his natural foe.

The world of *Jekyll and Hyde* is one of sharply etched moral opposition. Its most pervasive imagery is that of light and shadow. There is very little sense of gradation in its moral perception; the words 'good' and 'evil' are constantly on the lips of the characters. The conflict of Jekyll is pondered almost melodramatically by Utterson long before the truth is known; his disturbance must be provoked by 'the ghost of some old sin, the cancer of some concealed disgrace', the terrible legacy of his wild youth (p. 58). Jekyll sees himself in the same kind of dramatised, antinomial perspective: 'You must suffer me to go on my own dark way', he tells Dr Lanyon. 'If I am the chief of sinners, I am the chief of sufferers also' (p. 58). As his crisis approaches he cries out upon the name of God, weeps like a lost soul; after his death a pious work is found 'annotated, in his own hand, with startling blasphemies' (p. 71). His confession unfolds the separation of light and darkness, good and evil, in his tortured consciousness.

Jekyll finds the genesis of his division in an aspect of that familiar incubus of the divided man, pride. Unable to reconcile 'my imperious desire to hold my head high' with the natural gaiety of his disposition, he endeavoured to hide his frivolous and irregular side, and found himself early committed to a 'profound duplicity of life'. It was thus 'the exacting nature of my aspirations', dictating a systematic repression of every natural impulse, which 'severed in me those provinces of good and ill which divide and compound man's dual nature' (p. 71). Both sides of his personality were, however, equally real to him, equally in earnest, and he disowns the name of hypocrite. Persistently conscious of this Pauline 'war among my members', he came to see 'that man is not truly one, but truly two'; and he became the victim of that primitive duality because he was unable to decide between his two natures, knowing that he was 'radically both'. So he began to daydream about the possibility of separating the warring and incompatible elements: 'It was the curse of mankind that these incongruous faggots were thus bound together – that in the agonized womb of consciousness, these polarities should be continuously struggling' (p. 81).

Jekyll succeeds in concocting a drug which suppresses the rule of his natural body over his spirit and substitutes a second form and countenance, 'none the less natural to me because they were the expression and bore the stamp, of lower elements in my soul' (p. 83). As soon as he has screwed up his courage sufficiently to administer this drug to himself, and has emerged from the agonies of transition, he knows himself 'to be more wicked, tenfold more wicked, sold a slave to my original evil' (p. 84). Yet the contrast between Jekyll and Hyde is not, as is popularly often supposed, a straightforward opposition of good and evil. In the first place, as Masao Miyoshi has shrewdly pointed out, Hyde is at the beginning 'merely Jekyll's unrepressed spontaneous existence'.[8] The transformed 'I' feels at once younger, lighter, happier and free in soul. Even on first seeing the image of the second self in the mirror, in spite of the 'imprint of deformity and decay' left upon it by evil, he feels no repugnance: 'This, too, was myself. It seemed natural and human. In my eyes it bore a livelier image of the spirit, it seemed more express and single, than the imperfect and divided countenance I had been hitherto accustomed to call mine' (pp. 84–5).

This is the second and more important point. Although Hyde is a projection of what Stevenson calls pure 'evil', Jekyll remains mixed, the same 'incongruous compound' as before. The overall movement is therefore 'wholly towards the worse'. Jekyll has projected his evil and inferior second self as Hyde, his psychic balance has been lost, and faced with this double he is at a disadvantage: evil and weakness still persist in Jekyll, and Hyde, freed from Jekyll's countervailing good qualities, can exploit the weakness to gain the upper hand. This is the acutest psychological point which the tale makes, the feature which gives it its originality and fidelity to experience. It is the dissociation and autonomy of the complex that is Hyde which allow it to dominate, and eventually to arrogate, the personality of Jekyll. 'At that time my virtue slumbered,' he explains, 'my evil, kept awake by ambition, was alert and swift to seize the occasion' (p. 85).

The Frankenstein monster which Jekyll has released is an expression of pure *id*, of savage instinctual life, of self unrestrained by any socialisation, anarchic and primitive, 'the brute that slept within me': 'This familiar that I called out of my own soul . . . was a being inherently malign and villainous: his every act and thought centred on self . . . relentless like a man of stone' (p. 86). The fatal development is that Jekyll can now, when in his old form, think of Hyde as a separate being over whom he has no control and for whom he has no responsibility; Hyde alone is guilty, while Jekyll's conscience is relaxed and slumbers. One morning, however, having gone to bed as Henry Jekyll, he wakes to see lying before him on the bedclothes the lean, dark, swarthy and hairy hand of Edward Hyde. The balance is being lost; Jekyll will gradually lose the power of voluntary change, and become irrevocably Hyde: 'I was slowly losing hold of my original and better self, and becoming slowly incorporated with my second and worse' (p. 89). This double, too, is a usurper.

Jekyll's dilemma really consists in this, that while there is always a part of himself that wants to be Hyde, there is nothing in Hyde that wants to be Jekyll, no inducement sufficient to encourage him to undergo the reverse transformation. Indeed, this is a conceptual weakness in the basic idea: since Hyde is pure self, why should he, even on the first occasion, have chosen to revert to Jekyll? Eventually, when he is being hunted, he does so out of expediency, and remembers Jekyll 'as the mountain bandit remembers the cavern in which he conceals himself from pursuit', but this will not suffice for the original inducement. To account for this behaviour we would have to assume that he retains in himself some kind of 'Jekyll-consciousness', some admixture of good, but this is explicitly and repeatedly stated not to be the case. It is really only the vividness and the dramatic quality of the image of transformation which allow Stevenson to override this difficulty.

The argument which Jekyll conducts with himself is conceived in a form which again refers back to St Paul's divided will. 'Strange as my circumstances were, the terms of this debate are as old and commonplace as man; . . . I chose the better part, and was found wanting in the strength to keep to it' (p. 89). When, after abstaining for two months, he once more takes the fatal draught, Hyde is like a caged wild beast set free: 'Instantly the spirit of hell awoke in me and raged' (p. 90). It is then that Sir Danvers Carew is murdered. After this Jekyll decides that Hyde is henceforth impossible; but it is not to be. Here Stevenson introduces the subtlest and most delicate touch in his story. Jekyll does not succumb to the temptation of resuscitating Hyde, but, afflicted still with 'duality of purpose', he falls victim 'as an ordinary secret sinner' to an inner motion of pride. He is sitting on a park bench on a fine winter's day, the vigilance of his conscience a little relaxed, and a 'vainglorious thought' comes to him; he compares himself favourably to other men. This 'brief condescension' to evil finally destroys the balance of his soul; no sooner has he thought the thought than the transformation overtakes him and he finds himself instantly Hyde (p. 92).

Jekyll knows that his days are numbered. When 'he' is Hyde, like Chamisso's shadowless man he can come out only in the dark, a terrified and hunted beast, haunted by the gallows. As Jekyll he knows no peace, for ever tormented by the horror of his second self. As G. K. Chesterton shrewdly pointed out, 'The real stab of the story is not in the discovery that the one man is two men; but in the discovery that the two men are one man.'[9] Both selves now loathe each other, Hyde experiencing Jekyll as a prison in which he has to retreat to accept once more the role of a 'part instead of a person'; while Jekyll detests Hyde as 'something not only hellish but inorganic', abhorring the fearful truth that 'what was dead, and had no shape, should usurp the offices of life' (p. 95). (Here once more we find a fiction writer giving supporting testimony to the insight of Augustine, that evil is in itself nothing, merely negativity, death, privation – what Ivan Karamazov's Devil called 'the indispensable minus sign'.) This mutual loathing of the two selves can end only with the dissolution of the one man who is both. With the supply of his drug finally run dry, Jekyll becomes irreversibly Hyde; and it is left to Hyde to perform, on behalf of both of them, the ultimate crime of self-destruction.

## OSCAR WILDE

Five years after *Dr Jekyll and Mr Hyde* there appeared another book, influenced by its example, in which the approach to the double is equally allegorical, and which struck upon a central image which has held a continuing fascination for the public imagination only a little less striking than that of Stevenson's metaphor of the double life. Oscar Wilde's *The Picture of Dorian Gray* (1891) is, however, a less satisfactory work in almost every respect. This is not because its allegorising is in itself clumsier or less convincing than Stevenson's. The metamorphosis of Dorian's picture is effected through some unexplained supernatural means which the reader is, of course, obliged to take on trust or to accept as purely symbolic in its mode of operation; there is no question here of a 'willing suspension of disbelief', and the reader accepts this premise from the outset. Wilde also resorts, in the episode of Campbell's disposal of Basil Hallward's body, to a laboratory scientism very similar to that of *Jekyll and Hyde*, and this again the reader is prepared to take on trust. It is not the novelist's allegorical method which causes unease, but the unavoidable question-mark which hangs over his fundamental artistic sincerity.

Masao Miyoshi has rightly pointed to the derivativeness of most of the key elements in *Dorian Gray*: the idea of the portrait borrowed from Maturin's *Melmoth the Wanderer*, Lord Henry Wotton one more in a long line of Mephistophilean tempters, Dorian's prayer a 'rudimentary devil-compact', the ending directly dependent on Poe's 'William Wilson'.[10] Derivativeness, however, is nothing new in the history of the double theme and of the various Gothic devices on which it draws. Melmoth itself owes a deep debt of gratitude to *The Monk*, and so too does *The Devil's Elixirs*, while the work of Hogg and the culminating achievement of Dostoevsky could scarcely have been possible without the decisive and pervasive presence of Hoffmann. And although it is true that Wilde obtained both the catastrophe of sudden ageing and the notion of portrait-identity (itself a primordial folk motif) from Maturin, his combination of these elements is both ingenious and original, for in *Melmoth* they are two discrete and separate ideas.

Miyoshi reaches closer to the heart of the matter when he indicates that, in vociferously expounding the 'terrible moral' of *Dorian Gray* and arguing defensively for its moralistic intention, Wilde is in direct contradiction of his own celebrated dicta in the book's Preface.[11] There Wilde states that 'There is no such thing as a moral or an immoral book. Books are well written or badly written, that is all'; again that 'No artist desires to prove anything'; and once more that 'No artist has ethical sympathies. An ethical sympathy in an artist is an unpardonable mannerism of style.'[12] 'Those who read the symbol do so at their peril', he adds – which is precisely what Wilde does himself when he writes that his novel will be 'ultimately recognised as a real work of art with a strong ethical lesson inherent in it'.[13]

Wilde's aesthetic doctrine begs endless questions. What exactly is to be understood by a well or a badly written book? Is this merely a matter of style, or does, for instance, a book's content and the way a writer handles it come into the matter? What is an 'ethical sympathy'? Does he intend to suggest that the artist, alone of mortals, does or should live in a moral vacuum? If so, why should he have found it necessary to defend the morality of his intention as an artist?

The view is attributed by Wilde to Lord Henry Wotton that 'Even the cardinal virtues cannot atone for half-cold *entrées*', and Wilde, or the narrative voice, goes on to opine that 'there is possibly a good deal to be said for his view'. Insincerity, it is suggested, is an essential ingredient of form. 'Is insincerity such a terrible thing? I think not. It is merely a method by which we can multiply our personalities' (p. 158). The multiplication of personality, we must then assume, is not a terrible event that may overwhelm the soul, but a convenient means of dispelling the *ennui* of bored artists, 'the elect to whom beautiful things mean only Beauty'. (What, one wonders, do beautiful things 'mean' to the non-elect?) Having said this, however, Wilde revealingly goes on to hedge his bets: 'Such, at any rate, was Dorian Gray's opinion' (p. 159).

That ambivalence is precisely the weakness of *The Picture of Dorian Gray*. Since insincerity is proclaimed as a virtue, we are entitled to draw the conclusion that the book is sincerely insincere. Self-love is the sin by which Dorian falls, but the tone of the writing repeatedly attests Wilde's complicity in Dorian's self-love. A subtle transposition of values is continually at work. Sin and vice are not essentially reprehensible because they are evil, but because they are *ugly*; or rather, evil is seen almost solely in terms of ugliness. And after all, is there not a kind of beauty in ugliness, and therefore a kind of beauty in sin? It is impossible to escape the impression that at times Wilde finds Dorian's sin attractive. There is, of course, retribution. But in what does retribution consist? In ugliness; not simply to die, but to die ugly. What worse retribution could there possibly be for an exceptionally beautiful young man?

Self-love, the vanity of physical beauty which epitomises the self-absorption of the soul, is the whole character of Dorian Gray. If this is the particular variety of pride which constitutes the *hubris* of the novel's traditional moral framework, or overt moral framework, it is also what makes Dorian attractive to his creator, and thus subverts what we would have assumed to be his intention, had we not first been assured that the artist has no intention (the contradiction of this quoted above being *post facto*). This is reflected in the language. For Dorian the picture is 'the shadow of his own loveliness', he is 'in love with it' precisely because it is 'part of [him]self' (pp. 33, 35). The mutual attraction between Dorian and Lord Henry is represented, from the point of view of each, in narcissistic terms. They are more than just Platonic soul-mates. The influences which Gray feels working within him when he first meets Lord Henry seem to him 'to have come really from himself' (p. 26). For Wotton, 'To project one's soul into some gracious form . . . to convey one's temperament into another as though it were a subtle fluid or a strange perfume' is the most satisfying joy available in a vulgar age, an impulse to domination and absorption (p. 44). We are told that it was the portrait which 'taught [Dorian] to love his own beauty' (p. 114), but we might be forgiven for feeling that he needed little encouragement. As the portrait changes and becomes evil and ageing, he titillates himself with contemplation of the contrast: 'He grew more and more enamoured of his own beauty, more and more interested in the corruption of his own soul' (p. 143).

Dorian's prayer which turns the portrait into his double, the repository of his evil (or ugly) second self, is really a magic invocation. Although he exclaims, 'I would give my soul for that' – that is, for the picture to grow old and himself to stay young – he does not explicitly pray to the Devil. Certainly the request is scarcely one which he could properly make to God, but we can no doubt assume that he scarcely believes in either God or Devil. The magical invocation is successful and the transference which takes place is essentially sympathetic magic. The women in the opium dens which Dorian will later haunt give him the nickname of 'the devil's bargain'; but the Devil himself, unless he be Lord Henry, is nowhere to be seen. He can have little part to play in a context in which evil is most of all a deplorable lapse in taste. Dorian is bound to the portrait in a 'secret love of strange affinity', even as its beauty degenerates into repulsive squalor. He loves his sin for the same reason that he loves his beauty, that both are aspects of himself, both are his own (p. 120). Yet, as an externalised image of himself, the portrait is dissociated from Gray. 'There is something fatal about a portrait', he tells Basil Hallward. 'It has a life of its own' (p. 131).

Witnessing the first change in the portrait, Dorian tells himself that (like the mirror which Markheim saw as a 'hand-conscience') it will become for him 'the visible emblem of his conscience', 'the most magical of mirrors' (pp. 105, 120). As a symbol (which, we must remember, we read at our peril), the portrait has a heavy load to bear: it is to be 'a guide to him through life . . . what holiness is to some, and conscience to others, and the fear of God to us all . . . a visible symbol of the degradation of sin . . . an ever-present sign of the ruin men brought upon their souls' (p. 109). It is 'his own soul . . . looking at him from the canvas and calling him to judgment' (p. 134). However, the attempts of Dorian to profit from the lessons the portrait has to teach him are sadly evanescent and ineffectual. When Basil learns the truth about what has happened to the portrait he painted, he urges repentance on Gray: 'The prayer of your pride has been answered. The prayer of your repentance will be answered also' (p. 110). The sobbing Dorian replies that it is too late, and Basil, taking the role of Faustus's Good Angel, assures him that it is never too late and suggests that they kneel and pray. Gray will have none of it, and when Hallward in protest appeals to the reproach of 'that accursed thing leering at us', Dorian, filled with an uncontrollable hatred of his former friend and admirer, plunges a knife into the back of his neck.

Dorian genuinely believes that 'The soul is a terrible reality. It can be bought, and sold, and bartered away' (p. 238). He tells Basil, too, that each of us has Heaven and Hell in him. Yet his fleeting impulse, early in his career of vice, to pray that the 'horrible sympathy between himself and the picture might cease' is quickly dispelled by the thought that he would then have to age like every other mortal (p. 119). Even at the last his guilt seems unreal to him, and he falls back on blaming the dead Basil for having created the portrait that he considers the origin of all his woe. He destroys the portrait because it is evidence against himself: this act 'would kill this monstrous soul-life, and, without its hideous warnings, he would be at peace' (p. 247).

In his inability to repent of his pride Dorian Gray is certainly well in the tradition of the divided protagonist who has come face to face with his separated evil self. What is striking, however, is the merely notional status of the moral conflict in which he is said to be involved. His most real emotion is the *pity* which he feels for the portrait, because it is becoming ugly. The reader's uneasy feeling of the author's half-conscious complicity in some of both Dorian's and Lord Henry's attitudes is encouraged by the self-indulgence of the language they use, which is not adequately 'placed', and in the lack of any device which might distance him decisively from his characters.

An example is the conversation between the two friends which takes place after the suicide of Sybil Vane, in which the event is discussed in terms of the 'terrible beauty of a Greek tragedy', 'artistic elements of beauty', the 'sense of dramatic effect' and so on. It is true that Lord Henry is said at this point to be 'playing on the lad's unconscious egotism'; but Dorian's words to Sybil, 'Without your art you are nothing', and the philosophical conclusions which Wotton derives from the melancholy outcome, are too close for comfort to the perspective of the book's Preface (p. 114). This is a case where a definite authorial distancing or disclaimer would be in order (indeed almost a moral and artistic necessity), one that would be built into the way the episode was structured; and the absence of anything of the sort makes the discussion morally repellent.

The evil which is projected by Dorian's psyche is conceived almost entirely in terms of hideousness, and moral turpitude is finally ugliness. Dorian smiles 'with secret pleasure at the mis-shapen shadow that had to bear the burden that should have been his own', even though he has to hide from all other eyes the degeneration which mirrors that of his soul. He feels keenly 'the terrible pleasure of a double life' (pp. 156, 194). Under the influence of a novel (evidently Huysmans' *A Rebours*) about a young Parisian whom he sees as 'a prefiguring type of himself', he throws himself into a restless intellectual experimentation which is clearly Faustian but which is also reminiscent of the life of Rimbaud, whose terrifying seriousness, however, makes Dorian look frivolous in the extreme. He imagines himself as 'those strange terrible figures that had passed across the stage of the world and made sin so marvellous, and evil so full of subtlety', achieving the ultimate in solipsism in supposing 'that the whole of history was merely the record of his own life' (pp. 142, 161). The monstrosity of his soul is thus turned into an aesthetic experience. All this, we are told, springs from 'that pride of individualism that is half the fascination of sin' (p. 156). But, as Mario Praz long ago acutely remarked, 'the author's real interest is in the decorative . . . Wilde's point of view, in fact, is always scenic.'[14]

There is an ironic moment early in the novel when Basil, unhappily aware that Dorian is drawing away from him, pulled by the counter-attraction of Lord Henry, says sadly, 'I shall stay with the real Dorian', meaning the just-completed portrait (p. 37). The irony goes deeper than Wilde intended, though, for the Dorian whose originality, freshness and unspoilt simplicity are so much insisted upon is in reality no more than a painted picture. We are not vouchsafed any convincing display of these qualities in action, and we have to conclude that they are simply deduced by his admirers from the fact of his physical beauty. Dorian is simply beauty personified, and his shadow-self is, with complete consistency, projected as ugliness. For all the high moral tone which the narrative voice often assumes, the tale's moral dimension is therefore wavering, ambiguous and uncertain. The book's habit of stylistic overkill serves partly to cover this uncertainty. If 'To reveal art and conceal the artist is art's aim' (p. 5), *Dorian Gray* cannot be said to succeed, for the artistic end is vitiated by the element of the *poseur* that it reveals in the artist.

## KIPLING, MAUPASSANT AND CHEKHOV

*Dr Jekyll and Mr Hyde* represented, for all its brilliant simplicity of conception and the dramatic power of its central metaphor, somewhat of a falling away from the highest achievements of earlier writers who took the double as their theme, in that its allegorical approach was not capable of accommodating the depth, range and acuity of perception available to the tradition of psychological realism pioneered by Hoffmann and Hogg and brought to its highest development in the work of Dostoevsky. *The Picture of Dorian Gray*, also an allegorical novel, is in a real sense a decadent work, underpinned as it is by an aesthetic doctrine which gives sanction to artistic insincerity, a sanction of which we may feel that Wilde did not fail to avail himself.

Kipling's very short story 'The Dream of Duncan Parrenness' (1891) combines the allegorical approach with the Dostoevskyan theme of night visitation by a demonic *alter ego* and tempter.[15] Duncan, a young employee of the East India Company in the era of Warren Hastings, has been celebrating at the Governor-General's annual ball a year's survival in the India which has already claimed the lives of so many of his fellows. It has been a year that has aged him through debauchery, 'burnt and seared [his] mind with the flames of a thousand passions and desires'. As he lies in post-alcoholic insomnia he broods on the sweet girl at home who has jilted him, and the temptress he now pursues, 'whom only my devilish pride made me follow'. Falling asleep at last in drink-induced delusions of grandeur, he is awakened by a drunken man who sits down at the foot of his bed and keeps repeating to him his own arrogant self-description: 'Writer in the Company's service and afraid of no man.' At first the visitor's appearance wavers from that of Parrenness himself grown older to that of the Governor-General, and then Duncan's father; but when he comes to see it clearly in the moonlight he understands, with terror and beyond doubt, that it is the face he once saw in the mirror when very drunk: 'my very own, but marked and lined and scarred with the furrows of disease and much evil living'.

'Myself', as he comes to call him, has called in order to persuade Parrenness to pay the required price for the aspirations of which he has been dreaming, which is to render up those attributes which will only be a hindrance to him in India: his trust in man, his trust in women, and finally his 'boy's soul and conscience'. In each case he puts up only a token resistance, and as his double lays his hand on his heart he feels there a 'deadly coldness'. In one night he has lost all conscience and all innocence and passed to the 'sorrowful state of manhood'. The apparition fades with the dawn, 'as my mother used to tell me is the habit of ghosts and devils and the like'; but as he fades Parrenness asks him with chattering teeth what is his return for the price he has paid. In reply his cynical and world-weary *Doppelgänger* presses into his hand a symbolical parting gift: 'a little piece of dried bread'.

Duncan's double is close kin to Markheim's 'hand-conscience' and Dorian Gray's portrait. He is presented not as conscience but as the thief of conscience, but in so far as his appearance in itself betokens the surviving activity of conscience within the primary self, the *alter ego* represents the degeneration of the concept of conscience to mere fear of retribution, consciousness of the 'price to pay' for evil living: the debauchee conjures up an image of what he is fated to become, and it is the degeneracy of his future self which reproaches him. The idea has little depth or complexity and indicates a relapse of the double theme into comparative triviality.

Kipling's story, though within the limits of its ambition quite successful, illustrates rather vividly the restrictiveness inherent in the allegorical stance.

The two remaining stories which we shall consider are not allegorical, but they testify to the decline of the double as a fictional theme in a different, but no less telling way. Maupassant's 'The Horla' (1887) can be read either as a ghost story with a difference, or as a study of a man descending into madness. These possible interpretations cannot be made to interpenetrate, and the tale has almost no moral or spiritual dimension. Dostoevsky's investigations of the double life also deal with characters who are succumbing to mental breakdown, and already in his work the independent, autonomous supernatural element has almost, though not entirely, disappeared. The sickness of both Mr Golyadkin and Ivan Karamazov, however, is conceived primarily as a *spiritual* sickness. Their nervous collapse is seen as issuing from the conflicting passions of their moral lives and as expressing the psychic chaos to which they have been reduced by the divisions in their natures. Advances in medical psychology towards the end of the nineteenth century now begin to encourage in creative writers a more clinical and hence a more reductive understanding of such conditions. The narrator of 'The Horla', if he is not simply haunted by supernatural beings, is less spiritually sick than mentally ill.

The story is written in the form of a journal. Its author appears to be a single man, a gentleman of leisure, living in a country house on the Seine near Rouen. Of his antecedents and his past history we learn almost nothing; his psychic condition remains a closed book to the reader. The first entry describes an idyllic day by the river. He watches a number of boats pass down the Seine past his property; among them is a Brazilian three-master which gives him such pleasure that he salutes her. But a few days later he is depressed and saddened by a vague nervous fever. 'Where do they come from, these mysterious influences which turn our happiness into gloom and our self-assurance into distress? It is as if the air, the invisible air, were full of unfathomable powers, whose mysterious proximity affects us.'[16]

The man's illness worsens. He is afflicted with a sense of imminent danger, even of approaching death. One night, knowing that he is asleep, he seems to feel someone climb on to him, kneel on his chest and try to strangle him; this dreadful experience is repeated night after night. Then, on a country walk, he is fearfully haunted by an unseen presence: 'All of a sudden it seemed to me that I was being followed, that somebody was hard on my heels, very close, near enough to touch me' (p. 317). This is the very same numinous experience to which Coleridge refers in 'The Ancient Mariner':

> Like one, that on a lonesome road
> Doth walk in fear and dread,
> And having once turned round walks on,
> And turns no more his head;
> Because he knows, a frightful fiend
> Doth close behind him tread.
>
> (ll. 446–51)

Attributing his visitations to his nervous condition, the narrator decides to go away for a few weeks, and returns 'cured'.

Maupassant orchestrates the developing tension, the alternating hope and fear, the relief of sanity and normality followed by the sickening return of the mysterious hauntings, with great delicacy and skill. The victim's suggestibility is fed by, and seizes on, external confirmations of his fearful imaginings. On a visit to Mont St Michel during his holiday the narrator meets a monk who tells him a supernatural story. In the face of his scepticism the monk asks, 'Do we see a hundred-thousandth part of all that exists?' (p. 319). As soon as he returns home the man's condition returns. The invading being has now become vampire-like, 'pressing his lips against mine and drinking my life through my lips' (p. 320). One night he finds his water carafe has been emptied while he slept: has he been sleepwalking? He believes he has: 'unknown to myself I was living that mysterious double life which makes us wonder whether there are two creatures in us or whether, when our mind is asleep, some alien being, invisible and unknowable, takes control of our captive body' (p. 321). When this experience is repeated the narrator begins to suspect that he is going mad, so he performs experiments which appear to prove the objective reality of his nocturnal visitor.

Once more he flees from the psychic invasion, this time to Paris. Once again he believes himself cured, and that he has merely peopled 'the void with phantoms'. But immediately his susceptibility is reactivated by a conversation at his cousin's house with Dr Parent, a nerve doctor, whose hypnotic experiments demonstrate graphically the possibility of the human mind being entered and taken over by a power outside itself. On his return home he 'sees' not the visitor, but the effects of its activity: an invisible hand plucks a rose and the broken stem remains behind to bear witness. Still he has 'detailed, well-founded doubts' of his sanity. Or does he suffer from hallucinations while remaining perfectly sane? Walking by the river, he feels an intense joy and love of life, but little by little some 'occult force' obliges him to turn back: 'I can feel him near me, spying on me, watching me, penetrating me, dominating me' (p. 332).

Increasingly the hero of the story appears to be in the grip of a paranoid delusion: he is possessed. Some psychic force from within his own nature has separated itself off and assumed autonomy, and has begun to control his will as if from without. Now, when he wants to go away, he cannot do so: 'I can no longer will anything; but someone wills things for me – and I obey.' He is thus reduced to the status of a mere spectator of his own actions: 'Someone is in possession of my mind and controlling it!' (p. 333). He can no longer act without the other's permission or resist his prompting. He feels like his hypnotised cousin, 'in the power of an alien will which had entered into her, like another soul, a parasitic, tyrannical soul. Is the world coming to an end?' (p. 334).

As his possession becomes established and unrelenting he becomes entirely convinced of the real existence of his tormentor. He reads Hermann Herestauss's book on the invisible beings of the world, and comes to believe that man is about to be displaced by an alien and more powerful being. His state of mind now exactly resembles that of Mr Golyadkin in the face of his double: he will appear 'humble, servile, submissive. But a time will come . . .' (p. 336). Reading of an outbreak of mass madness in Brazil, where the inhabitants claim they are similarly possessed, he concludes that one of these beings has reached him from the Brazilian ship whose passage he noted in his first journal entry. The mesmerists, he believes, 'have played with this weapon of the new Lord, the imposition of a mysterious will upon the enslaved minds of man. They call it magnetism, hypnotism, suggestion'. *He* calls it 'The Horla' (pp. 337–8).

With the progression of his madness, if such it is, the narrator becomes intent on the destruction of the alien being who is robbing him of identity and will. This invader has now symbolically obliterated his self-image, for he can no longer see himself in the mirror: the Horla's invisible body, of an 'opaque transparency', has swallowed up his reflection. Believing that he has succeeded in locking his tormentor in his room, he sets fire to the house; but in the blindness of his obsession, which we can now see also as a moral blindness, he forgets about his servants, who perish in the flames. But he believes the Horla is dead . . . or is he? Is 'that transparent, unknowable body, that spiritual body' subject to the forces which injure and destroy the human body? 'No . . . no . . . I know beyond a doubt that he is not dead. . . . In that case . . . in that case . . . I shall have to kill – myself' (p. 344). As in so many of the tales of the double which we have encountered, the dissociated second self has first invaded and controlled, then swallowed up and finally destroyed the psyche from which it has become detached.

Though the ghost of a possibility of a purely supernatural interpretation is offered the reader in the shape of the experiments carried out by the narrator which seem to point to the objective existence of some spiritual being, the balance of probability must be that these are illusory and that the subject is indeed going mad. Such a conclusion is lent added weight by the fact that at the time he wrote 'The Horla' Maupassant, who earlier had described hallucinatory visions of his *alter ego*, was himself succumbing to insanity, of syphilitic origin; he died in an asylum six years later.[17] The story is particularly interesting in being perhaps the first fictional dramatisation of a form of madness which has become increasingly common with the twentieth century and the space age: the belief that one's personality and will have been 'taken over' by an alien being from outside the human world.[18]

'The Horla', consummately crafted and chillingly convincing story though it is, is thus conceived simply as a study of psychological disintegration with no wider implications, and supported by no elucidatory moral framework. The double that is projected is quite devoid of content, anything to relate it to the totality of the psychic context from which it detaches itself. This may well reflect the purely infective causation of Maupassant's own illness; but it is also part of a new tendency to see madness in merely clinical terms which fail to establish its relation to the moral life of the soul.

The case of Chekhov's story 'The Black Monk' (1893) is related but somewhat different. Here the nature of the main character's delusional illness is clearly seen to be in close relation to his whole way of life and to his conception of himself and his role in the world, yet there is an almost stubborn insistence that he is simply mad, the implication being that we should not be tempted to draw any metaphysical conclusions from his mania. As Karl Miller has pointed out, Chekhov described 'The Black Monk' as 'a medical story, the case history of a disease. The subject is megalomania.'[19] The apparition of the Black Monk which comes to Kovrin is a true double, a projection of dissociated psychic contents, but it is a double which, in a break with the central tradition which we have been discussing, is wholly secularised. Ivan Karamazov's Devil embodies his internal struggle with the forces of evil within him, and their confrontation involves a far-reaching argument about whether or not this evil corresponds to a separately existing and autonomous spiritual principle. Kovrin's Black Monk, by contrast, has the status only of a symptom.

Kovrin, a scholar engaged in the study of psychology and philosophy, goes to the country with unsettled nerves to stay with Yegor Semionovich, the foster father by whom he was raised, and his daughter, Tanya. In the country, however, he continues to live 'the same nervous and untranquil life as he had lived in town'.[20] Emotionally exhausted, he becomes obsessed with the legend of a black monk in ancient Syria or Arabia who is reproduced endlessly by a mirage: 'From the first mirage was produced another mirage, from the second a third, so that the image of the Black Monk is eternally reflected from one stratum of the atmosphere to another' (p. 9). After a thousand years the mirage will again show itself in the world, and this is now imminently expected. Full of expectation Kovrin walks out at nightfall, and the Monk duly materialises.

On this occasion the floating apparition merely nods to him and smiles 'kindly and at the same time slyly'. Kovrin keeps his own counsel, but is delighted that he alone has seen the mirage, and, though suspecting himself of hallucinating, returns home wearing 'an expression of ecstasy and inspiration' (p. 11). Kovrin's introspection is contrasted with Yegor's healthy enthusiasm for gardening and his dedication to manual work; but Yegor and Tanya too are unquiet and irritable characters who echo his nervous sensitivity. The Monk reappears to Kovrin, and this time sits down beside him and converses. 'The legend, the mirage, I – all are products of your excited imagination', he tells him. 'I am a phantom . . . I exist in your imagination, and as your imagination is a part of Nature, I must exist also in Nature' (p. 17). This establishes the

Monk's status clearly enough, and nothing that later occurs imparts to him any more substantial objectivity.

The Monk reflects back to Kovrin his own inflated self-image. He is pleased with him, 'For you are one of the few who can justly be named the elected of God. You serve eternal truth'. His life bears 'the stamp of divinity'. A little warily, Kovrin asks if he is not 'psychically diseased'. 'What if you are?' replies the hallucination. Men of genius see visions, and genius is akin to insanity (pp. 18–19). 'How strange that you should repeat what I myself have so often thought!' exclaims Kovrin ecstatically. Chekhov continues, 'What the Black Monk had said to him flattered, not his self-love, but his soul, his whole being' (p. 19).

Everything that the Black Monk tells Kovrin has an intensely familiar ring to it. In essence it is what Mephistophilis told Faustus, what his pride spoke to Ambrosio, what the Devil's elixirs induced in Medardus, what Gil-Martin imparted to Robert Wringhim. This time, however, we are offered not a spiritual but a medical diagnosis. This is what used to be called spiritual pride, a sin, and is now dubbed megalomania, a mental illness.

Tanya meets Kovrin in his enraptured condition and he impetuously declares his love. Tanya responds, but feels an instinctive foreboding. 'She was overcome, bent, withered up, and seemed suddenly to have aged ten years. But Kovrin found her beautiful, and loudly expressed his ecstasy' (p. 20). He is drawn to her 'like a magnet', and a marriage is arranged. The unreality in Kovrin's soul has imparted itself to those around him like an infection.

With the celebration of his marriage to Tanya, their situation moves towards tragedy. When the Monk appears at his bedside, Tanya tells him that he is psychically ill, and, for the first time squarely recognising the truth that he is mad, he agrees to undergo a course of treatment. He recovers; but with his comforting delusions of grandeur he has lost all his joy in life. Deprived of his 'mania of greatness', he is forced to acknowledge to himself his irremediable mediocrity, and, bitterly resenting the loss of his illusions, he begins to weary of life. He takes revenge in his appalling treatment of Tanya and her father, whom he turns into scapegoats for his disappointment and frustration.

Time passes; Kovrin receives a Chair, but is already ill with consumption. He has left Tanya for another, older, woman who mothers him, but is consumed by guilt that he has 'avenged on people in no way guilty his spiritual vacuity, his solitude, his

disenchantment with life' (p. 30). He receives an accusing letter
from Tanya, full of hate: his treatment has been responsible for
the death of her father. Kovrin now fears to see again the 'unknown
power' that has wrecked their lives. He believes himself reconciled
to his mediocrity; but once again a kind of restless terror stirs
within him. Standing on the balcony of his room in the Crimea,
where he has gone for his health, he hears voices below singing a
song he had heard once before on a night of ecstasy; 'the magical
ecstatic rapture which he had long forgotten trembled in his heart
again' (p. 33).

The Black Monk returns, telling Kovrin that all his troubles have
been due to loss of faith in his message. 'Kovrin again believed
that he was the elected of God and a genius' (p. 33); but this return
of his ecstasy heralds the hour of death, and he suffers a fatal
haemorrhage. He cries out to Tanya, calls out to 'the life that had
been so beautiful', and is filled with irrepressible joy. So Kovrin
dies in happy illusion, leaving behind him a legacy of misery and
lives wrecked by his deluded self-idealisation.

'The Black Monk' is a very sensitive and a very moving story,
beautifully modulated and, taken as a whole, psychologically
convincing. It does, however, exhibit the double motif in a state
of decline. The figure of the Monk is deprived of resonance by his
own insistence on his hallucinatory character, an insistence that
does not even seem to be particularly true to experience. It is as if
Chekhov were rather perversely making certain that he should
build into his story a safeguard against its being taken as anything
other than, or beyond, 'the case history of a disease'. Had the
Black Monk not been forced thus to insist on his own illusoriness,
he would have retained the resonating flexibility which is proper
and natural to the figure of the double. By representing the
phantom as a purely clinical phenomenon, Chekhov paradoxically
robs it of its psychological truth and depth.

With this secularisation of the traditional double, its assimilation
to a rationalist perspective, the dualistic mainstream is about to
move away from fiction and into formal psychology. As the fictional
double separates in the eighties and nineties into the divergent
streams of allegory and scientific rationalism, the Dostoevskyan
synthesis is lost and the theme tails off into comparative margina-
lity. In the early years of the new century Henry James (in 'The
Jolly Corner') and Joseph Conrad (in 'Heart of Darkness', 'The
Secret Sharer' and 'The Shadow Line') were yet to make important

contributions to the genre, and the motif recurs frequently enough in twentieth-century novels and stories, but it seldom occupies the position of centrality that it held in the nineteenth-century works we have discussed.

# 9
# Into Psychology

Throughout the history of the fictional exploitation of the theme of the double, psychology and art have gone hand in hand. We have seen how the German Romantics, and most decisively Hoffmann, were incalculably influenced by the psychological researches of G. H. Schubert, and especially by his idea of the shadow-self, a dark and hidden counterpart of, or supplement to, the daytime consciousness. Later Dostoevsky was to be similarly affected by the work of C. G. Carus, who in the middle of the century interpreted new psycho-physiological theories in terms of the old idealist metaphysics. Even more profound and long-lasting was the legacy of Mesmer, whose theory of the magnetic union of souls, developed by Schubert as 'animal magnetism', harks back to the occultist teachings about spiritual affinity and thence to the Platonic urge to bring together the severed halves of the human soul. In the magnetic trance, the forerunner of hypnotism, novelists found an endlessly suggestive source of secondary personalities, and thrilling confirmation of the insight that the human mind could be entered and controlled by an alien will. We have noticed that allusions to Mesmer abound in tales of the double right up to the end of our period, and indeed the effect continues well into the twentieth century.

It was suggested towards the end of the previous chapter that the developing spirit of scientific rationalism was much less sympathetic to the areas of psychological perception which could be expressed through the medium of the double. In the early nineteenth century, there was no sense of cleavage between literary and scientific psychology. The appearance of matter from the void, and evolution from the merely material through the organic to the animate and spiritual, was a commonplace of Romantic science, and the process of human growth from unconsciousness to consciousness was often viewed as an analogous process. Kleist believed that by reapproaching himself from his hidden side man could return to a state of 'grace'. Schelling found it natural to proceed from the philosophy of nature to metaphysical speculation,

153

and Carus remained at mid-century entirely within this unitive tradition.[1] 'Literature and science', as Karl Miller observes, 'collaborated in spreading the gospel which enjoined the plurality of the mind', whether double or multiple.[2]

As the nineteenth century advanced, however, this bond was progressively obscured, if not loosened. Although in reality Freud as well as Jung built on Romantic psychology with only slight modifications, the debt was often not recognised and sometimes not fully acknowledged, and as science became marked off as a domain of 'fact' which was seen as distinct from, and even alien to, the subjectivity of literature, the abstraction of metaphysics and the mythology of religion, there grew up an alternative romanticism of the factual which was sometimes at odds with the deeper insights of 'literary' psychology as expressed, for instance, in the work of Dostoevsky.

This new romanticism of scientific fact can be seen in the scientism of *Dr Jekyll and Mr Hyde*, and further down the scale of literary distinction its sources are less hidden and absorbed, if also less remote from reality. W. H. Mallock's *An Immortal Soul*, for instance, which appeared after the turn of the century in 1908, mixes theological quibbling with scientific scepticism in its dramatised confrontation between traditional belief and clinical rationalism; the duality of the schizoid heroine is investigated by a believable nerve doctor, and the Preface appeals for its authority directly to 'phenomena observed and recorded by scientific students during the last quarter of a century, and especially during the last ten years'. Mallock probably had particularly in mind the work of the French psychologist Charcot.[3]

Charcot investigated the role of amnesia in hysterical conditions, while his compatriot Janet defined multiple personality in terms of the malfunctioning of the associative system. In 1886 Frederic Myers' essay 'Multiplex Personality' elaborated a mechanical model of the evolutionary maladaptation of psychic responses, and of the art of 'self-modification' which might be developed to counteract this failure.[4] With the infiltration into popular consciousness of the new psychological theories, the literary treatment of psychic dividedness took a more rationalist and materialist turn. Robbed of a spiritual dimension, the theme of the double loses much of its resonance, its flexibility and its fruitful ambiguity.

The phenomenon of the double was not neglected by the Freudian school. Otto Rank, for instance, basing himself on Freud's insights, devoted an important study to the subject. In practice, however, critics have found it difficult usefully to apply the findings of Freudian psychology to the actuality of what is contained in dualistic fictions. Masao Miyoshi, for example, referring particularly to the work of Rank, while acknowledging that 'There is a plausibility in the notion that the use of the double may indicate the author's fear of sex, or perhaps his irrational desire for immortality', tactfully pushes this material aside as an unhelpful critical resource.[5] Karl Miller, again, commenting on Sylvia Plath's application, in an undergraduate thesis, of Rank's theories to Dostoevsky's *The Double*, doubts their relevance. Rank, he explains, referred Freud's category of primary narcissism to the modern neurotic's incapacity for sexual fulfilment, linking this to a change in the signification of the double from the immortal self which denied the power of death, to a fear of and defence against death which itself becomes deathly. 'It is doubtful, however,' comments Miller, 'whether these postulates have much bearing on Dostoevsky's novel, which has nothing memorable to say on the subject of immortality.'[6]

In defence of Rank it should certainly be said that the appearance of a double does often, in the works of fiction which we have examined, result eventually either in actual death or in the psychic disintegration, the loss of identity, which is a symbolic annihilation of the self; and as Chizhevsky has said in discussing the Dostoevskyan double, 'the ethical function of the appearance of the double is obviously the same as the ethical function of death, i.e. the loss of existence of the subject'.[7] It does not clearly follow, however, that loss of identity is feared less in itself than because it symbolises death. To see the symbology of the double as referring primarily to the fear of death the critic must read a subtext derived from psychological theory and is consequently in danger of finding not what is actually in the text but what he would perhaps prefer to be there. For the present writer, at least, the ideas of Jung offer insights into the psychological symbolism of the double which have a clearer, more obvious and more definite application to its use in fiction than those of the Freudian school.

Just after the turn of the century, an important counterweight to the more reductive elements in the rationalist tendency in psychology had been provided in William James's *The Varieties of Religious Experience*, originally the Gifford Lectures delivered at Edinburgh University in 1901–2. James, who had published his

*Principles of Psychology* in 1890, was sympathetic to the theories of Janet and admired the work of Myers, but he refused to interpret their findings from a purely materialist perspective. He introduced his observations in the later work by dissociating himself from such attitudes as that underlying Taine's view that 'Vice and virtue are products like vitriol and sugar.' 'It seems to me', he remarks, 'that few conceptions are less fruitful than [the] re-interpretation of religion as perverted sexuality.' Referring to 'medical materialism', he asks, 'how can such an existential account of facts of mental history decide one way or the other upon their spiritual significance? . . . To plead the organic causation of a religious state of mind . . . in refutation of its claim to possess superior spiritual value, is quite illogical and arbitrary, unless one has already worked out in advance some psycho-physical theory connecting spiritual values in general with determinate sorts of physiological change.'[8]

James devoted one of his lectures to 'The Divided Self, and the Process of its Unification'. Here he deals with precisely the forms of self-division which, in the fictions we have discussed, are embodied and dramatised in the figure of the double. 'The psychological basis of the twice-born character', he observes, 'seems to be a certain discordancy or heterogeneity in the native temperament of the subject, an incompletely unified moral and intellectual constitution.' He points to the example of Alphonse Daudet, quoting from his *Notes sur la Vie* where Daudet laments his 'horrible duality', his 'terrible second me' which is detached, observant, dissociated from the active and suffering self.[9] He instances also Bunyan's obsession with the words 'Sell Christ', countered by the retort, 'I will not, I will not', as an example of blasphemous obsessions often experienced by saints and holy men and invariably ascribed to the direct agency of Satan; and connects the phenomenon with the life of the subconscious self.[10] James further points to the classic expression of the divided will in St Augustine's *Confessions*, which we discussed in the first chapter of this book. These crises of self-division, he argues, are frequently resolved by the phenomenon of conversion, but not necessarily religious conversion: James cites, for instance, a particularly interesting example of a conversion from profligacy to avarice.

The principal heir to the tradition which sees in psychology and religion mutually supportive and complementary understandings of the human soul is C. G. Jung. Jung's view that the self is not ultimately distinguishable from the image of God in man, is adumbrated in William James's concluding lecture in *Varieties of Religious Experience*, in which, building on the work of Frederic Myers, he identifies the 'subconscious self', understood as a psychical entity whose extent cannot be delimited, as the mediating term which will allow psychologists to recognise as real what he calls the 'more', the final goal of religious union.[11] This, again, harks back to Schelling's understanding of God as the Universal Unconscious.

The aspect of Jung's psychology which has the most obviously relevant application to the phenomenon of the double is his work on the archetype of the shadow. In Jung's formulation, the second self which G. H. Schubert unearthed, dwelling in the night-side of the personality, is understood as a universal form existing within the self and corresponding ultimately to the entire personal unconscious life of the psyche. As well as affording a great deal of retrospective illumination of the theme of the literary double, this Jungian construct is itself an imaginative structure which, in important ways, takes up the torch of the double as, for complex cultural reasons, its dominant expression passes from imaginative fiction into psychology proper.

In *Memories, Dreams, Reflections* Jung describes a dream of his own about Siegfried in which there appears the figure of a 'small, brown-skinned savage' who, he states, 'was an embodiment of the primitive shadow'.[12] The shadow he defines elsewhere as 'the "negative" side of the personality, the sum of all those unpleasant qualities we like to hide, together with the insufficiently developed functions and the contents of the personal unconscious'.[13] Everyone possesses such a shadow, and 'the less it is embodied in the individual's conscious life, the blacker and denser it is . . . if it is repressed and isolated from consciousness, it never gets corrected, and is liable to burst forth suddenly in a moment of unawareness'.[14] This is particularly liable to happen, for instance, in 'highly moral people'. We can immediately recognise features to which we have become accustomed in investigating the double in fiction: Mr Hyde has the typical physical characteristics of the shadow; its definition at once recalls the relation of Smerdyakov to Ivan Karamazov; its irruption when repressed can be identified in the startling moral reversals of a dozen elect or self-consciously righteous protagonists.

Jung describes the shadow as consisting of 'inferiorities', which 'have an *emotional* nature, a kind of autonomy, and accordingly an obsessive or, better, possessive quality'.[15] This autonomy and this obsessive quality are highly characteristic of the doubles we have seen projected by our fictional acquaintances. The shadow, Jung asserts, is not obviously evil, it is 'merely somewhat inferior, primitive, unadapted, awkward; not wholly bad'.[16] In another context he maintains that the lowest levels of this inferior personality are 'indistinguishable from the instinctuality of an animal'.[17] Often these inferiorities are projected on to others, and then it is almost impossible for the subject to recognise them for what they are. There is a certain ambivalence, however, about Jung's view of the nature of the inferior personality. Sometimes he does clearly imply that the psychotherapeutic confrontation between certain people and 'their blackest shadow' *is* a confrontation with the power of evil. The patient must not be inactive, he asserts, but must endeavour with all his might to do the right thing, 'in order to prevent the pressure of evil from becoming too powerful for him'.[18]

This ambivalence can be resolved by considering the case of Stevenson's Mr Hyde, in so many ways the purest fictional representation of the shadow. We saw that when Hyde first materialises he does so as the embodiment of Jekyll's suddenly released instinctual nature. But the instinctual nature is also pure self, and this is what Hyde really is. In the context of human affairs, of the individual in relation to other individuals and to society, the assertion of the unrestrained demands of the self amounts to what, in the language of morality, is called evil; 'for good and evil are ultimately nothing but ideal extensions and abstractions of doing'.[19] When Hyde is inactive, latent, he expresses a sense of lightness, joy, spiritual freedom; but as soon as he comes into contact with the other, with anything which interferes with the importunity of self, his instinctuality finds expression in moral evil.

There is another aspect of confrontation with the shadow which casts a rich light on the psychology of the double. 'Projections', writes Jung, 'change the world into the replica of one's own unknown face.' The unattainability of the dream world thus created breeds a frustration and sense of unfulfilment which in turn is projected as 'the malevolence of the environment', that is, as fate.[20] '"My fate" means a daemonic will to precisely that fate – a will not necessarily coincident with my own (the ego will). When it is opposed to the ego, it is difficult not to feel a certain "power" in it, whether divine or infernal. The man who submits to his fate calls it the will of God; the man who puts up a hopeless and exhausting struggle is more apt to see the devil in it.'[21] This sense of hopelessness in the teeth of fate is repeatedly professed by morally divided protagonists – Ambrosio, Clithero, Nathaniel, Medardus, Wringhim, Golyadkin spring at once to mind. It is a projection which is at once expressed and embodied in, and then reinforced by, predestinarian theology, and helps to explain another characteristic which we have noticed in these individuals, the inability to repent, or at the least the great difficulty experienced in repenting.

Jung indicates that the alternative to getting rid of the shadow by means of projection is that of 'casting our sins upon a divine mediator'. 'I wish everybody could be freed from the burden of their sins by the Church', he comments. 'But he to whom she cannot render this service must bend very low in the imitation of Christ in order to take the burden of his cross upon him.'[22] William James had also stressed the psychological importance of the 'critical religious act' of repentance, so long as it is what he calls 'healthy-minded' repentance, that is, *getting away* from sin, not groaning and writhing over its commission. The Catholic practice of confession and absolution is in one of its aspects little more than a systematic method of keeping healthy-mindedness on top . . . any Catholic will tell you how fresh and free he feels after the purging operation.'[23]

Jung sees very clearly the importance for psychological health of taking the part of 'the sinner who is oneself': 'as little as we would accuse Christ of fraternizing with evil, so little should we reproach ourselves that to love the sinner who is oneself is to make a pact with the devil. Love makes a man better, hate makes him worse – even when that man is oneself.'[24] This insight is entirely in line with the central Catholic theology of the Christian Church: it is essential for the sinner to believe that he is never too wicked for God's mercy, and when, through Christ, that mercy has been obtained, it is a particularly deleterious form of pride to be unable or unwilling to forgive oneself. But this, as we have found, is notoriously the case with our divided heroes of dualistic fiction.

These are, typically, morally riven characters whose overweening pride, and belief in their own righteousness and election, cause the complete repression of their dark shadow-self. The repressed shadow then irrupts and asserts itself in moral reversal, separates itself from the conscious ego and is projected as a double. The subject's powerlessness in the face of his double's baleful activity and control of his will is then projected as 'fate' or infernal destiny, and this projection attaches itself to, and is reinforced and confirmed by, a fatalistic theological position which, by suggesting to the subject that he is predestined to reprobation, effectively limits God's mercy and makes repentance, and integration of the dissociated shadow-self, impossible.

Jung takes exception to the Augustinian theology of evil as the *privatio boni*, and, indeed, to the much wider Christian view of God as the *summum bonum*.[25] For him, good and evil are simply complementary opposites, each the necessary condition for the existence of the other, and he is insistent on the necessity for the reintegration of the dark face of God in the Divine image; indeed, he emphasises the importance of the question 'whether in this very power of evil God might not have placed some special purpose which it is most important for us to know'.[26] Jung sees the Self as a *complexio oppositorum*, and though he treats Christ as an image of the Self, holds that this image is weakened by the separation from it of its own dark side in the inferior and subordinated figure of Satan. The burden of *Answer to Job* (1954) is that the repression of the dark or evil side and its subordination to a faultless good is liable to issue in an 'enantodromia' (the conversion of a thing into its opposite), at the societal level a disastrous development which he believes to have been prophetically adumbrated in the Revelation of St John the Divine.

Jung's position on this issue is somewhat paradoxical, for it can be argued that his own imagery of the shadow very profoundly suggests the inferiority of the dark side of the Self, and that this can be taken as implying its subordinate status. A counter-argument could be that Jung in this imagery is using 'inferior' in a strictly spatial sense: the unconscious lies 'below' the threshold of the ego consciousness, and it is only in this sense that inferiority can be ascribed to it. The embodiments of the shadow which Jung finds spontaneously expressed in dream imagery suggest otherwise, however: the shadow is characteristically a small, stunted, physically inferior being, like Mr Hyde. The evidence of the fictional double indeed repeatedly confirms the danger of repression of the shadow, in the phenomenon of the personal enantiodromia or moral reversal; but there are also suggestions that might lend support to the Augustinian view of the ultimate nullity of evil, its final non-entity. We have seen, for instance, how the suicide of Smerdyakov in *The Brothers Karamazov* can plausibly be interpreted in such a light.

The insights of Jung bring into focus the central argument of this book, that the form of the double as a literary device cannot be understood in a psychological way or in socio-historical terms without reference to its contents, which are predominantly concerned with religious questions, with dilemmas of man's moral life, and especially with the irruption of repressed or denied evil tendencies in the human mind and soul. Form and content here exactly reflect each other and are aspects of a single meaning. As Chizhevsky has insisted, 'The problem of "stability", of the ontological "fixity" of an ethical being is the real problem of the nineteenth century.'[27] The writers who, exercised with this problem, took the double as their theme, were steeped, whether fully or partly consciously, in the theological traditions of the Christian West; and, especially at the beginning of the period surveyed, embodied their insights in terms of traditional theological concepts and imagery.

As the nineteenth century progressed and scientific understanding of the mechanisms of the mind became more developed, these ways of perceiving the questions involved interpenetrated with a more 'psychological' fictional approach. *Psyche*, however, means simply 'soul', and as long as this correspondence seemed natural to the writers concerned, a harmonious synthesis of the religious and psychological ways of understanding and using the motif of the double remained possible. The finest works which arose from this fruitful synthesis offer unique creative insights into the troubled and divided soul of man.

# Notes

For the primary texts discussed, only the first reference, citing the edition used, is included in the Notes; all subsequent page references are placed in the body of the text. All references to secondary sources are in the Notes.

## Notes to Chapter 1: The Psychological and Theological Background

1. St Augustine, *Confessions*, tr. E. V. Rieu (Harmondsworth, Middx, 1961; 1964 reprint) p. 171.
2. For a more extended discussion of these origins of the double see Ralph Tymms, *Doubles in Literary Psychology* (Cambridge, 1949) Ch. i. I follow Tymms in part here.
3. Aniela Jaffé, *Apparitions: An Archetypal Approach to Death Dreams and Ghosts*, with a foreword by C. G. Jung (Irving, Tx, 1979) pp. 143–55.
4. F. A. Mesmer's *Mémoires sur la découverte de magnetisme animal* was published in Paris in 1779.
5. Tymms, *Doubles in Literary Psychology*, p. 26. G. H. Schubert's influential work *Die Symbolik des Traumes* was published in Bamberg in 1814.
6. See Tymms, *Doubles in Literary Psychology*, pp. 26–7, 35–6.
7. Luke 22.42 RSV. See also Matthew 26.39, Mark 14.36.
8. Romans 7.14–19, RSV.
9. See Romans 7.21–5, RSV.
10. For Gnosticism, see R. M. Grant, *Gnosticism: An Anthology* (London, 1961), and *Gnosticism and Early Christianity* (2nd edn, New York, 1966).
11. See article, 'Gnosticism', in *The Oxford Dictionary of the Christian Church*, 2nd edn, ed. F. L. Cross and F. A. Livingstone (London, 1974).
12. Irenaeus, *Adversus Haereses*, ed. W. W. Harvey (Cambridge, 1857) ii.39.1.
13. See 'Gnosticism', *Oxford Dictionary of the Christian Church*: also Harry Levin, *The Overreacher: A Study of Christopher Marlowe* (London, 1954) p. 131.
14. C. G. Jung discusses the phenomenon of 'enantiodromia' in relation to Christianity especially in *Answer to Job* (London, 1954; paperback edn 1979).
15. For Manichaeism see F. C. Burkitt, *The Religion of the Manichees* (Cambridge, 1925).
16. Galatians 5.17, RSV.
17. John 15.5, RSV.
18. For Augustine and Pelagianism, see Gerald Bonner, *St. Augustine: Life and Controversies* (London, 1964); G. R. Evans, *Augustine on Evil*

(Cambridge, 1982); R. F. Evans, *Pelagius: Inquiries and Reappraisals* (London, 1968).

19. For the Cathars, see A. Borst, *Die Katharen* (Stuttgart, 1953); M. D. Lambert, *Medieval Heresy* (London, 1977); G. Leff, *Heresy in the Later Middle Ages*, 2 vols (Manchester and New York, 1967); R. I. Moore, *The Birth of Popular Heresy* (London, 1975).

20. T. R. Wright, *Theology and Literature* (Oxford, 1988) p. 178.

## Notes to Chapter 2: The Emergence and Development of the Double Theme

1. Edwin M. Eigner, *Robert Louis Stevenson and Romantic Tradition* (Princeton, NJ, 1966) p. 23.
2. Ralph Tymms, *Doubles in Literary Psychology* (Cambridge, 1949) p. 33.
3. Ibid., p. 29.
4. Angela Carter, *The Sadeian Woman: An Exercise in Cultural History* (London, 1979; 1983 reprint) pp. 78, 80; see also Mario Praz, *The Romantic Agony*, tr. Angus Davidson (London, 1933; 2nd (revised) edn Oxford, 1951) pp. 102–7.
5. Joseph Frank, *Dostoevsky: The Seeds of Revolt 1821–1849* (London, 1977) p. 311.
6. Muriel Spark, *Mary Shelley* (London, 1988) pp. 161, 173–4.
7. John Gross, 'A Tale of Two Cities', in *Dickens and the Twentieth Century*, ed. John Gross and Gabriel Pearson (London, 1962) p. 189.
8. Eigner, *Robert Louis Stevenson and Romantic Tradition*, p. 31.

## Notes to Chapter 3: Terror, Pursuit and Shadows

1. William Beckford, *Vathek*, ed. with an introduction by Roger Lonsdale (Oxford, 1970) p. 3.
2. John Livingston Lowes, *The Road to Xanadu* (London, 1927; 2nd edn 1951; paperback edn 1978) p. 230.
3. M. G. Lewis, *The Monk*, ed. with an introduction by Howard Anderson (Oxford, 1973; 1987 reprint) p. 18.
4. Mario Praz, *The Romantic Agony*, tr. Angus Davidson (London, 1933; 2nd edn Oxford, 1951) pp. 58–9.
5. Masao Miyoshi, *The Divided Self: A Perspective on the Literature of the Victorians* (New York and London, 1969) p. 33.
6. Mario Praz, in his Introduction to *Three Gothic Novels (The Castle of Otranto, Vathek, Frankenstein)* (Harmondsworth, Middx, 1968; 1973 reprint) p. 34.
7. Charles Maturin, *Melmoth the Wanderer*, ed. with an introduction by Douglas Grant (Oxford, 1968; paperback edn 1972) p. 336.
8. See Miyoshi, *The Divided Self*, p. 312.
9. Isaiah 53.5; Philippians 2.12.
10. William Godwin, *Caleb Williams*, ed. with an introduction by Maurice Hindle (London, 1988) p. 3 (Preface).

11. See Hindle in the Introduction to Godwin, *Caleb Williams*, p. xi.
12. Godwin's account of the composition of *Caleb Williams* is included as Appendix II of the 1988 edition, pp. 347–54. The words quoted appear on p. 349.
13. Charles Brockden Brown, *Wieland*, ed. with an introduction by Fred. Lewis Pattee (New York, 1958) pp. 59, 62.
14. Charles Brockden Brown, *Edgar Huntly*, ed. with an introduction by Norman S. Grabo (London, 1988) p. 28.
15. Adalbert von Chamisso, *Peter Schlemihl*, tr. Leopold von Loewenstein-Wertheim (London, 1957) p. 10 (Introduction).
16. Karl Miller, *Doubles: Studies in Literary History* (Oxford, 1985; paperback edn 1987) pp. 125–6.
17. H. C. Andersen, 'The Shadow', in *Forty-Two Stories*, tr. M. R. James, illustrated by Robin Jacques (London, 1930; 1953 reprint) p. 236.

### Notes to Chapter 4: E. T. A. Hoffmann

1. E. T. A. Hoffmann, *Tales of Hoffmann*, selected and tr. with an introduction by R. J. Hollingdale (Harmondsworth, Middx, 1982) p. 7 (Introduction).
2. Ronald J. Taylor, *Hoffmann* (London, 1963) p. 8.
3. In *Tales of Hoffmann*, pp. 17–84.
4. Ralph Tymms, *Doubles in Literary Psychology* (Cambridge, 1949) pp. 27, 35.
5. Kenneth Negus, *E. T. A. Hoffmann's Other World* (Philadelphia, 1965) p. 24.
6. See Charles E. Passage, *The Russian Hoffmannists* (The Hague, 1963) pp. 168, 197.
7. *Tales of Hoffmann*, p. 89.
8. T. S. Eliot, 'Tradition and the Individual Talent', in *Selected Essays* (London, 1932; 1958 reprint) p. 19.
9. Quoted by Taylor in *Hoffmann*, p. 84.
10. E. T. A. Hoffmann, *The Devil's Elixirs*, tr. with an introduction by Ronald Taylor (London, 1963). Hoffmann's statement of his aims is quoted by Taylor in the Introduction, p. ix; and in the same author's *Hoffmann*, pp. 92–3, where the source is given as a letter to Kunz of 24 March 1814.
11. See Taylor, *Hoffmann*, p. 27.
12. Ibid., p. 104.
13. 1 Corinthians 1.18ff., RSV.
14. Negus, *E. T. A. Hoffmann's Other World*, p. 83.

### Notes to Chapter 5: James Hogg

1. John Carey, Introduction to James Hogg, *The Private Memoirs and Confessions of a Justified Sinner* (Oxford, 1969) pp. xxi–xxii.
2. See Louis Simpson, *James Hogg: A Critical Study* (Edinburgh, 1962)

pp. 190–2; also Karl Miller, *Doubles: Studies in Literary History* (Oxford, 1985; paperback edn 1987) pp. 3–4.

3. James Hogg, *The Private Memoirs and Confessions of a Justified Sinner*, ed. with an introduction by John Wain (Harmondsworth, Middx, 1983; 1986 reprint) p. 30.

4. Douglas Gifford, *James Hogg* (Edinburgh, 1976) p. 165.

5. From 'The Marriage of Heaven and Hell', in William Blake, *Poetical Works*, ed. John Sampson (Oxford, 1913; 1960 reprint) p. 249.

6. See Gifford, *James Hogg*, p. 170.

7. Ibid., p. 167.

8. In James Hogg, *Selected Stories and Sketches*, ed. Douglas S. Mack (Edinburgh, 1982) pp. 158–68.

9. Gifford, *James Hogg*, p. 139.

## Notes to Chapter 6: Edgar Allan Poe

1. Harry Levin, *The Power of Blackness: Hawthorne, Poe, Melville* (London and New York, 1958; paperback edn 1960) p. 7.

2. See Palmer Cobb, 'The Influence of E. T. A. Hoffmann on the Tales of Edgar Allan Poe', *Studies in Philology*, III (1908).

3. 'Dostoevsky on Edgar Allan Poe', a translation by Vladimir Astrov, *American Literature* XIV (1942) p. 74.

4. In Edgar Allan Poe, *The Fall of the House of Usher and Other Writings*, ed. with an introduction by David Galloway; originally entitled *Selected Writings of Edgar Allan Poe* (Harmondsworth, Middx, 1967; 1988 reprint) p. 194.

5. In Poe, *The Fall of the House of Usher*, pp. 110–26.

6. Ibid., pp. 350–9.

7. In Edgar Allan Poe, *Tales of Mystery and Imagination* (London, 1908; 1962 reprint) pp. 21–30.

8. In Poe, *The Fall of the House of Usher*, pp. 320–9.

9. See Karl Miller, *Doubles: Studies in Literary History* (Oxford, 1985; paperback edn 1987) p. 155.

10. Poe, *The Fall of the House of Usher*, p. 159.

## Notes to Chapter 7: The Russian Double

1. N. Gogol, *Diary of a Madman and Other Stories*, tr. with an introduction by Ronald Wilks (Harmondsworth, Middx, 1972; 1974 reprint) p. 50.

2. See Charles E. Passage, *The Russian Hoffmannists* (The Hague, 1963) pp. 166–8.

3. Joseph Frank, *Dostoevsky: The Seeds of Revolt 1821–1849* (London, 1977) p. 311. See also Dmitri Chizhevsky, 'The Theme of the Double in Dostoevsky', in *Dostoevsky*, ed. René Wellek (Englewood Cliffs, NJ, 1962) pp. 112–13.

4. See Passage, *The Russian Hoffmannists*, p. 197.

5. Quoted by Frank in *Dostoevsky: The Seeds of Revolt*, p. 300.

6. F. M. Dostoevsky, *The Double* (published in one volume with *Notes from Underground*) tr. with an introduction by Jessie Coulson (Harmondsworth, Middx, 1972; 1973 reprint) p. 127.
7. See Joseph Frank, *Dostoevsky: The Seeds of Revolt*, pp. 160–8; and *Dostoevsky: The Stir of Liberation 1860–1865* (London, 1987) p. 9.
8. Chizhevsky, 'The Theme of the Double', p. 116.
9. Passage, *The Russian Hoffmannists*, p. 201.
10. Frank, *Dostoevsky: The Seeds of Revolt*, p. 311.
11. Chizhevsky, 'The Theme of the Double', p. 114.
12. Joseph Frank, *Dostoevsky: The Years of Ordeal 1850–1859* (London, 1983) pp. 172–4.
13. C. G. Carus, *Psyche, zur Entwicklungsgeschichte der Seele* (Pforzheim, 1846) p. 1.
14. Harry Levin, *The Overreacher: A Study of Christopher Marlowe* (London, 1954) p. 138.
15. George Steiner, *Tolstoy or Dostoevsky* (New York, 1959; rev. edn 1967) p. 141.
16. F. M. Dostoevsky, *The Idiot*, tr. with an introduction by David Magarshack (Harmondsworth, Middx, 1955; 1971 reprint) p. 265.
17. Quoted by Chizhevsky in 'The Theme of the Double', pp. 117–18.
18. F. M. Dostoevsky, *The Devils*, tr. with an introduction by David Magarshack (Harmondsworth, Middx, 1953; 1971 reprint) pp. 676, 677.
19. Chizhevsky, 'The Theme of the Double', p. 119.
20. Ibid., p. 120.
21. The case of Stavrogin has also been interestingly discussed by Karl Miller in *Doubles: Studies in Literary History* (Oxford, 1985; paperback edn 1987) pp. 137–42.
22. C. G. Jung, *Psychology and Alchemy* (*Collected Works*, vol. 12) (London, 1953; 2nd (rev.) edn 1968; paperback edn 1980) p. 26
23. C. G. Jung, *Aion* (*Collected Works*, vol. 9, part II) (London, 1959; 1981 reprint) p. 253.
24. Jung, *Psychology and Alchemy*, pp. 26–7.
25. Jung, *Aion*, p. 225.
26. F. M. Dostoevsky, *The Brothers Karamazov*, 2 vols, tr. with an introduction by David Magarshack (Harmondsworth, Middx, 1958; 1972 reprint) p. 13.
27. See Passage, *The Russian Hoffmannists*, pp. 219, 244.
28. Ralph Tymms, *Doubles in Literary Psychology* (Cambridge, 1949) p. 98.

**Notes to Chapter 8: The Double in Decline**

1. See Edwin M. Eigner, *Robert Louis Stevenson and Romantic Tradition* (Princeton, NJ, 1966) especially Ch. I.
2. Ibid., p. 37.
3. See John Gibson, *Deacon Brodie: Father to Jekyll and Hyde* (Edinburgh, 1977).
4. R. L. Stevenson, *The Master of Ballantrae* (published in one volume

with *Weir of Hermiston*; London, 1925; 1984 reprint) p. 99.

5. R. L. Stevenson, 'Markheim', in *The Merry Men and Other Tales*, vol. VIII (London, 1924) p. 91.

6. John Kelman, in his Introduction to the Collins Library of Classics edition of *Dr. Jekyll and Mr. Hyde* (London and Glasgow, undated) pp. 12–13.

7. R. L. Stevenson, *Dr. Jekyll and Mr. Hyde and Other Stories*, ed. with an introduction by Jenni Calder (Harmondsworth, Middx, 1979; 1986 reprint) p. 38.

8. Masao Miyoshi, *The Divided Self: A Perspective on the Literature of the Victorians* (New York and London, 1969) p. 299.

9. G. K. Chesterton, *Robert Louis Stevenson* (New York, 1928) p. 54.

10. Miyoshi, *The Divided Self*, p. 312.

11. Ibid., pp. 317ff.

12. Oscar Wilde, *The Picture of Dorian Gray* (Harmondsworth, Middx, 1949; 1961 reprint) p. 5. Page references to the text are to this reprint.

13. Quoted by Peter Ackroyd in his Introduction to *The Picture of Dorian Gray* (Harmondsworth, Middx, 1985 reprint) pp. 7–8.

14. Mario Praz, *The Romantic Agony*, tr. Angus Davidson (London, 1933; 2nd edn Oxford, 1951) pp. 344, 345.

15. Rudyard Kipling, 'The Dream of Duncan Parrenness', in *Life's Handicap* (London, 1907; 1920 reprint) pp. 399–407.

16. Guy de Maupassant, 'The Horla', in *Selected Short Stories*, ed. with an introduction by Roger Colet (Harmondsworth, Middx, 1971; 1986 reprint) p. 314.

17. See Colet, Introduction, ibid., p. 12.

18. For a particularly odd example see Arthur Janov, *The Primal Revolution* (New York, 1973) pp. 143ff.

19. See Karl Miller, *Doubles: Studies in Literary History* (Oxford, 1985; paperback edn 1987) pp. 144–5.

20. A. Chekhov, *The Black Monk and Other Stories*, translator unidentified (Gloucester, 1985) p. 8.

## Notes to Chapter 9: Into Psychology

1. See Gerald Gillespie, Introduction to *Die Nachtwachen des Bonaventura* (Edinburgh, 1972) p. 19.

2. Karl Miller, *Doubles: Studies in Literary History* (Oxford, 1985; paperback edn 1987) p. 329.

3. I am indebted to Arthur Sale for pointing this out to me.

4. See Miller, *Doubles*, pp. 331, 242.

5. Masao Miyoshi, *The Divided Self: A Perspective on the Literature of the Victorians* (New York and London, 1969) p. xvii.

6. Miller, *Doubles*, p. 135.

7. Dmitri Chizhevsky, 'The Theme of the Double in Dostoevsky', in *Dostoevsky*, ed. René Wellek (Englewood Cliffs, NJ, 1962) p. 128.

8. William James, *The Varieties of Religious Experience* (London, 1960; 1963 reprint) pp. 32, 33n., 35–6.

9. Ibid., p. 173.
10. Ibid., p. 175.
11. Ibid., pp. 486–7.
12. C. G. Jung, *Selected Writings*, introduced by Anthony Storr (London, 1983) pp. 81–2.
13. Ibid., p. 87.
14. Ibid., p. 88.
15. Ibid., p. 91.
16. Ibid., p. 90.
17. C. G. Jung, *Aion* (*Collected Works*, vol. 9, part II) (London, 1959; 1981 reprint) p. 233.
18. Jung, *Selected Writings*, p. 279.
19. Ibid., p. 280.
20. Ibid., p. 92.
21. Ibid., p. 279n.
22. Ibid., pp. 279, 281.
23. James, *Varieties of Religious Experience*, p. 138.
24. Jung, *Selected Writings*, p. 281.
25. Jung, *Aion*, pp. 40–53.
26. Jung, *Selected Writings*, p. 279.
27. Chizhevsky, 'The Theme of the Double', p. 122.

# Select Bibliography

Brown, Peter, *Augustine of Hippo: A Biography* (London, 1967).
Carter, Angela, *The Sadeian Woman: An Exercise in Cultural History* (London, 1979).
Carus, C. G., *Psyche, zur Entwicklungsgeschichte der Seele* (Pforzheim, 1846).
Chadwick, Henry, *Augustine* (Oxford, 1986).
Cobb, Palmer, 'The Influence of E. T. A. Hoffmann on the Tales of Edgar Allan Poe', in *Studies in Philology*, III (1908).
Eigner, Edwin M., *Robert Louis Stevenson and Romantic Tradition* (Princeton, NJ, 1966).
Ellmann, Richard, *Oscar Wilde* (London, 1987).
Evans, G. R., *Augustine on Evil* (Cambridge, 1982).
Fiedler, Leslie A., *Love and Death in the American Novel* (New York, 1960).
Frank, Joseph, *Dostoevsky: The Seeds of Revolt 1821–1849* (London, 1977).
Frank, Joseph, *Dostoevsky: The Years of Ordeal 1850–1859* (London, 1983).
Frank, Joseph, *Dostoevsky: The Stir of Liberation 1860–1865* (London, 1987).
Gibson, John, *Deacon Brodie: Father to Jekyll and Hyde* (Edinburgh, 1977).
Gifford, Douglas, *James Hogg* (Edinburgh, 1976).
Grant, R. M., *Gnosticism and Early Christianity*, 2nd edn (New York, 1966).
Groves, David, *James Hogg: The Growth of a Writer* (Edinburgh, 1988).
Jaffé, Aniela, *Apparitions: An Archetypal Approach to Death Dreams and Ghosts* (Irving, Tx, 1979).
James, William, *The Varieties of Religious Experience* (London, 1902).
Julian, Philippe, *Oscar Wilde* (London, 1971).
Jung, C. G., *Answer to Job* (London, 1954).
Jung, C. G., *Aion* (*Collected Works*, vol. 9, part II) (London, 1959; reprint 1981).
Jung, C. G., *Psychology and Alchemy* (*Collected Works*, vol. 12) (London, 1953; 2nd (rev.) edn 1968).
Jung C. G., *Selected Writings*, introduced by Anthony Storr (London, 1983).
Levin, Harry, *The Overreacher: A Study of Christopher Marlowe* (London, 1954).
Levin, Harry, *The Power of Blackness: Hawthorne, Poe, Melville* (London and New York, 1958).
Lowes, John Livingston, *The Road to Xanadu* (London, 1927; 2nd edn 1951).
Mesmer, F. A., *Mémoires sur la découverte de magnétisme animal* (Paris, 1779).
Miller, Karl, *Doubles: Studies in Literary History* (Oxford, 1985).
Miyoshi, Masao, *The Divided Self: A Perspective on the Literature of the Victorians* (New York and London, 1969).
Moore, R. I., *The Birth of Popular Heresy* (London, 1975).
Negus, Kenneth, *E. T. A. Hoffmann's Other World* (Philadelphia, Pa, 1965).

Passage, Charles E., *The Russian Hoffmannists* (The Hague, 1963).

Passage, Charles E., *Dostoevski the Adapter: A Study in Dostoevski's Use of the Tales of Hoffmann* (Chapel Hill, NC, 1954).

Praz, Mario, *The Romantic Agony*, tr. Angus Davidson (London, 1933; 2nd (rev.) edn Oxford, 1951).

Praz, Mario, *The Hero in Eclipse in Victorian Fiction*, tr. Angus Davidson (London, 1956).

- Rank, Otto, *Der Doppelgänger (Psychoanalytische Studien)* (Leipzig, Vienna and Zurich, 1925).

Reber, Natalie, *Studien zum Motiv des Doppelgängers bei Dostoevskij und E. T. A. Hoffmann* (Giessen, 1964).

Sanford, John A., *The Strange Trial of Dr. Hyde* (San Francisco, Cal. 1981).

Schubert, G. H., *Die Symbolik des Traumes* (Bamberg, 1814).

Simpson, Louis, *James Hogg: A Critical Study* (Edinburgh, 1962).

Steiner, George, *Tolstoy or Dostoevsky* (New York, 1959; rev. edn 1967).

Taylor, Ronald J., *Hoffmann* (London, 1963).

- Tymms, Ralph V., *Doubles in Literary Psychology* (Cambridge, 1949).

Wellek, René (ed.), *Dostoevsky* (Englewood Cliffs, NJ, 1962).

Wright, T. R., *Theology and Literature* (Oxford, 1988).

# Index

Page numbers referring to passages in which authors, texts or topics are discussed at considerable length are noted in italics.

| | DATE DUE | | |
|---|---|---|---|
| AUG 19 1998 | | | |
| | | | |
| | | | |
| | | | |
| | | | |
| | | | |
| | | | |
| | | | |
| | | | |
| | | | |
| | | | |